John Edwin Gurr, S.J.

John Edwin Gurr, S.J., academic vice president and dean of the graduate school of Seattle University, was graduated from Gonzaga University in 1943 and received his doctor's degree in philosophy from St. Louis University in 1955. He received the degree of Licentiate in Sacred Theology in 1949 from Weston College, Weston, Massachusetts.

Father Gurr was born in Yakima, Washington. He attended parochial and public schools in southeastern Alaska and was graduated from Gonzaga high school, Spokane, in 1930. He entered the Jesuit Novitiate of St. Francis Xavier, Sheridan, Oregon in 1937.

One year after his graduation from Gonzaga University, Father Gurr received his Master of Arts degree from the same institution and for the next year he taught English and philosophy there. He was ordained to the priesthood in 1948, after which he spent a year in the study of ascetical theology at Manresa Hall, Port Townsend, Washington.

After completing work on his doctorate degree at St. Louis University Father Gurr was appointed to the faculty of Seattle University where he is now an associate professor of philosophy.

From 1955-57, Father Gurr was director of pre-major guidance at Seattle University. He is also a member of the University's Board of Trustees.

Father Gurr is the author of articles appearing in the *Proceedings of the American Catholic Philosophical Association*. "Genesis and Function of Principles in Philosophy" was published in 1955; "Some Historical Origins of Rationalism in Catholic Philosophy Manuals," in 1956.

Father Gurr is presently a member of the American Catholic Philosophical Association, the Jesuit Philosophical Association, the American Studies Association, the National Catholic Educational Association, the Jesuit Educational Association, and the Council for Basic Education.

The Principle
of Sufficient Reason
in Some Scholastic Systems
1750-1900

by JOHN EDWIN GURR, S.J.

THE MARQUETTE UNIVERSITY PRESS · MILWAUKEE

IMPRIMI POTEST

Alexander F. McDonald, S.J.
Praepositus Provincialis
Provinciae Oregonensis
die 7 mensis Iulii, 1959

NIHIL OBSTAT

John A. Schulien, censor librorum
Milwauchiae, die 14 Iulii, 1959

IMPRIMATUR

Gulielmus E. Cousins
Archiepiscopus Milwauchiensis
Milwauchiae, die 21 mensis Iulii, 1959

To

MY FATHER AND MOTHER

Preface

ALTHOUGH the chapters of this book constitute a unity, the basic materials of the study have been drawn from a century and a half of philosophical writings. As an aid to the sense of direction and as a basis for patient reading to the end, it may help to realize from the beginning that this study is primarily a kind of philosophical induction derived from the historical material under examination. For this reason, it is necessary to present the evidence as fully as possible before making any final summary or pointing up in detail the suggested insights. Yet the historical portions do not stand separated from the critical; the method used here aims precisely at combining these two dimensions. Taking stock together with the assessment of the inventory constitutes the result.

With this procedure it is hardly possible to formulate at the start a simple thesis in a few words and designate it from the beginning as the "precise problem" of investigation. The problem is far from precise. Rather, it involves a complexity of historical, apologetical, and philosophical factors which must be patiently, if summarily, examined as a source for whatever insights accrue from the experience. At some points, perhaps, this method of study may appear as a massive digression from the announced subject of investigation—the Principle of Sufficient Reason. Some readers may wish for more definitions, greater delimitation by clear and distinct ideas chosen ahead of time for "verification." For example, the word *ratio*—could it not have been carefully examined and its many meanings indicated?

Certainly it could have. Only I have not found this in the manual authors under consideration. The meaning of *ratio* in St. Thomas or in Maritain may aid the reader to evaluate its meaning in Wolff or Stattler. But I have confined my presentation to meanings current from 1750 to 1900 and leave to others the interesting task of comparison and evaluation in a larger framework. Also, while indicating in each chapter the basic movement of the study, I have tried to leave the reader free to make his own assessments as he goes through the presentation of the data, and thus enable him at least to view more objectively the critique of the final chapter.

Necessarily, in a study such as this some philosophical position has to function as a point of reference. The meaning of "essence" and "existence" and the focus drawn on the "primacy-of-essence" context may therefore be subject to question and challenge by readers whose viewpoint is other than that of "Thomistic existentialism." Many perhaps will agree in the rejection of rationalism and essentialism, but be in radical disagreement as to what should be substituted in their place. Or some may feel that anti-abstractionism can be carried too far toward a form of "dogmatic empiricism" which buries its starting point so deeply in sense experience that it must then introduce surreptitiously the whole content of metaphysics somewhere alone the line.

But in any case, the evidence presented in these pages from the old manual philosophy itself seems to indicate that we are only recently beginning to realize how profound a change Leo XIII must have had in mind when he called for a return to St. Thomas. This work, then, is presented with the hope that those who are particularly bothered by the interpretation I have read from the evidence of the meaning and use of the Principle of Sufficient Reason in eighteenth- and nineteenth-century Scholasticism will subject my textual findings to scrutiny from their own point of view and give, in the light of the textbook evidence itself, their own reading of the matter. There is a large body of fact about the Principle of Sufficient Reason which is independent of the doctrinal norms used to assess it. This study will be a success if these facts become widely known. The resolution of mutual differences in their interpretation can safely be left to others.

I am indebted to many people both for the opportunity to pursue and for aid in completing this work which began as a doctoral dissertation in philosophy at St. Louis University. The pleasure of acknowledging this debt and thus in a small way expressing my gratitude involves one difficulty: there are so many names which should be mentioned individually for the expression to be a complete one.

But to be satisfied with what is possible, I am particularly grateful, first, to the members of many library staffs, secondly, to my religious superiors and, thirdly, to Rev. William L. Wade, S.J. He must be credited with asking the original questions and posing the problems which ultimately led to initiating research. Finally and especially I am grateful to Dr. James Collins of St. Louis University for criticism, suggestions and indispensible aid received toward the accomplishment of the venture.

Seattle University, Sept. 26, 1958   John E. Gurr, S.J.

Contents

Chapter I

৯ Introduction

T ITLES are like telescopes: they must be expanded for focused vision. Hence, this introduction, by elaborating briefly on "The Principle of Sufficient Reason in Some Scholastic Systems, 1750-1900," intends to furnish the reader a preliminary focus on the field to be investigated in the pages that follow. This elaboration is threefold: (1) the period chosen, 1750-1900, (2) the meaning of "some Scholastic systems," and (3) the Principle of Sufficient Reason as a subject of investigation.

The Chronological Framework

There is in the source material itself a genetic reason for the choice of 1750 as the *terminus a quo* of this study. As we shall see, the actual references to Leibniz and Wolff which occur in those eighteenth- and nineteenth-century philosophy manuals using the Principle of Sufficient Reason suffice to determine this mid-eighteenth-century boundary. By approximately 1750 the impact of German rationalism, as delivered by its two classical expositors, had had its full thrust, and the story of its influence on Scholastic writings can begin at this point.

The choice of 1900 as the chronological terminus of investigation, on the other hand, is more arbitrary, yet not without reason. For one thing, the twentieth-century pattern of use worked out for the Principle of Sufficient Reason had taken a definite outline by the end of the nineteenth, so that further accumulation of evidence would be unduly repetitious. Secondly, after the exposition of the question's historical aspects, some cognizance is taken, in the chapter devoted to critique, of the later variations in the Principle's use from 1900 to the present.

Within this period (1750-1900), there is a further subdivision at fifty-year intervals: the first from 1750 to 1800, and then a division of the nineteenth century roughly into its two halves.

These period-divisions are not a mere artificial freezing of the ever-fluid movement of time and thought into static compartments. They are made because the history of Scholasticism in these three half-centuries presents a real basis for fifty-year units.

In the latter half of the eighteenth century, for instance, the influence of Wolff (and/or Leibniz) characterized a considerable portion of the Scholastic product. But in the period from 1800 to 1850, a certain Cartesian predominance, at least reductively, can be singled out of the hodgepodge of doctrine and format in the then current manuals. Finally, beginning at mid-century, there is the famous revival of Scholasticism and the surge of Neo-Thomistic "innovators."

Once the chronological limits of this study were determined, and some exploration of the selected area had been made, the next immediate need was to narrow the field by specific selection of individual treatments of the Principle of Sufficient Reason. Numerically, there are dozens of authors and compilers of textbooks and manuals in this century and a half, and the survey actually touches upon more than three hundred single works as source material.

The first step in selection was one of elimination. Only passing use was made of manuals specifically theological in purpose and content, or of particular philosophical studies centered on distinct single problems not involving the Principle of Sufficient Reason. Actual research has been concentrated on the books of various shapes and kinds which were used as formal textbooks of philosophy in Catholic seminaries, houses of study and colleges from 1750 to 1900. Except for a brief glance at names prominent in the history of sufficient reason among the Germans, the non-Scholastic appearances of the Principle during this period have been left to other studies.

The Meaning of "Scholastic"

With the chronological and purely physical limits of investigation decided upon, a more intrinsic problem of classification is posed by the meaning of "some Scholastic systems," as taken in the context of this survey. The "some" is easily explained. It means simply, *sensu aiente,* the selection made and embodied in these chapters. There has been no attempt to give an exhaustive chronological account of the Principle of Sufficient Reason nor to define the limits and the extent of its use. Neither has its genetic history been traced conclusively from one manual to another in an effort to show in every instance the chain of borrowings or the line of influence that may or may not exist from period to period and flow from school to school. The simple purpose here is to present: 1. a reliable record of the Principle's appearance and function in selected authors, and 2. an objective appraisal of the meaning and use accorded it generally in philosophy manuals.

As to the meaning of "Scholastic," the manual-writers themselves are of little help in justifying the application of this adjective to their works. In earlier divisions of this period under study there is a definite anti-Scholastic trend in the compendia; in the next century "Neo-Scholastic" embraces such a mixture of elements that a common definition is not readily accessible.

But common to all the writers of our period is at least one characteristic on which, with some foundation, we can base the appellation "Scholastic." This was the attention they paid to theology. At least negatively, theological considerations functioned to establish the ultimate frame of reference in all their manuals, even when the authors tended logically and doctrinally to heresy or suffered actual censure. At least the apologetical character common to so many philosophical manuals tends to support the view that, as applied to most of these authors, this theological orientation is a safe generalization.

"Scholastic," therefore, is a descriptive adjective which includes a wide range of Catholic philosophy textbook authors, be they Wolffian, Cartesian, or Ontologist, Thomistic, Scotistic, or Suarezian; Benedictine, Sulpician, or diocesan in their inspiration and use. Most of them bear little or no genetic and historical relation to the older Scholastic philosophy.

The Principle of Sufficient Reason as a Subject for Investigation

Finally, an account must be given of the prime focal point of this investigation: the Principle of Sufficient Reason. At first glance, it appears as a subject too narrow and self-evident to sustain a prolonged study of its meaning and use. After all, common sense supplies us with the very obvious notion that things are explained by "reasons," and it is generally a fairly evident judgment of the normal mind that there must be a sufficiency of reasons before there is anything to explain. Moreover, even as viewed here in a setting furnished by the philosophy manuals, the subject does not take on any great stature of commanding import because in the textbooks themselves there is an unassuming simplicity about a principle which merely states that *Nothing is without a sufficient reason.* For many readers, then, the first question that calls for an answer is: "Why bother about a principle so simple to enunciate and so easy to explain?" Some defense, therefore, of this choice of subject matter is in order.

From the way men talk in the non-technical idiom of every day speech, it is noticeable that the ordinary use of "sufficient reason," while clear and communicative in the practical order, offers material for professional reflection to the philosopher who is interested in the more ultimate meanings involved. In such questions as "What was your reason for that?" "Is there any reason why this won't work?" "Can you convince him with that kind of reason?" very little analysis is required to show that the meaning of "reason" is not the same in each usage.

In the first example, it more often indicates the motive or purpose that the agent had in mind to guide choice and finalize action. In the second usage exemplified, the answer sought could be in terms of material or efficient or even formal causality. It will not work, there is no efficient response because, for instance, there is no electricity, the tube is broken, the connections are bad, there is not enough energy available, the design is faulty. As to speaking of reasons in regard to conviction, it means argument or demonstration and might involve formal structure, over-all purpose, choice of source material, or the psychology of purposeful appeal. Combined with "sufficient," these various usages of "reason" indicate a relation to an effect which follows or fails to follow the "cause" or reason posited.

Now this kind of analysis may not go far beyond the purely linguistic aspects of the word, where etymology and the history of language are more appropriate than metaphysics and the analysis of meaning. But even at this level of spontaneous experience it is clear that "sufficient reason" has about it an accommodating neutrality which is charged with significance by the existential context of each particular usage. In itself, "sufficient reason" seems to pertain more to the realm of the possible, the essential, the logical, whereas in the context of actual use it takes on a causal, existential connotation.

To the philosopher, then, this ordinary neutrality of "sufficient reason" in a kind of no-man's-land between essence and existence is interesting, and this interest alone justifies a more technical examination.

There is, however, a deeper level of speculation where, in a definite context of historical use and technical meaning, the Principle of Sufficient Reason presents itself for philosophical analysis and evaluation. There is a *principle* of sufficient reason which comes to our attention against the complex background of the history of modern philosophy and its relation with Scholasticism—a principle involving something more than the idea or notion of sufficient reason that belongs to "common sense."

This latter has been with us a long time and can be asserted as at least implicitly present even in technical philosophical contexts of the remote past. As a *concept* or *notion,* "sufficient reason" arises from the common experience of man and has its place in ordinary language. But the *Principle* of Sufficient Reason takes its origin, or at least is given particular and unique prominence, in the philosophical milieu of the seventeenth and eighteenth century where it is embedded in the systematic context of the philosophy of Leibniz and Wolff.[1]

To one accustomed to think of the Principle of Sufficient Reason merely as a simple statement of common-sense experience, its systematic function and technical meaning in Leibniz are amazing. And amazement always justifies the interest of the philosopher whose starting point is well taken when it begins in wonder.

A further source of amazement to those who have seen the Principle of Sufficient Reason defined and used exclusively in the context of the nineteenth-century Scholastic manuals of philosophy (and theology) is a question raised by the history of philosophy and formulated as a problem of origin: When did the Principle of Sufficient Reason appear in systematic philosophy? Was it in-

---

[1] Gerard Esser, S.V.D., in his *Metaphysica generalis in usum scholarum* (Techny, Ill.: Mission Press, S.V.D., 1952), P. 355, does not hesitate to say: "Enuntiatio principii modo data scholasticis medii aevi prorsus ignota erat. Ipsa philosophia rationalismi auctore Leibniz, primo instituta est, deinde apud omnes fere philosophos, etiam apud scholasticos, accepta est." Cf. also J. De Vries, S.J., "Zur Frage der Begründung des Kausalitäts-Prinzips," *Stimmen der Zeit,* CXXIII (1932), p. 389. On Leibniz' debt to Sebastien Izquierdo, S.J., for antecedent influence in a doctrine of moral necessity, cf. Gaston Grua. *Jurisprudence universelle et Théodicée selon Leibniz* (Paris: Presses Universitaires de France, 1953), p. 302. This book will henceforth be referred to as *Jurisprudence.*

vented and injected into philosophical content by any one individual, or did it, like Topsy, just grow into prominence without
any assignable origin?

Such a question can stir wonder because of a rather wide-spread
assumption that the existence and use of the Principle of Sufficient
Reason in philosophy goes back to Aristotle and is found in St.
Thomas and Suarez. Two reasons explain the currency of this
general impression. One partial explanation is the lack of clear
distinction between the common sense *notion* and the systematic
Principle of Sufficient Reason. Secondly, textbook manuals, especially after 1850, simply repeat the formulation of the Principle
and outline its use, without relating it to the original systematic
context or examining the history of its use.

When it is, as a matter of history, vaguely associated with Leibniz, the technique of textbook scholarship also includes footnote
reference to Aristotle and St. Thomas. For beginners who do not
always have time to track all the sources, these references seem to
lead from an author's treatment of the Principle of Sufficient Reason to the great classics of philosophy. But too often the cited
texts of Aristotle or St. Thomas are merely treatments of the "Principle of Causality" or of principles in general; selection has been
made on the basis of the manual-writer's own implied interpretation. Upon examination, little or no trace is to be found even of
the term *ratio sufficiens,* let alone a technical principle akin to
that of Leibniz, Wolff and their imitators.[2] Further problems concerning what the Principle of Sufficient Reason adds to the Principle of Causality, or what is meant by saying that God is His own
sufficient reason, the free will is its own sufficient reason for choos-

2 An example of reading "sufficient reason" into a text of St. Thomas is found
in the widely-used work of R. Garrigou-Lagrange, O.P., *God: His Existence and His
Nature; A Thomistic Solution of Certain Agnostic Antinomies,* trans. from the fifth
French edition by Dom Bede Rose, O.S.B., (2 vols., St. Louis: B. Herder Book Co.,
1939), I, 112: " 'The word *intelligence,*' says St. Thomas (*Sum. Theol.* II-II, q. 8, a. 1),
'signifies a certain intimate knowledge, for it is derived from *intus legere,* which means
to read what is within *(to read in anything its sufficient reason for existing).* And
this is evident when we observe the difference between the intellect and the senses
. . ." (Italics within the parentheses are mine.) The Latin Text of St. Thomas is as
follows: "Respondeo. Dicendum quod nomen intellectus quandam intimam cognitionem importat; dicitur enim intelligere quasi intus legere. Et hoc manifeste
patet considerantibus differentiam intellectus et sensus; . . ." The words added to
this Latin Text by Garrigou-Lagrange should be indicated by the square bracket
as an addition and thus avoid confusing the reader with the impression that St.
Thomas explains *intus legere* as "to read in anything its sufficient reason."

ing to do this rather than that—these seem to be of secondary import until a clearer grasp is had of the origin and history of the Principle itself.

Whatever may have been the absolutely first time of its appearance in a philosophical function, the Principle of Sufficient Reason, on the testimony of the manual-writers themselves, certainly has a relative origin in the writings of Leibniz and Wolff whose works are the source for its adoption by many subsequent philosophers.[3] Details of this relationship and examination of nineteenth-century Scholastic dependence on the rationalists furnish a third justification for this study.

There is a fourth and final motive which may be brought in defense of this choice of subject matter—a motive drawn more from the history of philosophy and the methodology of research than from any technical analysis, but a motive which in the long run keeps analysis out of ivory-tower speculation and in contact with the experience of the individual philosopher. This historical justification of a full length study of the Principle of Sufficient Reason among some Scholastics from 1750 to 1900 may be briefly sustained by an analogy with the historical study of medieval Scholastic philosophy.

For years it had been the custom to lump the medieval philosophers into one general category of "Scholastic" and to view Scho-

---

[3] We are not entering into the question either of the absolute origin of the Principle of Sufficient Reason or of the specific formulation of the Principle which Pius XII had in mind when he says of philosophy acknowledged and accepted by the Church that it "safeguards the genuine validity of human knowledge, the unshakable metaphysical principles of sufficient reason, causality and finality, and finally the mind's ability to attain certain and unchangeable truth." Encyclical of August 12, 1950, *Humani Generis,* trans. by Gerald C. Treacy, S.J. (New York: The Paulist Press, 1950), p. 15.

Since the Church demands instruction in philosophy "according to the method, doctrine and principles of the Angelic Doctor" (*ibid.,* p. 16, quoting Canon 1366, p. 2), and since formulation of principles involves the context of the system in which they function, there is no question here of the brain-child of Leibniz belonging to the patrimony of sound philosophy. Therefore, criticism of his Principle of Sufficient Reason and an examination of Scholastic relations with it in no way involves disrespect for such formulations as would be acceptable to perennial Scholasticism. From a more positive viewpoint, one safeguard against the error condemned in *Humani Generis* of scorning the philosophy honored by the Church as "outmoded in form and rationalistic" (*loc. cit.*), is to know something of the effect Continental Rationalism had on some eighteenth- and nineteenth-century Scholastic manual-writers. This knowledge helps us to see the distinction between rationalism and Thomism and prevents the rejection of the latter under the mistaken assumption that it is the former.

lastic philosophy as a kind of monolithic formation in the history of ideas. But as scholars took up one by one the individual thinkers and writers who had disappeared under the abstract label of "Scholastic," it was possible to rewrite, or write for the first time, the history of philosophy in the Middle Ages.

So also, although in a lesser degree and with much less intrinsic importance, the history of nineteenth-century Scholastic philosophy may be as yet buried in such over-all classifications as "Christian philosophy," "Neo-Scholasticism," or "Thomistic Revival," or even under the national labels of "German," "French," "Italian," or "Spanish" Scholasticism. Here also the monograph is the great deliverer from monolithic generalizations in history. Only in this case it will be employed more profitably in exploring, not the individual *writers,* but individual *problems* of systematic import. Followed through the works of many individuals who in themselves have not made any great contribution, these problems bring into focus the pressure points of interest and the division of schools so useful for evaluating the depth and direction of the century's philosophical current.

One of these problems is the Principle of Sufficient Reason. In itself it may not be a very weighty chunk of the metaphysical structure; the importance of its function outside of an epistemological use, rooted in the persistent rationalistic dichotomy between reason and experience, may relegate it to the list of minor topics in any division of philosophical subject matter. But place and function it does have in systematic philosophy, where analysis of reality and synthesis of knowledge about reality tend to a unity in which the smallest parts and the most minor functions involve and are involved in the integration of the larger elements.

Even if only a back-door entry into the mansion of philosophy, the Principle quickly leads to the main rooms where the business of the day is always transacted. Part of our procedure in this study will be to follow the Principle of Sufficient Reason through the doors marked: "induction," "methodology," "essence and existence," "causality," and "existence of God" to see what goes on there.

And if it be asked why we delay along minor by-paths when the main highways are open and at hand, let us say, *mutatis mutandis,* about such a subject as the Principle of Sufficient Reason what Balz says in reference to his scholarly studies of certain 'obscure' followers and opponents of Descartes:

If the student stray from the great highway of philosophy's history, to wander in its collateral byways, he may be sure of adventures. Quite possibly he will attain, here and there, a vantage point from which the highway itself may be viewed in a new perspective. The highway itself and the world through which it leads may be glimpsed from a bypath that in itself leads nowhere.[4]

The Principle of Sufficient Reason may lead nowhere. That remains to be determined. It may have come from somewhere into the system of Leibniz. That question of origin will not directly concern us here. We will begin our straying and our adventure with the formulation of the principle as it appears in Leibniz and is taken up for propagation by Wolff, and from there follow its trail through nineteenth-century Scholasticism.

To contribute to the historical knowledge of that period of philosophy and to strengthen our grasp on the perennial elements that must be accounted for in all truly philosophical speculation, this history of the Principle of Sufficient Reason among some Scholastics from 1750 to 1900 has been written.

[4] Albert G. A. Balz, *Cartesian Studies* (New York: Columbia University Press, 1951), p. 218.

Chapter II

ᘒᕫ The Point of Departure
in Leibniz and Wolff

T O ESTABLISH a point of departure for the Scholastic manuals of 1750-1900 it is necessary to begin with the Principle of Sufficient Reason as it appeared in Leibniz and Wolff. Whatever may have been the absolute origin of the Principle in general, with Leibniz we possess the source relative to the writers we are studying, and with Wolff we have a carrier of the doctrine and a systematizer of the context in which Leibniz made the Principle function.

Whatever other sources the manual-writers may have drawn upon in the pre-Leibnizian Scholastics, Leibniz remains a classical point of reference. Beneath the details of his monadological system there is a core of metaphysical doctrine and assumptions which is of classical proportion in the philosophical experience of modern philosophers, Scholastic and non-Scholastic alike. Basically, this core, in a sense to be made clear as we progress, is that of the primacy of essence. This is the ubiquitous *context* of the Principle of Sufficient Reason during the one hundred and fifty years under examination; any understanding of the Principle's meaning, any insight into its function must keep it in view. Wolff especially merits attention because he took this primacy-of-essence core into a theory of method, which resulted in that concrete physical format of a philosophy textbook where the Principle of Sufficient Reason received its local habitation and name.

First, then, we propose to note the textual history of the Principle of Sufficient Reason, that is, its appearance in the *Monadology* and the *Primae Veritates,* and a brief outline of its over-all *de facto* context in Leibniz. In the *Monadology,* the Principle of Sufficient Reason functions in a mature synthesis of doctrine peculiar to its author and well known to later Scholastic manual-writers. In the less well known *Primae Veritates,* unpublished until this century, the Principle is seen to be at the heart of the analytic origin of this monadological metaphysics; in this function it is in a frame of reference which shows more clearly and directly the meaning of "sufficient reason."

Following this, our interest is drawn to Wolff in whose works this basic metaphysics was systematized at the practical level of pedagogical presentation. He is especially interesting as to his divisions of the science of philosophy and the role given to the Principle of Sufficient Reason in the establishment of an analytic system.

This study of Leibniz and Wolff is designed to illustrate that "sufficient reason" is neutral enough for transplanting into another system and that the Scholastics who did so manipulate it faced the necessity of first disengaging it from the more glaring implications of German rationalism and then giving it a content adjusted to their own positions. To evaluate the degree of success achieved by compilers of Scholastic textbooks in this process of setting aside the context of the monadology for their own, we must subject this rationalist context to some historical and systematic examination.

The Sources in Leibniz

Louis Couturat, in the preface of his *Opuscules et fragments inédits de Leibniz,* notes shortcomings in the various editions of Leibniz' works.[1] He outlines the ultimate and as yet unrelieved need for a systematic publication of every single scrap of writing still unedited in the Archives of Hanover, and he issues warning against rash and hurried attempts meanwhile to make definitive interpretations of the great German's systematic philosophy. Since the Principle of Sufficient Reason plays such an important role in this system, it would seem to be included in this warning and precluded therefore from any attempts at other than mere descriptive analysis of its meaning and use in Leibniz.

However, there are three factors which make it both possible and profitable for our study of the Scholastics to outline briefly the Leibnizian Principle of Sufficient Reason as it functions in the *Monadology.* First, there is a scholarly opinion to the effect that

[1] Louis Couturat, *Opuscules et fragments inédits de Leibniz* (Paris: Alcan, 1903).

any further publication of the unedited writings of Leibniz would not bring any substantial change in our understanding of the essentials of his philosophy. As Couturat himself points out, there is such integration and cohesion in the thought of Leibniz, scattered though it is in fragments as well as formal treatises from his early years to his last, that on the basis of what is available to us of his writings the essentials of his system have been sufficiently well determined. Gaston Grua, enjoying over Couturat the discovery and publication of even more material in the last half-century, echoes this opinion. The *quality* of Leibniz' thought has been grasped; the problem now is purely *quantitative*. Any further unfolding of his principal conceptions will contribute more to the study of how that thought actually evolved to its mature formulation in the *Monadology* and *Theodicy* than to any major restatement of that formulation itself.

Secondly, the restricted circulation of much of Leibniz' writing and the lack of printed editions of his work until late in the eighteenth century narrow the sources to those which were actually known and most referred to by later manual-writers.

Thus in the first half of the eighteenth century (1700-1750), the principal works of Leibniz enjoying public circulation as printed books were: the *Theodicy,* the *Correspondence with Clarke* and the *Monadology*. Of these, the *Theodicy* (1714) was his only work published before his death in 1716. In 1717 Samuel Clarke brought out an edition of the *Correspondence,* while a German translation of the *Monadology* (the original French edition did not appear in print until 1840) appeared in 1720.

Often associated with the name of Leibniz in later references to its origin, the Principle of Sufficient Reason was probably best known in connection with these three works, of which the *Monadology* appears most frequently as a source given in references to sufficient reason in Scholastic texts. Systematically and as a mature formulation of his metaphysical system, the *Monadology* is most important. Historically, and as a setting for the "crisis of conscience" with which Leibniz' thought and writing were so constantly concerned, the *Theodicy* is most famous. Somewhat in the middle between these two is the *Correspondence with Clarke,* combining as it does the apologetical motive of the *Theodicy* with the systematic character of the *Monadology*. In these letters he attempted not only to justify God and His ways but also to rescue

that justification from arguments he deemed falsely based on Newtonian science.

To these three published works of Leibniz must be added, for
our purposes here, the important opuscule Couturat made available, the *Primae Veritates*. As for the later publication of his
New Essays Concerning Human Understanding (1765), edited
by Raspe, and his "collected" works (1768), edited by Dutens,
their systematic effect on Scholastic writers, to judge from the
paucity of references to them, seems to have been negligible.
This is probably explained by the fact that Wolff's influence
and authority had risen to its zenith before 1765 and drew away
from Leibniz the interest that might otherwise have been focused
directly upon his writings. The very effort we shall make to keep
to the evidence of the textbooks will free us for the most part from
any obligation of exploring the prodigious stream of Leibniz'
manuscripts and correspondence because such a consideration is
a task which the Scholastics themselves seem never to have under-
taken.

By detaching ourselves from a direct evaluation of the monadological system as such and by viewing Leibniz' system as a kind of
stage on which the Principle gives its best performance, we are
able to place the Principle of Sufficient Reason itself under scrutiny
in order to discover the characteristic features which pertain to it
generally as a principle and not merely as an element in Leibniz'
philosophy.

Apologetical Context of the Principle

There are as many approaches to the Principle of Sufficient
Reason in Leibniz as there are viewpoints for the examination of
his systematic thinking as a whole. But one simple way to undertake the subject from an angle corresponding to the ultimate purpose of this study is to distinguish two aspects of the Principle which
must be carefully noted and at times compared, in order to appreciate fully its appeal to the manual-writers, Catholic and non-
Catholic alike, and to understand their motives for its use.

Historically, sufficient reason is involved in the almost desper-
ate apologetics of an era where the accusation of atheism fell like
a sword on the neck of any philosopher who left himself open to it.
In accordance with the methodology of accusation, censure and
counter-accusation of the times, it was almost impossible to avoid
vulnerability somewhere. Hence, it is curious as well as instructive

to see how Leibniz and the Principle of Sufficient Reason are at one time on the side of the angels in defending the proof for the existence of God by natural reason, while at another they are cast into exterior darkness for affiliation with the cause of Fatal Necessity.

Leibniz was a thinker and writer of enormous prestige. His efforts to find middle ground between Catholics and Protestants, to defend religion against skeptic and libertine, and his friendly gleanings from the Scholastic tradition of Catholic Europe made him widely accepted and perhaps saved his system from the kind of scrutiny that brought down the charge of atheism on the heads of Descartes and Spinoza. In an atmosphere charged with contempt for any philosophy that involved final causes, formal causes, distinctions between essence and existence, and yet tense with the dangers which the new science carried for old beliefs in the existence and providence of God, the use which Leibniz made of the Principle of Sufficient Reason to prove the existence of God made him a welcome ally in the battle with atheism.

The facility with which paragraphs can be found in his writings eulogizing the Scholasticism of the past, his alleged "Catholicity," amounting at times to the rumor of his conversion—all these made it apologetically profitable for Scholastics to reach into the *Monadology* or the *Theodicy* for corroboratory material. While disavowing or simply ignoring the deeper metaphysical doctrines on substance, pre-established harmony, extension, and the origin of the soul, it was easy for these manual-writers to hold up before an audience, which was more interested in apologetics than metaphysics, in argument rather than discussion, magic formulae like *Nihil est sine ratione sufficiente* to establish proof for the existence of God and to point up the absurdity of materialistic atheism.[2]

---

[2] The Sulpician, Eymery, points out in his preface to *Exposition de la doctrine de Leibnitz sur la religion* that his arrangement and publication of selections from Leibniz were guided by the pious design of making known more and more "combien sincère, constante et profonde étoit la religion de Leibnitz, et par-là de fortifier un témoignage en faveur de la religion aussi précieux et aussi imposant aux yeux de nos incrédules modernes que celui de ce grand philosophe. Nous savons effectivement que notre ouvrage a fait sur plusieurs de ces messieurs une impression salutaire. Et un ministre protestant, plus zélé pour la défense de la religion, que ne le sont aujourd'hui plusieurs de ses confrères en Allemagne, a cru servir advantageusement la religion contre les impies, en le traduisant dans la langue de ses compatriotes . . . Ce traducteur est M. Brung, premier prédicateur et consulteur du consistoire calviniste de Stettin." M. Eymery, S.S., *Exposition de la doctrine de Leibnitz sur la religion*

On such questions as freedom of the will and divine liberty to create, the going was a little harder. But even here the *Theodicy,* for instance, was a gold mine for Scholastic arguments, phrases and well-wrought criticism of the position which men like Bayle in Leibniz' time and Voltaire in the later age of the Enlightenment sought to establish.[3]

Certainly from this it is not hard to appreciate why an author of a text designed more as a handbook of apologetics than as a manual of philosophy should be loathe either to drop out of circulation such a time-honored device as the Principle of Sufficient Reason or to expose its systematic context in continental rationalism, for the purpose of protection or correction. Wolff and his successors had also enhanced its apologetics value and helped to enshrine it as accepted doctrine common to all right-reasoning men.

The Problem of Intelligibility and Necessity

From the *technical* standpoint, there was an underlying continuity of problems and points of contact between apologetics and metaphysics that made a complete break with rationalism, and especially with the "corrected" brand selected from the stock of Leibniz and Wolff, almost impossible. In fact, it was not attempted by most Scholastics until the nineteenth-century revival of Thomism. Only then was there any re-examination of the very starting points and assumptions of rationalism, which for generations it was good apologetical strategy either to accept or at least to ignore.[4]

suivie de pensées extraites des ouvrages du même auteur (Paris: Tournachon-Molin and H. Seguin, 1819), p. viii. Cf. Jean Felix Nourrison's long note on Leibniz as a Catholic in *La philosophie de Leibniz* (Paris: Hachette, 1860), pp. 5-7. During the deliberations of the Vatican Council, Bishop Strossmeyer referred once to Leibniz as a help to Catholics. Cf. Dom Cuthbert Butler, *The Vatican Council; The Story Told from the Inside in Bishop Ullathorne's Letters* (London: Longmans, Green & Co., 1930), p. 290. Other influential testimony is that of Cardinal Zephyrinus Gonzalez, O.P., in his *Histoire de la philosophie,* trans. by P. de Pascal (Paris: P. Lethielleux, 1891), IV, pp. 310-318.

[3] The *Theodicy* was the culminating masterpiece of Leibniz' life-long effort to validate the Christian tradition in the face of the age's scientific revolution. "Dans les premières années à Hanovre, et un ordre difficile à preciser, se multiplient les essais pour définer, à la fois contre le scepticisme et contre le fidéisme, la vraie piété enracinée dans la connaissance rationelle de Dieu . . ." Gaston Grua, *G. W. Leibniz, textes inédits d'après les manuscrits de la bibliothèque provinciale de Hanovre* (Paris: Presses Universitaires de France, 1948), I, 3. Cf. F. W. Meyer, *Leibnitz and The Seventeenth Century Revolution,* trans. by J. P. Stern (Cambridge, England: Bower & Bower, 1952), p. 141.

[4] W. T. Jones, *A History of Western Philosophy* (New York: Harcourt, Brace,

A quick resumé of two persistent philosophical problems which his system sought to solve will contribute to our methodological purpose of detaching the Principle of Sufficient Reason from its systematic context in Leibniz. Admittedly, this problem-approach to Leibniz has its pitfalls because he carried on a polemic which was as complex as the nature and number of the opponents with whom he engaged. The older Scholastics, Descartes, Spinoza, Newton, Locke, all came into his range of inquiry and fell under his powers of analysis. Nevertheless, certain basic themes appear and persist through the various patterns of his development, to be picked up by his successors and imitators who on some points merely repeat as a solution what actually is only a suppression of the problem entailed. One of these problems is that of intelligibility. The nature of necessity and contingency is the other. Both can be held in appropriate focus by the doctrine of substance.

Rationalism is characterized particularly by its unyielding commitment to the deductive *intelligibility* of the world. For Leibniz, this commitment constituted a general problem whose solution raised other and subsidiary questions of metaphysical theory. For example, both the problem of God's existence, which kept the Principle of Sufficient Reason apologetically alive in the battle with atheism, and the problem of certitude, which stimulated its use on the metaphysical front in the agitation over Pyrrhonism, are basically problems of intelligibility. Universal doubt destroys intelligibility and, without the latter, there is meaning in neither the idea nor the proof for the existence of God.

Now historically and systematically this fundamental commitment to intelligibility and the problems entailed therewith are often drawn into sharper focus at two crucial points: the nature of substance and the nature or relation of necessity and contingency

1952), II, 686-687, points out that Continental Rationalism resorted to a very useful device for avoiding any conflict between science and religion: keep mind (theology, values, freedom, universals, rational truth, thought) and body (physics, the scientific view, universal mechanism, the actual, existent particular, perception) *isolated* from each other, yet in relation along lines decreed by God as parallel from the beginning. (Who but God could do this? Therefore, the parallel harmony of the two realms in isolation not only avoids conflict but furnishes a proof for the wisdom and power of God.) This is worth noting because later it will help make clear why it simply was not enough for Scholastic manual-writers to drop parallelism in its various forms (Descartes, Malebranche, Leibniz) and yet keep the metaphysical context of a universe which ultimately needed a pre-established parallelism of some kind to render its operation intelligible and contingent.

in the universe. The Principle of Sufficient Reason has important
implications in both of these problems.

Leibniz' doctrine on substance and the role which the Principle
of Sufficient Reason plays therein are rooted in a context furnished
him by Spinoza in terms of the dichotomized world of Descartes.[5]
Descartes' radical fracture of the universe into material and spiritual substance appeared to many of his contemporaries and successors as resulting actually in a "duo-verse," which sinned griev-
ously against the unity on which ultimate intelligibility must depend. With unity thus rendered an acute problem in philosophy,
the systematic thinking of the period was always under the tension
of a threatened coalescence that would logically collapse matter
and spirit into one substance.

Whether this substance would be material and thus achieve
unity by sacrificing the spiritual, or vice versa, would depend
on the systematic choice of reasoning whereby one argued to
the nature of reality. With Spinoza the choice was for spirit and
the monism of one substance of many attributes.[6] In the case of
Hobbes and Gassendi, materialism won out and the ultimate intelligibility of the real world of experience lay in and was limited
to the mechanism of moving atoms. While highly speculative in
nature, these problems and the line of thinking they occasioned
had tremendous practical consequences which Leibniz, as a lawyer,

[5] Here also may be noted in passing two points of doctrine from Descartes which
belong to the historical background of the Principle of Sufficient Reason and while
constituting a study in themselves should be kept in mind. One is his basic distinction
of the object of human cognition into "things" and "eternal truths," a distinction
so sharp and profound that the cognition of the latter is independent of the cognition
of the former. (*Principiorum Philosophiae,* I, 48, 49). The other is his attenuation
of the notion of efficient causality to the point where it practically coincides with
formal causality, a context in which "cause" is reducible to "reason" and hence can be
treated in an entirely essentialist framework. (*Reply to the 4th Set of Objections*)
Cf. *Oeuvres de Descartes.* Edited by Charles Adam and Paul Tannery, (12 vols.
Paris, Cerf, 1897-1905), VII, 22-24; VII, 239.

[6] Descartes' postulate of a finite thinking self as an immaterial substance together with other finite selves, God and the various modes of material substance, made
a *universe* impossible. Spinoza kept the dualism between extension and thought
which Descartes had set up, but rejected any dualism between extended substance
and thinking substance. This resulted in One Universe or whole of one Substance,
many modes. Thus in Spinoza's concept of reality, everything follows from the first
principle or ground of the universe. *Causari* equals *sequi* and *causa* is *ratio,* or
reason, the logical essence or reason of a thing, a kind of rule or formula that generates a series. There is thus a Spinozan dimension to the Principle of Sufficient Reason
which belongs to the history of its origin in Leibniz. Cf. Susanna Del Boca, *Finalismo
e Necessità in Leibniz* (Florence: Sansoni, 1936), p. 26.

diplomat, roving reporter and practical apologist for Christianity, saw very clearly and strongly deprecated.

As a philosopher, however, he accepted the quandary of Descartes' theory of substance and, while leaving the original chasm between matter and spirit as wide as he found it, sought none the less to bridge the gulf with a new theory of substance. Its aim was to achieve the unity necessary for intelligibility, without having recourse to the unity of matter and form, potency and act, and other such Scholastic elements of solution. Spinoza in this matter had gone too far; Descartes had not gone far enough. Leibniz thought one way to strike a happy medium between the horns was to correct and strengthen the original insights of Descartes.[7] The latter had neglected to provide the demonstrations which would substantiate his assertions. What Descartes had already proposed as true now had to be *demonstrated* as such, and correction of Cartesian theory in many instances would consist for Leibniz in the addition of the demonstration hitherto neglected. *Thus the commitment to the intelligibility of the world is enlarged to include demonstration as the great source of intelligibility.*

Now intelligibility, whether attained by demonstration or otherwise, must be characterized by a certain universal *necessity* which gives stability to knowledge and sinew to the process of establishing it. Necessity is a requisite for demonstration. But this necessity must not be such that the experienced and equally obvious diversity of *contingent* reality is ignored or suppressed. Explanations that depend either on a spiritualistic monism or a mechanical atomism result in the disaster of a completely necessitated world where there is indeed reason for everything and therefore intelligibility, but where rational, ontological reality is static with a geometric necessity that actually destroys change and absorbs the individual. Change, the contingent, the multiple, are dynamic realities in which are rooted the realities of time and diversity.

---

[7] "Pour ce qui est des Disputes qui ont été entre Mr. *Gassendi* and Mr. *Descartes,* j'ai trouvé que Mr. Gassendi a raison de rejetter quelques prétendues demonstrations de Mr. Descartes touchant Dieu et l'Ame; cependant dans le fond je crois que les sentimens de Mr. Descartes ont été meilleurs, quoiqu'ils n'ayent pas été assez bien démonstrés. Au lieu que Mr. Gassendi m'a paru trop chancelant sur la nature de l'âme, et en un mot sur la Théologie naturelle." Leibniz, "Lettre IV à M.M. Remond de Montmort, Vienne, le 26 Aoust, 1714," in L. Dutens, *Gothofredi Guilielmi Leibnitii . . . Opera omnia, nunc primum collecta* (Geneva: Fratres de Tournes, 1768), V, 17.

Yet, without some element of the universal and the necessary, this segment of the real remains forever irrational and incomprehensible. In the order of knowledge there would be a chasm between knowledge of truth and knowledge of the individual as deep and unbridged as that between matter and mind in the order of being. If knowledge is the possession of the intelligible, and intelligibility belongs only to necessary propositions, then individuals and the concrete existent are meaningless.

Here again, the theoretical is projected into the realm of practical moral life, and the problem of making intelligible the relation between the necessary and the contingent ultimately deepens to the level where there is a question of saving freedom and responsibility in human acts. Brute necessity, whether induced by the geometric monism of Spinoza or the atomistic matter-in-motion theories of Hobbes and Gassendi, makes human freedom and therefore human moral action unintelligible.

On the other hand, to postulate contingency, as Descartes seems to do,[8] by rooting everything in the arbitrary will of God alone in such a way that necessity in things, events or even meaning itself is purely extrinsic to them and could be changed by God tomorrow, likewise bristles with practical consequences for the nature of truth and the stability of world order. The Principle of Sufficient Reason ultimately comes to rest in the center of this problem.

In a letter to Bourget, Leibniz makes a very clear statement of the issue and his contribution to its solution.[9] The solution, he thinks, is a happy medium between extremes and he thus accepts the dichotomy while trying to overcome it. Essentially, it consists in explaining the origin of the real as drawn neither from a brute necessity to exist nor from a purely arbitrary exercise of brute power to create, but rather from a certain convenience or suitableness which can be called the principle of the best and in a sense is the ultimate *ratio sufficiens* or final intelligibility of everything that is.[10]

To keep a balance between necessity and contingency, neither of which can be denied, Leibniz' theory depends upon a distinc-

[8] Cf. the letters to Mersenne in the *Correspondance de Descartes*, ed. C. Adam and G. Milhaud (Paris: Alcan, 1936 ff.), I, 135-36; 139-42.

[9] Cf. Leibniz' "Second Letter to D. Bourguet, Hanover, 11 April 1710," in Dutens, *op. cit.*, VI, 207-208.

[10] James Collins, *A History of Modern European Philosophy* (Milwaukee: The Bruce Publishing Co., 1954), p. 261.

tion that appears frequently in his writings and is of crucial importance both as a principle and a consequence in his system. It is also basic to the monadological context of the Principle of Sufficient Reason. This is the distinction between *necessary* and *contingent truths;* it is one way of escape from entanglement in the consequences of Descartes' dual substance theory. With it, Leibniz can keep both the necessity needed for the intelligibility of essence and the contingency experienced in the succession of existents.

His union of these two, essence and existence, is achieved by a theory of substance in a universe where pre-established harmony is the ultimate root of intelligibility. The systematic principle that enabled Leibniz to unite the essential nature of things and the natural succession of existents which come and go in an order completely necessitated yet eternally contingent is the Principle of Sufficient Reason.

The Systematic Context of Sufficient Reason in Leibniz

In this process of peeling off onion-wise the contextual layers of the system in which Leibniz uses the Principle of Sufficient Reason, we now turn from a statement of problems to an investigation of the system designed to solve them. In the *Monadology* occurs one of the basic texts on the Principle of Sufficient Reason and the one probably most often quoted. But, since it is so readily accessible, this work of Leibniz will receive no more than passing attention here on the way to a consideration of the *Primae Veritates.* The *Monadology's* classic text on the Principle of Sufficient Reason reads as follows:

> Our reasonings are founded on two great principles, *that of contradiction,* in virtue of which we judge that to be *false* which involves contradiction and that *true,* which is opposed or contradictory to the false. And *that of sufficient reason,* in virtue of which we hold that no fact can be real or existent, no statement true, unless there be a sufficient reason why it is so and not otherwise, although most often these reasons cannot be known to us.[11]

[11] *The Monadology; Leibniz Selections,* ed. P. Wiener (New York: Scribner, 1951), Nos. 31-32, p. 539. Where Descartes had started with the *cogito* that had survived doubt, and Spinoza had begun with God and the ontologically linked universe of one substance, Leibniz began with the obvious existence of a manifold and diverse reality as the fundamental certitude and all-important concrete starting point. He accepts Descartes' dichotomy of matter and spirit as a valid problem to be solved

This text is one of the easiest to lift from its immediate context, and it is precisely this monadological context which one must leave behind, or attempt to leave behind, when taking it into a Scholastic framework. This necessity, of course, was clearly seen by the textbook authors, and they had little patience with monads and a "force" notion of substance. What they did not see so clearly is the fact that the *Monadology* is itself part of the larger context of a primacy-of-essence orientation which remains and must be reckoned with even after the Principle of Sufficient Reason has been purged of more proximate Leibnizian connotations. Hence, any use of these texts in other systems must be carefully justified or run the risk of being sheer nominalism.[12]

The meaning of "our reasonings" has been previously determined in the careful step-by-step evolvement of what *monad* means. So also the full impact of "sufficient reason" depends upon this previous development as well as upon the subsequent distinction of truths and the further complex analysis of activity in both God and the monads that systematically depend upon Him. In the *Monadology,* the Principle of Sufficient Reason is an integral part of the key doctrine of pre-established harmony. Since the monads do not act upon one another but nevertheless are adapted to each other and to the universe as a whole, some law or laws must govern their connection and adaptation, if pre-established harmony is to be effected.

by a theory of substance which will preserve multiplicity (against the monism of Spinoza) and yet achieve unity in diversity (against the dualism of Descartes). By beginning with the compound and arguing to the presence of the simple, Leibniz takes the existence of the monad, a simple substance capable of action, as a demonstrable starting-point. One of the key points at which the doctrine in *Primae Veritates* takes on its full ontological reference is Leibniz' notion of the monad as containing within itself the *sufficiency* of its internal activities. Another crucial contact between his ontological theory of substance and his logical or metaphysical doctrine on truth and the subject-predicate relation is made when he considers "every present state of a simple substance is naturally the consequence of its preceding state, so its present is big with its future." *The Monadology,* No. 22, in Wiener, p. 537. Cf. Leibniz, *Discourse on Metaphysics* (1686), No. 13, I, in Wiener, p. 305. The monad contains the series and is the principle or law of succession.

12 Thus in manipulating the Leibnizian Principle of Sufficient Reason as a means to prove the existence of God, the following points of the context in the *Monadology* must be drained of technical monadological meaning for adjustment to Scholastic use: "the immense variety of the things in nature," and the division of bodies *ad infinitum,* the distinction between efficient and final causes, "our reasonings;" the nature of the *series,* and God as a pure consequence of possible being.

Thus, the intelligibility which accrues to "sufficient reason" comes from a systematic context dominated by Leibniz' basic concept—pre-established harmony. That this in turn is not ultimate in its intelligibility is evident from the function performed by the Principle of Sufficient Reason in establishing the meaning of pre-established harmony itself. By extension of monadological doctrine "upward" to God and "outward" to phenomena, Leibniz produced the other two basic works: the *Theodicy* and the *Correspondence with Clarke.* In both of these works the same problem-context is present, and the Principle of Sufficient Reason has the same general utility in rendering a combination of necessity and contingency intelligible.

More particularly, in the *Theodicy* the Principle functions in a setting dominated by contingency and freedom, while in the *Clarke Correspondence* it is involved in Leibniz' theory of contingent secondary causality in the world of phenomena. There remains a third aspect: contingency and the notion of truth. It is with this context that the Principle of Sufficient Reason is more properly concerned in a rationalistic world, and in reference to which it has been probably most often conceived. One of the clearest and more direct presentations of this analytic function of the Principle is given by Leibniz in his *Primae Veritates,* a manuscript from those "day book" fragments which were the workshop of his philosophical mind. Here the more analytic and explanatory developments of fundamental positions are found, out of which the later synthesis and elaboration were to issue.

Couturat, who published this little work in his *Opuscules et fragments,*[13] judged it to be a resumé of the whole of Leibniz' philosophy in its genetic sequence and in its true perspective.[14] The importance of this opuscule for our study lies in its brief but classical formulation of the subject-predicate relation, which provides the context of the Principle of Sufficient Reason. Written in 1686, the piece is short and the reasoning direct and clear, with the metaphysics of the monad deduced from the Principle of Sufficient Reason.

Leibniz begins with a definition of First or Primary Truths as those which "enunciate the same of itself or the opposite of its op-

[13] Couturat, *op. cit.,* pp. 518-523.
[14] Couturat, "Sur la métaphysique de Leibniz," *Revue de métaphysique et de morale,* (1902), X, 1-23. This article includes both text and commentary.

posite," that is, *A* is *A; A* is not *non-A*. All other truths whatsoever
are reduced to primary truths and this reduction is by means of
definition. Definition is the resolution by analysis of the notions
which constitute a particular complex truth or true proposition.
It is *a priori* proof, or proof independent of experience.[15]

From this it is clear in what the nature of logical or essential
truth consists. Truth is the connection between the subject-predicate terms of an enunciation. Since this connection is always a
connection of inclusion, predicates are always in their subject,
consequents are always in the antecedent. Thus, truth, ultimately
rooted in the definition of first truths, is always an identity either
expressed or implied. To prove, therefore, the truth of a proposition is to demonstrate the *ratio* or nature of truth which consists
in a connection *(nexus)* between subject and predicate.[16]

Unfortunately, continues Leibniz, the nature of truth so conceived has not been sufficiently considered by philosophers, with
the result that consequences of no small magnitude have been
overlooked. The first of these is the PRINCIPLE OF SUFFI-
CIENT REASON, which immediately arises *(statim nascitur)*
from a consideration of the nature of truth as a nexus between a
subject and its contained predicate. "Certainly," he says, "the most
immediate consequence is that commonly accepted axiom: *nihil
esse sine ratione* or *nullum effectum esse absque causa.*"[17]

If there were no Principle of Sufficient Reason, he continues
to explain, then there would be some truths which could not be
proven *a priori,* that is, truths not reducible to identical propositions. This "is contrary to the nature of truth, which is always
either expressly or implicitly identical."[18] As a corollary of this
Principle of Sufficient Reason or, rather (and Leibniz lets his
hesitancy stand here), as an example of the Principle of Sufficient

[15] "Primae *veritates* sunt quae idem se ipso enuntiant aut oppositum de ipso
opposito negant. Ut A est A, vel A non est non A. Si verum est A esse B, falsum est
A non esse B vel esse non B. Item unumquodque est quale est. Unumquodque sibi
ipsi simile aut aequale est. Nihil est majus [aut minus] se ipso, aliaque id genus,
quae licet suos ipsa gradus habeant prioritatis, omnia tamen uno nomine identicorum
comprehendi possunt . . . Omnes autem reliquae veritates reducuntur ad primas
ope definitionum, seu per resolutionem notionum, in qua consistat *probatio a priori,*
independens ab experimento." Leibniz, *Primae Veritates,* in Couturat, *Opuscules
et fragments inédits de Leibniz,* p. 518.

[16] *Loc. Cit.*

[17] *Ibid.,* p. 519.

[18] *Loc. Cit.*

Reason, is Archimedes' postulate on the principle of equilibrium that in the case of the free arms of a balance, equal weights having been placed on both sides, all will remain in equilibrium.[19]

With the Principle of Sufficient Reason clearly established and its validity guaranteed by the very nature of truth itself, Leibniz is now in a position to deduce the principal tenets of the *Monadology*, beginning with the important *identity of indiscernibles* and using the precise notions of substance and substantial action to reach the *hypothesis of concordance* and a detailed theory of phenomena in the physical world.[20]

Hence, as Couturat points out, the later and more technically developed work, the *Monadology*, takes its point of departure from a notion of the monad which is itself the result of a long process of reasoning, at the very beginning of which stands the Principle of Sufficient Reason.[21] This axiom here stands midway as it were between a principle of identity, which says that every identical proposition (analytic) is true, and a principle of universal intelligibility, which states that everything is demonstrable. What the Principle of Sufficient Reason itself says is that *every true proposition is identical* (analytic).[22]

[19] *Loc. Cit.*

[20] Some of the apologetical implications of Leibniz' theory of dynamics or physics are brought out in his *Correspondence with Clarke*. Samuel Clarke (1675-1729) was an Anglican divine, more theologian than philosopher, who combatted the irreligious tendencies in the materialism and deism of Hobbes and Locke. Leibniz agreed with Clarke against materialism, and abhorrence for its contribution to impiety was common to the two men. But, as he pointed out in his second paper, Leibniz felt it was useless to fight these materialistic principles of philosophy with the mathematical principles of the philosophy of Newton which, in his estimate, are reducible to the very materialism they were to combat. Therefore, he offered as the only effective opposition to materialism his own metaphysical principles, known somewhat to Pythagoras, Plato and Aristotle but which he claims "to have established . . . demonstratively in [his] Theodicy, although . . . done [there] in a popular manner." *Second Paper,* in Wiener, p. 217. Clarke seems to have set the example of admitting the Principle of Sufficient Reason and at the same time trying to avoid admitting all that Leibniz means by it. The latter complains of this in his third paper: "The author [Clarke] grants me this important *principle*: that *nothing happens without a sufficient reason, why it should be so, rather than otherwise*. But he grants it only in *words* and in *reality* denies it. Which shows that he does not fully perceive the strength of it . . ." *Third Paper,* in Wiener, p. 222. Leibniz made no effort in this correspondence to justify his principle as we have seen in *Primae Veritates;* when pressed by Clarke to do so he falls back on its axiomatic nature. Cf. last part of the *Fifth Paper,* in Wiener, p. 280.

[21] Couturat, *Revue de métaphysique et de morale,* 1902, X, 9.

[22] *Loc. Cit.*

Drawing for a moment on other writings of Leibniz, two important precisions can well be made here as to the nature and meaning of the Principle of Sufficient Reason. This discussion of the Principle in the *Primae Veritates* may be considered as a logical development within Leibniz' theory of truth. But it would be a serious mistake to overlook the combination effected by the genius of Leibniz between this approach and the metaphysical theory of substance. In his fundamental context of pre-established harmony and with the fruitful doctrine of perceptual action in substance itself systematically worked out to explain the facts of diversity and "causality," logic and metaphysics are so unified in Leibniz' existential problems that what he says about truth is true of what he regards as the real.[23]

Moreover, the Principle of Sufficient Reason was an essential element in Leibniz' solution of his basic dichotomy between the essential and the existential which is found at every level of his system. Since he holds that the human mind cannot know the true formal *ratio* of existence and can only approach the truth of contingent things in a process of convergence to infinity, then he postulated that God has installed permanently in the mind a principle by which enough universality and necessity can be grasped in the contingent to render it intelligible, that is, make its inclusion within a system possible. This innate principle is that of Sufficient Reason, and it supplies a sufficient motive for whatever judgments we make of existent contingents, whose *a priori* truth escapes us.[24]

---

[23] In the *Letters to Arnauld* (1686), Leibniz argues his whole view of the nature of substance as following from a basic principle of logic to which he gives the status of an ontological axiom: *Verae propositionis semper praedicatum inest subjecto.* Cf. Genevieve Lewis, *Lettres de Leibniz à Arnauld d'après un manuscrit inédit* (Paris: Presses Universitaires de France, 1952), p. 39. When a logical subject or single proposition is erected into substance, then its attributes or predicates become "accidents" inherent in the essence of the substance. "This is the nature of an individual substance or of a complete being, namely, to afford a conception so complete that the concept shall be sufficient for the understanding of and for the deduction of all the predicates of which the substance is or may become the subject." *Discourse on Metaphysics, op. cit.,* p. 300.

[24] "Quia non possumus cognoscere veram rationem formalem existentiae [, vicarium nobis Deus concessit, et experimentis perpetuis stabilivi insitum] <in ullo casu speciali, involvit enim progressum in infinitum, deo sufficit nobis veritatem contingentium nosse a posteriori nempe per experimenta; et tamen illud simul [discere] tenere in universum vel generatum, quod et ratione et experientia ipsa [stabilitur] (quantum nos in res penetrare datum est) firmatur, insitum divinitus> menti nostrae principium, nihil fieri sine ratione, et ex oppositis semper illud fieri, quod plus rationis habet." *De contingentia* (1686), in Grua, *G. W. Leibniz, textes inedites,*

Since existence never has an unconditionally necessary connection with essence (lest the world remain within the framework of Spinoza), then the Principle of Sufficient Reason is quite essential to Leibniz' fundamental understanding of existence and existential judgment.

Failure to consider this point explains many of the efforts made in the late eighteenth century to combine Leibniz and Locke. What will particularly interest us will be the degree of consciousness exhibited by later Scholastic manual-writers of this predicament involving the existential judgment, as well as the extent and success of their attempts to meet it.

Now out of this doctrinal situation around Leibniz' theory of truth and his use of the Principle of Sufficient Reason arises a problem which returns us to our original consideration of the distinction between *contingent* and *necessary* truth. Is "truth" used with the same meaning in both these areas? In other words, is *every* true contingent proposition, for example, "Nero fiddles while Rome burns," ultimately reducible to identity.[25] Since all

---

I, 304-305. Leibniz rightly sees that the reason or cause for contingent existents must be found outside their definition; otherwise not to exist would imply a contradiction and the necessitated world of Spinoza would be back on the scene again. "**Omnes Existentiae** excepta solius Dei Existentia sunt contingentes. Causa autem cur res aliqua contigens <prae alia> existat, non petitur ex <sola> eius definitione, [sed praeterea ex aliqua ratione. Quia scilicet ratio fuit eam existere potius quam non existere] sed comparatione cum aliis rebus. Cum enim infinita sint possibilia quae tamen non existunt, ideo cur haec potius quam illa existant, ratio peti debet non ex definitione, alioqui non existere implicaret contradictionem, et alio non esset possibilia, contra hypothesin, sed ex principio extrinseco quod scilicet ista sunt aliis perfectiora . . ." *De libertate,* Grua, *G. W. Leibniz,* I, 288.

It is beyond human power to make the infinite analysis of contingent facts necessary to reduce them to complete unity of truth and intelligibility. But we can reduce them to at least one indemonstrable primitive truth, the principle of sufficient reason, innately present to us, and thus take them into the intelligibility of the total system. Cf. *Introductio ad Encyclopaediam Arcanam,* in Couturat, *Opuscules,* p. 514.

25 "Si omnes propositiones etiam contingentes resolvuntur in propositiones identicas, an non omnes necessariae sunt? Respondeo non sane, nam etsi certum sit exiturum esse quod est perfectius, tamen, minus perfectum nihilominus possibile est. In propositionibus facti involvitur existentia. Existentiae autem notio est talis, ut existens sit talis status universi qui DEO placet. DEO autem libere placet quod perfectius est. Itaque involvitur demum actio libera. At nonne ipsius actionis liberae reddi ratio potest? Utique si actionem liberam sumamus ut in tempore, erit ejus ratio alia actio DEI praecedens aeque libera, et sic porro. Si sumamus actionem liberam aeternam, quaenam ratio cur DEUS potius [elegerit] talem semper formaverit? Est utique ipsa natura seu perfectio divina, dicendumque est in contingentibus non quidem demonstrari praedicatum ex notione subjecti, sed tantum ejus rationem reddi, quae non necessitet, sed inclinet." *Phil.* VII, C, 68, in Couturat, *Opuscules,* p. 405.

truth is analytic and thus demonstrable by analysis, is the predicate "fiddling while Rome burns" included in the subject "Nero"
so that by an analysis of the subject the nexus with its predicate
will ultimately appear? And if so, then how can contingent truth
escape being necessary, which would mean the destruction of
contingency and the revival of the original fatalism of Spinoza,
although somewhat camouflaged by monadological distinctions?

Leibniz does not flinch from the consequences of his analytic
conception of truth. Even true contingent propositions are reducible to identity. They are analytic, not synthetic. But there
must be, none the less, an escape hatch from the pressure of such
a position that threatens logically to crush the world into a
necessity of consequences that render forever impossible the contingency required for freedom in man's moral choice and God's
creative act. There must be a difference between necessary and
contingent truth, if they are to remain distinct.

This difference Leibniz attributes to the *different ways* in
which contingent and necessary truths reduce to identity; the difference is in terms of infinity. The reduction of necessary truths
is a finite process, while that of contingent truths is infinite.[26]
Both, to be true, are and must be demonstrable. But only in the
case of the necessary truths is demonstration ever finished by the
human mind. Here there is a reduction or analysis of terms which
is finite in its process and terminated by arrival at the identity
of propositions by means of the principle of contradiction.

---

[26] "Et hoc arcano detegitur discrimen inter veritates et necessarias et contingentes, quod non facile intelliget, nisi qui aliquam tincturam Matheseos habet, nempe
in propositionibus necessariis analysis aliquousque continuata devenitur ad aequa-
tionem identicam; et hoc ipsum est in geometrico rigore demonstrare veritatem; in
contingentibus vero progressus est analyseos in infinitum per rationes rationum, ita
ut numquam quidem habeatur <plena> demonstratio [perfecta] ratio tamen veritatis <semper> subsit, et a solo Deo perfecte intelligatur, qui unus seriem infinitam
uno mentis ictu pervadit. Exemplo apposito ex Geometria et numeris res illustrari
potest: . . . Uti in propositionibus necessariis per continuam analysin praedicati et
subjecti res eo tandem reduci potest . . . ut appareat notionem praedicati inesse
subjecto, ita in numeris per continuam analysin (alternarum divisionum) tandem
pervenire potest ad communem mensuram, sed quemadmodum in <ipsis> incom-
mensurabilibus <quoque> datur proportio sive comparatio; etsi resolutio procedat
in infinitum, nec unquam terminetur, [saltem enim ipsa quemadmodum] uti ab
Euclide est demonstratum; ita in contingentibus datur conexio [relatioque] terminorum sive veritas, etsi ea ad principium contradictionis sive necessitatis per analysin
in identicas reduci nequeat." *De Contingentia* (1686?), in Grua, *G. W. Leibniz*,
I, 303-04.

Although contingent truth depends upon the contingency of God's choice making it to *be,* still, to be true, its subject must contain the predicate, and the fact that only at infinity is this inclusion discovered does not change the necessary and absolute identity of the subject and predicate. Therefore, Nero's contingency of action is ultimately real only from the viewpoint of a human, finite mind and, hence, not *really* real, not *really* contingent, not *really* free.

To extricate himself from this difficulty, Leibniz defines contingency ultimately in terms of an infinity of possibles; he puts the root of contingency in the infinite. As long as the opposite is possible without contradiction, then the thing or event is contingent.

Leibniz explains this possibility of the opposite by recourse to the mind of God where everything which already does exist is seen in view of the infinite number of unrealized, unchosen possibles which will never be in existence. Here the opposite to the present realized possibility (i.e., this existing universe) is also possible, which by definition means that our actual universe is contingent.

His answer to a final question, Why does a possible exist? is that the existence of this world, for instance, was a more sufficient reason for God's choice than that of any other possible world.[27] And this reason is rooted ultimately in the *richness of reality* contained in the system of compossibles which wins out in its bid for God's gift of existence.[28]

In other words, all essence calls for existence, but existence comes only to the essence with the strongest call. Existence is the exigency of essence realized; and, if it were anything else than this exigency or call of essence, there would be no sufficient reason in essence for existence, nor would any judgment of existence have a sufficient reason for its assent.[29] Actually, therefore, ex-

---

[27] The universe itself is a system of compossibles, and out of an infinite number of such systems it has been chosen to exist. It is a universe precisely because all of its possibilities are filled. The full is the best.

[28] "Principium primum circa Existentias est propositio haec: *Deus vult eligere perfectissimum.* Haec propositio demonstrari non potest; est omnium propositionum facti prima, seu origo omnis existentiae contingentis. Idem omnino est dicere Deum esse liberum, et dicere hanc propositionem esse principium indemonstrabile. Nam si ratio reddi posset huius primi divini decreti, eo ipso Deus hoc non libere decrevisset." *Reflexions sur Bellarmin* (1680-82?), in Grua, *G. W. Leibniz,* I, 301.

[29] "From the conflict of all the possibles demanding existence, this at once

istence is inscribed in advance and contained as exigency in essence itself and thus is deducible by simple analysis.

God is a divine combiner who sees each possible as a combination of certain *first possibles* and therefore as endowed with a certain degree of reality, which is a sufficient reason for its existence. By calculating the relative exigency of the possible systems of creation, God sees which one of them all is entitled to existence as the best.[30] To see this is to see the *ratio* for giving existence. Thereupon, the divine will, being determined, is inclined to create. "Cum Deus calculat . . . fit mundus."[31]

Erdmann points out clearly that

> . . . the transition from the possibility of the monads to their actual existence may be called, with reference to Leibniz' own terminology, a transition from his *metaphysics* to his *physics*. His essay of 1697, *De rerum originatione radicali,* is particularly important on this point. Here, as elsewhere, Leibniz makes use of what he calls sometimes *principium rationis sufficientis,* sometimes, *principium melioris* . . . All the infinite number of conceivable monads and combinations of monads press forward to come into existence; and absolutely no change takes place in their essential nature when they are brought from the *regio idearum* into actual existence . . .[32]

Of particular reference to the Principle of Sufficient Reason is the fact that, where metaphysics and physics are contrasted in terms of the possible and the existential, then the ultimate intelligibility of contingent (physical) things and therefore of existence must be found in the order of possibility. This transition from metaphysics to physics or, to speak more ontologically, the

follows, that there exists that series of things by which as many of them as possible exist; in other words, the maximal series of possibilities . . . And as we see liquids spontaneously and by their own nature gather into spherical drops, so in the nature of the universe the series which has the greatest capacity (*maxime capax*) exists." In Wiener, *op. cit.,* pp. 91-92.

30 Since perfection or the maximum of essence is a sufficient reason for existence, "reason" means "essence" and "sufficient reason" means "the most perfect or best essence." Hence, the Principle of Sufficient Reason ultimately means the Principle of the Best.

31 "Cum Deus calculat et cogitationem exercet, fit mundus." In Grua, *G. W. Leibniz,* I, 259. It is here, in the theory Leibniz holds as to the nature of the divine essence and its relation to contingent existents, that we find the roots of the essentialist philosophy in which the Principle of Sufficient Reason figures so prominently.

32 John E. Erdman, *A History of Philosophy,* translation edited by Williston S. Hough (London: Sonneschein, 1892), II, 183.

relation conceived to exist between essence and existence, is the point at which we can best turn to the peculiarities of this situation as exposed by Wolff.

Wolff's New Manuals and Theory of Method

In a letter to John Fabricius in 1710, Leibniz once complained that

> We are lacking today in good compendia of Logic, Physics and the other parts of philosophy, not to mention mathematics, but my friend Wolff at Halle in Saxony, writing in German, has recently done not a bad job in this regard.[33]

Although at the time of this complaint there was no lack of textbooks written in the old tradition of school philosophy, the new science and its method were making these outmoded, while at the moment compendia in the new style had not yet appeared.

These older manuals had a venerable history, and the evolution of the philosophical *Cursus* up to the eighteenth century must be kept in mind in order to preserve in proper perspective Wolff's response to this need of the hour.[34] In Protestant Germany

---

[33] "Epistola CIII Ad Johannem Fabricium" in L. Dutens, *op. cit.*, V. 291. Cf. also Lettre IV to De Montmort, *ibid.*, V, 15.

[34] In general, these older philosophy textbooks belonged to the school philosophy of "Peripateticism"; their format and method, the differences within the "school" and the evolution stimulated by the new science after Descartes would constitute a study in itself. Max Wundt in his *Die deutsche Schulmetaphysik des 17. Jahrhunderts* (Tübingen: J. Mohr, 1939), pp. x-xxvi, lists nearly two hundred individual titles in use at German universities from 1600 to 1700. There were dozens of others in use throughout Europe. Leibniz and Wolff were both quite familiar with Catholic authors as well as with the seventeenth-century German schoolmen.

The commitment of these philosophers to the Physics of Aristotle against the new science, their method of procedure according to *Liber, Tractatus, Dissertatio, Disputatio, Dubitatio, Quaestio, Opinio* instead of an unbroken chain of definitions and demonstrations from clear and distinct concepts marshalled in numerical order of paragraphs—all this was reason enough for Leibniz' lament over the lack of good compendia written according to mathematical method and from the standpoint of the Cartesian dichotomy of matter and spirit. The following authors may be consulted as examples of the old format in contrast to the new method of Wolff: Bartholomew Amicus, S.J., *In universam Aristotelis philosophiam notae ac disputationes* . . . (Naples: L. Scorigium, 1623); John Poncius, O.F.M., *Philosophiae ad mentem Scoti Cursus integer* (Lyons: L. Arnaud & P. Borde, 1672), 1st ed. (1648); Phillipus a Sanctissima Trinitate, O.C.D., *Summa philosophiae ex principiis Aristotelis d. Thomae doctrina juxta legitimam scholae Thomisticae intelligentiam* (Lyons: S. Jullieron, 1648); Thomas Compton-Carleton, S.J., *Philosophia universa* (Antwerp: J. Meursiun, 1649); Augustus Laurentius, S.J., *De triplici ente cursus philosophicus in tres tomos divisus: I. De ente logica; II. De ente physica; III. De ente metaphysica*

about 1700, Melanchthon (1497-1560) was still the soul and chief of school doctrine and doctors, but attempts were being made to found a national school in Germany which would be neither Latin, like Melanchthon's, nor French, like that of Ramus and Descartes. Christian Wolff (1679-1754) consummated this revolution. No iconoclast, he kept what he thought good from the past and concentrated on correction and completion of work already done.[35]

By 1717, the year in which he wrote an eulogy of the great Leibniz, "Mr. Wolff, professor at Halle [who] is very diligent and teaches there with great public acclaim,"[36] had taken some of the preliminary steps toward fulfilling the need for good compendia in philosophy. He had produced a German Logic in 1713, and in 1720 he began his production of philosophy texts written in the German language.[37] Eight years later came *Philosophia rationalis sive logica, methodo scientifica pertracta* (1728).[38]

In the preface to this work, Wolff bemoans two deficiencies in philosophy. First, its writers have not been presenting the kind of evidence which of itself renders the assent of the mind certain and unshakable in philosophical matters. Secondly, the

(Liége: W. Streel, 1688); Louis Babenstuber, O.S.B., *Philosophica Thomistica Salisburgensis . . .* (Ausburg: G. Schlisteri, 1706); Bartholomeus Maestrus de Meldula, et Bonaventura Bellutus de Catana, O.F.M.Conv., *Philosophiae ad mentem Scoti cursus integer* (Venice: N. Pezzana, 1708).

[35] The heritage of the past which Wolff set out to correct and utilize has a long history. Cf. Etienne Gilson, *Being and Some Philosophers* (Toronto: Pontifical Institute of Mediaeval Studies, 1949), pp. 108-119; also his "Historical Research and the Future of Scholasticism," *The Modern Schoolman*, XXIX (1951), 1-10. At the time of Wolff, St. Thomas was considered by Peripatetics as well as the Moderns to be a theologian who wrote philosophy mainly in his commentaries on the works of Aristotle. A. Touron, O.P., in his division of the philosophical and theological works of St. Thomas illustrates this identification with Aristotle. Cf. his *La Vie de S. Thomae d'Aquin, de l'ordre des Fréres Prêcheurs, Docteur de l'Eglise, avec un exposé de sa doctrine et des ses ouvrages* (Paris: Gissey, 1740).

[36] Leibniz' "Lettre II à Monsieur Marioni," in Dutens, *op. cit.*, V, 537.

[37] For a complete list of the works of Wolff, cf. Mariano Campo, *Cristiano Wolff e il razionalismo precritico* (Milan: Vita e Pensiero, 1939), II, 672-676.

[38] For a discussion of the relation between the German and the Latin editions, cf. Max Wundt, *Die deutsche Schulphilosophie im Zeitalter der Aufklärung* (Tübingen: J. Mohr, 1945), pp. 183-199 (especially 183-184). Wundt indicates the popularity of the German works in terms of the many editions they enjoyed. For Wolff's comment on his own German Compendia, see *Philosophia rationalis sive logica methodo scientifica pertractato, et ad usum scientiarum atque vitae aptata* (Editio novissima; Verona: M. Moroni, 1779), No. 895. References to the works of Wolff in this chapter will be according to paragraph numbers.

material treated in philosophy has not been sufficiently practical and in touch with the needs of human life.[39]

The reason for these failures, he affirms, is the same in both cases: the notions and propositions in use by philosophers are not sufficiently explained and demonstrated. Therefore, it will be his aim and purpose to reduce confused and vague terms to distinct and fixed meaning and to construct sound and demonstrable propositions not yet achieved by philosophers. Truth will be separated from falsehood, and truths which have an interconnection among themselves will be arranged in systematic harmony. Using Euclid and his reduction of all the principles of mathematics to a system as a model, Wolff aimed at a similar collection of the first principles of all knowledge into a system.

The basic law of this new application of scientific method to philosophy was that each single item be treated in that particular spot in the process of system-building where it could be understood and demonstrated from the preceding established demonstrations.[40] Three rules implement this law: (a) no term can be used unless explained by an accurate definition; (b) no principles can serve as starting points unless sufficiently proved; (c) no proposition can be admitted unless accurately determined and legitimately deduced from principles already sufficiently proved.[41]

The carrying out of this simple purpose led Wolff into the bi-lingual production of some forty volumes of systematic philosophy. Leibniz had indeed chosen his words well when he described Wolff as "very diligent."[42] Wolff himself felt that where

---

[39] Cf. both the 1728 Preface to his *Philosophia rationalis* and the 1729 Preface to *Philosophia prima sive ontologia methodo scientifica pertractata qua omnis cognitionis humanae principia continentur* (Editio novissima; Verona: M. Moroni, 1779).

[40] *Philosophia prima*, Preface.

[41] *Ibid.*, No. 7.

[42] Part of Wolff's success and the result that "good compendia" became abundant in Germany were due to the fact that from the beginning of his career, he had disciples who propagated his system in other universities of the Empire. Prémontval, no friend of the Wolffians, compared Wolff to a vine clinging for support to the oak which was Leibniz, and on the vine the brightest leaf was Baumgarten. Cf. Christian Bartholmèss, *Histoire philosophique d l'Académie de Prusse depuis Leibniz jusqu'à Schelling, particuliérement sous Frederic-Le-Grand* (Paris: Marc Ducloux, 1850), I, 213. Bartholmèss also notes that "la chaire evangélique elle-même parlait le langage wolfien, appelant le Christ *une adorable monade, une entéléchie surnaturelle.*" *Ibid.*, I, 117. Besides Alexander Baumgarten (1714-1762), author of a *Metaphysica* in both German and Latin (the latter for the sake of foreign students at Halle in 1766), other bright leaves were: George Bülffinger (1693-1750), *Dilucidationes*

his system ended, there Leibniz' could be said to begin in the sense that he had supplied (as Leibniz in turn had corrected Descartes) what the system needed to endure.

This was particularly true of the Principle of Sufficient Reason. If it was Leibniz who had given it classical formulation in the metaphysical context of the monad that involved it deeply in the perennial matrix of essentialist philosophy, then it was Wolff who, by uniting metaphysics and method for a distinctly pedagogical purpose, gave the Principle the place in his textbooks where its transmission to posterity was assured.[43]

philosophicae de Deo, anima humana, mundo et generalibus rerum affectionibus (Tübingen: J. & C. Cottae, 1725); Ludwig Phil. Thumming, *Institutiones philosophiae Wolfianae, in usus academicos adornatae* (Editio nova; Frankfurt: 1799) 1724 Preface from edition of 1725-26; Friedrick Christian Baumeister (1709-1785), *Institutiones metaphysicae ontologiam cosmologiam, psychologiam, theologiam denique naturalem complexae methodo Wolfii adornatae* (Editio nova; Wittenberg: S. Zimmermann, 1744). These disciples of Wolff, all his contemporaries, influenced subsequent Wolffians like Garve, Nicolai, Reimarus, Sulzer, and were often quoted in later Scholastic textbooks. Jean des Champs, in his *Cours abrégé de la philosophie Wolffienne* (Amsterdam: Arkstee et Merkus, 1743-47), I, dedicatory epistle, credits three French writers with having broken the ice for Wolff's entry into their country: Madame la Marquise du Chatelet, Jean Henri Formey and Emer de Vattel. Frederick Klimke, S.J., *Institutiones historiae philosophiae* (Rome: Gregorian University, 1923), refers to Polish Wolffians (the Saxon dynasty ruled Poland for a time) and to Russian. Spain, he says, always remained Scholastic, and Hungary offered no entry to Wolffianism. At Geneva, the prevailing influence was Cartesian. One of the services which his disciples and successors performed for Wolff's philosophy was to compress the master's interminable developments into classroom proportions.

[43] In contrast to the format of the older textbooks outlined in N. 34 above, Wolff proceeds from his distinction between the sensitive and the rational faculties in man (which is the psychological counterpart of that dichotomy of the universe inherited from Descartes through Leibniz) and accepts as a point of departure the chasm between experience and reason. This entails a basic division between empirical or historical and rational or philosophical science. In the wide sense this latter division includes physics and metaphysics. But more strictly, the philosophical is divided on the basis of a further distinction within man between the cognoscitive and appetitive powers into the theoretical and practical parts of philosophy.

This theoretical or cognitional knowledge is *metaphysics*. By means of a further breakdown into genus and species, a division so popular with Leibniz and so germane to the univocity of universal being under the primacy of essence, metaphysics becomes (1) *General Metaphysics* or *Ontology* and (2) *Special Metaphysics*, again divided into three parts: (a) *Cosmology* ("inauditum in Scholis"—cf. Preface to *Cosmologia),* (b) *Psychology,* and (c) *Natural Theology.*

Wolff's technical definition of philosophy as *Cognitio rationis eorum quae sunt vel fiunt (Philosophia rationalis sive Logica,* No. 6) is a generic definition which becomes specifically applicable to each division of philosophy according to the type of being under examination—God, man or matter—and the *possibilia* involved which yield *rationes.* Nor does knowledge of a connection between a reason and a fact constitute philosophy until this known connection is demonstrated as such (No. 9).

In this treatment of Wolff we will consider his use of the Principle of Sufficient Reason under three general headings suggested by his own arrangement of the matter, especially in the *Ontology*. 1. We shall see it presented as one of the twin pillars of philosophy, functioning as an axiom basic to his system, but subordinate to the Principle of Contradiction, and with the ultimate meaning of *ratio* derived from the system itself. 2. This will be followed by a quick glance at Wolff's history of the Principle and his theory of its origin. 3. The analysis will conclude with a view of the Principle in the over-all context of Wolff's metaphysics and method.

Twin Pillars of Philosophy: The Principles of Contradiction and Sufficient Reason

Wolff's explicit presentation of the Principle of Sufficient Reason occurs at the beginning of his *Ontologia*.[44] His approach to this Principle and the Principle of Contradiction is not by way of the notion of being and a deduction therefrom, although a cursory glance at the arrangement of his text might lead one to think so, especially after familiarity with later manuals which follow this development. Rather, Wolff makes these "twin pillars of philosophy" more intuitional than deductive; they are the *given* of the rationalistic mind generating its own data and starting points.[45]

What is merely known through experience is only historical knowledge; but if from this knowledge the *ratio* of other things can be explained then historical knowledge becomes a foundation for philosophy. Philosophy thus differs from history as knowledge of *reason for facts* differs from *knowledge of facts* (No. 10).

44 Wolff, *Philosophia prima*, No. 70 ff.

45 Part I of the *Ontologia* bears the title, "Concerning Being in General and the Properties Which Flow Therefrom." But this first part immediately divides into two parts: Section I, "Concerning the Principles of First Philosophy," and Section II, "Concerning Essence and Existence and certain related notions of being." Section I is composed of two chapters devoted to the two Principles, Contradiction and Sufficient Reason. It is only in Section II that he takes up the discussion of being and its notions, a discussion which proceeds by way of the possible and impossible, determined and indetermined, to Chapter III, "Concerning the Notion of Being."

It is within this framework as taken over by the successors of Wolff that we see the Principle of Sufficient Reason migrate back and forth as to relative position in the subject matter. In Bülffinger *(Dilucidationes)*, for instance, the Principles come after the treatment of the possible-impossible, necessary and contingent. In John G. Feder's *Institutiones logicae et metaphysicae* (Editio quarta; Göttingen: J. Dietrich, 1797 preface 1777), No. 63, they appear in the *Logic*, part II, "Concerning the right use of the intellect in seeking truth," Chapter I, "Concerning the principles of truth

Systematically, the Principle of Sufficient Reason is preceded by the Principle of Contradiction, and Wolff places the foundation of this latter in an obvious experience of mental life: *While we are judging something to be, it is impossible at the same time to judge it not to be.*[46] From this conscious experience of the nature of our minds, we concede without need of proof the proposition enunciated in general terms as the Principle of Contradiction: *It cannot happen that one and the same thing be and at the same time not be.* Or, another form of the same: *If A is B, it is false that the same A is not B.*[47]

To demonstrate the fecundity of this basic axiom, Wolff explores its logical implications and leaves little doubt that the principle for him is a purely formal one, a kind of *aliquid* to which subsequent concepts in his system may be tied. If it were not a true principle, he argues, then the same predicate could and could not pertain to the same subject under the same determinations, and the same proposition could be both false and true at the same time.[48] Besides "contradiction is simultaneity in affirming and denying,"[49] it is contained in two propositions, of which "one takes away what the other posits."

The important point is that the process of building concepts and working out demonstrations is insured by this principle against *logical* failure. Negatively, it is important to note that while this treatment is placed under ontology and the subject of being in general, yet with no systematic reference to or involvement of existential judgment or sensation, it is not possible to denote this principle as anything more than logical.

Proceeding next to the Principle of Sufficient Reason, Wolff does not make any detailed reference to the question of its relation

and the various modes of knowing them." To this migratory characteristic of the Principle of Sufficient Reason we shall return in Chapter Six.

[46] Wolff, *Philosophia prima, sive ontologia*, No. 27. So also with the Principle of Sufficient Reason, as we shall see below.

[47] "Naturae igitur mentis nostrae nobis conscii ad exempla attendentes sine probatione concedimus propositionem terminis generalibus enunciatem: *Fieri non potest, ut idem simul sit & non sit, seu quod perinde est, si A sit B, falsum est idem A non esse B*, sive A denotet ens absolute consideratum, sive sub data conditione spectatum." *Ibid.*, No. 28. "Propositio haec: Fieri non potest, ut idem simul sit & non sit, dicitur *Principium Contradictionis*, ob rationem mox adducendam. *Principium* autem *Contradictionis* jam olim *adhibuit* Aristoteles *eodem usi sunt Scholastici in philosophia prima instar axiomatis generalis.*" *Ibid.*, No. 29.

[48] *Ibid.*, Nos. 30, 31.

[49] *Ibid.*, No. 30.

to the Principle of Contradiction. To anyone following through within the system itself, the question of whether it reduces to the Principle of Contradiction is answered by the fact that the latter is the one systematically prior, and this priority makes reduction possible.[50]

Clearly, the dual sovereignty granted these principles by Leibniz no longer holds. Leibniz had located the relation between the Principle of Contradiction and the Principle of Sufficient Reason in the realm of the rational through his distinction between necessary and contingent truths. Wolff unified that realm of the rational around the Principle of Contradiction.[51] Again we can note the lack of existential reference in the fact that this realm remained distinct from that of the singular concrete sensible data of experience. Under the influence of Locke and the rise of empirical science, Wolff and his successors heightened the reality of this latter realm and deepened the realization and the value of its experience. But the systematic failure to incorporate it into an *existential* union with the realm of the rational will continue to haunt modern philosophy.

Unity in the order of *essence,* however, is impressively systematic. The possible as the non-contradictory, we shall see, gives to the Principle of Contradiction a primacy which it can share with no other. The *ratio* or reason whereby things are understood is ultimately explicable in terms of the opposition between "nothing" and "something," the latter being the systematic coherence of clear and distinct ideas whose right to, and precise determination of, a place in the system ultimately depends on the Principle of Contradiction. The Non-Contradictory is "something."[52]

This application of the primacy of essence to a theory of method grants priority to the Principle of Contradiction over the Principle of Sufficient Reason, and to the Principle of Sufficient Reason over causality. In other words, when Wolff has defined philosophy in

---

[50] Wilbur Urban, "The History of the Principle of Sufficient Reason: Its Metaphysical and Logical Formulations," *Princeton Contributions to Philosophy*, I, No. 3 April, 1900, p. 27. Urban sees in paragraphs Nos. 66-70 a statement of the Principle of Sufficient Reason as a logical law by means of deduction from the law of contradiction; he finds Wolff, in confusing real grounds with the grounds of knowledge, guilty of a *petitio principii*. Hans Pichler, *Über Christian Wolff's Ontologie* (Leipzig, Dürr'schen Buchhandlung, 1910), p. 7, calls Wolff's proof a word-play.

[51] Émile Bréhier, *Histoire de la philosophie* (Paris: Alcan, 1934), Vol. II, part II, 361.

[52] Wolff, *Philosophia prima,* Nos. 59-59.

terms of possibles rather than causes, he must use *ratio* instead of
causa to describe the object of the metaphysical search, and it is
one of the inevitabilities of such a system that "reasons grow more
rational and logical; causes, more empirical and real."[53] The deductive method of mathematics becomes the unique method of
philosophy, and here-and-now existential reference is obtained by
"common sense" joined sometimes with a pious use of Sacred
Scripture.

By "Sufficient Reason," Wolff meant whatever explains why
something is; it is "that whence it is understood why anything is."[54]
He gives two examples: The three sides of the triangle, or rather,
its *three-sidedness* is sufficient reason for the three angles because
this suffices for us to understand the triangle as having three angles.[55]
In the order of motivation and action he further instances the case
of a man rising to his feet out of respect for some person who has
just entered the room. From the fact of this entry, plus the rever-
ence due the newcomer, it can be understood why the man in the
room rises to his feet and hence a sufficient reason for the action
is assigned.

In keeping with his methodology of building notions and demonstrations from previously established concepts, it is now necessary to define the meaning of "nothing" and "something" as involved in the notion of "sufficient reason." This is very simply
managed in terms of the basic building block itself, the notion or
concept. We call that "nothing" to which no notion corresponds.
And "something" is that to which some notion can be attributed
or corresponds.[56]

All of this has been preliminary to a statement of the Principle
of Sufficient Reason, and in paragraph No. 70 Wolff states it as
follows:

[53] Norman Wilde, *Friedrich Henrich Jacobi: A Study in the Origin of German
Realism* (New York: Columbia College, 1894), p. 27.

[54] Wolff, *Philosophia prima*, No. 56.

[55] The triangle example is reminiscent of Spinoza, and a favorite example with
rationalists. Like Leibniz, Wolff was still faced with the threat of Spinozism. With
no systematic distinction between the true and the real that is supported by existential
reference, his only escape from being pushed into Spinoza's *universe*-version of "everything that exists has a cause or reason why it exists" was to *assert* as a starting point
the reality of the possible. The *primacy of essence* has a way of becoming the *primacy
of the logically necessary*, where what is not *impossible* is *necessary*, i.e., *is*.

[56] "Nihilum dicimus, cui nulla respondet notio." Wolff, *Philosophia prima*,
No. 57; cf. Nos. 59 and 60.

> *Nothing [no thing] is without a sufficient reason why it is rather
> than is not,* that is, if something is posited to be, then something
> must be posited whence it is understood why this is rather than
> is not.[57]

In his very first amplification of this proposition, Wolff returns for
a moment to the Principle of Excluded Middle and notes that either
no thing is without sufficient reason why it rather is than not; or
something is able to be without sufficient reason why it rather is
than not. If we posit A without a sufficient reason, then nothing is
to be posited whence it can be understood why A is.[58]

The long commentary Wolff makes on this passage is instructive
as to the meaning of Sufficient Reason and as an example of his
facility in gliding back and forth from the essential to the existential
sphere, from the realm of reason or explanation to that of cause or
existential change, to build up the meaning of a concept or proposition which his methodology compels him to deduce rigorously from
previous notions. For example, he says, take a cold rock becoming
warm: either there is some reason that explains (through which
it can be understood why) why the rock is hot now rather than cold,
or there is not. If there is no reason for this, then nothing is posited
in the rock or out of it to which the origin of heat can be ascribed,
which is absurd. Likewise is the case of a certain tree for which
there is a sufficient reason why it is in one place and not another.[59]

At this point, Wolff attempts to establish an ontological reference for the Principle of Sufficient Reason by "rising" from single
examples to a universal application of principle. He suggests that
"A" be substituted for the heat in the example given above and
argues that whether or not it signifies a non-existent mode in the
subject, or some attribute or even substance, this particular proof
of the absurdity of anything happening without a sufficient reason
becomes general. Examples from the world of natural bodies are
only for the sake of clarity. The general application is in so far as

[57] *"Nihil est sine ratione sufficiente, cur potius sit, quam non sit,* hoc est, *si
aliquid esse ponitur, ponendum etiam est aliquid, unde intelligitur, cur idem potius
sit, quam non sit.* Aut enim nihil est sine ratione sufficiente, cur potius sit, quam
non sit; aut aliquid esse potest absque ratione sufficiente, cur sit potius, quam non
sit No. 53." *Ibid.,* No. 70.

[58] Later, in Nos. 874-876, Wolff distinguishes three Principles of Sufficient Reason:
essendi, fiendi and *cognoscendi.*

[59] *Philosophia prima,* No. 70.

the rock or tree is a being.[60] He finds confirmation of this generalization in procedures of mathematics and physics, where demonstration by example or experiment yields a universal conclusion
applicable to all cases. There is no discussion of the implications
involved here, such as the validity of securing ontological reference
by logical universality, or the existential meaning of the rock or
tree "as a being." How does physical being become being in
general?

Before making a further and final brief exploration of this
systematic context of the Principle as it involves the object, method
and division of philosophy, two further aspects of the Principle as
presented by Wolff remain to be seen: his sketch of what he conceived to be its history, and his theory of its origin.

History of the Principle of Sufficient Reason and Theory of Its Origin according to Wolff

Wolff's history of the principle is quite brief. With less hesita-
tion than Leibniz showed,[61] he finds in Archimedes an early example of the Principle of Sufficient Reason used to establish the
principles of Statics. He also asserts that Confucius had acknowledged it as universally true and had extended it even to the realm
of moral truth.[62] The Scholastics had used the axiom "nothing is
without a cause," but since *ratio* and *causa* differ greatly, their
proposition must not be confused with the Principle of Sufficient
Reason. Descartes' elimination from philosophy of occult qualities
which could not be explained in an intelligible manner shows that
he had a clear notion of *ratio*, which is also apparent from the first
axiom he used to demonstrate by geometric method the existence
of God and the distinction of soul from body. Here, says Wolff,

[60] *Ibid.* Hans Pichler and Max Wundt unite in saying that this Principle of
Sufficient Reason in Wolff is ontological, and not logical—it applies to the reality of
things and not to mere abstract statements about things. But neither of these com-
mentators explains how Wolff makes his ontology *existential*, nor what the reality
of things means where truth is order and the more order the more truth; order here
means the nexus or connection between essences and definitions built upon concepts
which originate under the guidance of the logical Principle of Contradiction. Cf.
Pichler, *op. cit.*, 11, and Max Wundt, *Die deutsche Schulphilosophie im Zeitalter
Der Aufklärung*, (Tübingen: J. C. B. Mohr, [Paul Seebeck], 1945). p. 164.

[61] Leibniz in the *Primae Veritates* speaks of Archimedes' postulate as an example or corollary of the Principle of Sufficient Reason; cf. p. 45 *supra*.

[62] Wolff, *Philosophia prima*, No. 71. This version of the Principle's history by
Wolff becomes a stock account. For example, Dutens, *op. cit.*, p. 151, Note NN.

Descartes has at least a confused notion of the distinction between *ratio* and cause when he speaks of the immensity of God's nature as "cause or *ratio* which needs no cause for his existence."[63]

But it was the great Leibniz, concludes Wolff, who was the first to speak straightforwardly of the Principle of Sufficient Reason, and he used it as a principle in rectifying notions and demonstrating propositions."[64] Although Leibniz nowhere clearly exposed the difference between cause and reason, Wolff sees in the use he makes of the Principle of Sufficient Reason a distinction between the two which includes conformity with his own definition of sufficient reason as that whence it is understood why something is.[65]

As to the origin of the Principle, that is, an explanation of how we get it, together with a defense of its validity, Wolff relied on three points of argument to show that it is an axiom; he then goes on to confirm his position by an appeal to its "self-evidence." First, he states that the Principle of Sufficient Reason in no way contradicts experience. This is to say that no one can adduce an example where it is not operative. Any difficulties about freedom of the will and this Principle are only apparent, although he promises the question will receive further attention in *Psychology*.[66]

Secondly, he affirms that the Principle of Sufficient Reason can be abstracted as a universal from singular instances or examples of its use, and refers again to Archimedes and the equilibrium of the balance.[67] Finally, he argues that it is natural to the human mind because we are always asking "why," and it is repugnant to admit that anything can be without sufficient reason, that we are asking a question which has no answer.[68] Hence it is that the truth of this principle easily becomes known by attention to the confused notions which experience excites in our minds. Unless spoiled by perverse methods of study or by prejudice, the normal mind can accept the Principle of Sufficient Reason without proof and in the manner of an axiom.[69]

[63] *Ibid.* Cf. Descartes, *Reply to the 4th Set of Objections.*
[64] *Philosophia prima,* No. 71.
[65] *Loc. Cit.*
[66] *Ibid.,* No. 72.
[67] *Ibid.,* No. 73. Abstraction can only mean generalization for Wolff.
[68] *Philosophia prima,* No. 74.
[69] *Ibid.,* No. 75. Here Leibniz appears again as an example for Wolff's argument. He points out that in the Correspondence with Clarke, Leibniz, instead of attempting a proof of the Principle of Sufficient Reason simply appeals to the many cases of obvious experience, denies that any contrary example can be adduced and

Wolff confirms this analysis of the origin and axiomatic character of the Principle by a kind of *reductio ad absurdum,* which argues that this would be an absurd world if the Principle of Sufficinet Reason were not operative and its contrary were established. If everything was without a sufficient reason, then reality would be as fabulous as the world described in the old folk-tale, *Das Schlaraffenland* (Land of the Lazy), a kind of wishful existence where human willing takes the place of reasons for things.[70]

Although such absurd and crude tales are for the amusement of the populace, the philosopher can well afford to examine the idea embodied there of escaping from the laws of reason into a world of arbitrary desire which would be the logical result, *ad absurdum,* of no Principle of Sufficient Reason. In addition, the philosopher can see that in such a world where there would be no principle of possibility or principle of actuality extrinsic to man, neither would there be any reason for wishing one thing in preference to something else. Actually nothing would be taking place. Thus is manifest to the thinker, from the absurdity of its opposite, the strength and efficacy of the Principle of Sufficient Reason.[71]

Finally, the tale illustrates that in such a world where the human will would be the unique reason of whatever is or could be, man would be equally indifferent to wishing either side of a contradiction, with the result that in general two contradictories would be true together and the Principle of Contradiction would have no force except in a singular instance. Wolff promised to show in the

asserts that even where the sufficient reason itself is not actually known, it is still obvious that there must be one. Nor could Leibniz use the Principle to prove God's existence and foreknowledge as he does if it were not obvious. Thus, concludes Wolff, to accept the Principle of Sufficient Reason without proof is to follow the example of Euclid and other Geometricians who are unsurpassed in the rigor of their demonstrations, yet accepted the obvious truth of propositions such as *The Whole is greater than its parts,* since the truth of this latter, for example, appears in individual instances and is easily abstracted universally from single propositions, a procedure Wolff asserts Newton followed in establishing his law of inertia. (Wolff promises to show in his *Cosmology* that Newton's inertia axiom itself depends on the Principle of Sufficient Reason. Cf. *Philosophia prima,* No. 76.)

[70] Cf. *ibid.,* No. 77. In this Lubberland of Fable, whatever men desire immediately presents itself; a wish for fruit results in the immediate presence of a cherry tree, for example, and pigeons at dinner time make themselves available in edible form to the hungry eater. Note that Wolff's argument is a kind of generic one for meaning and intelligibility in the world. His adoption of it for the specific kind of intelligibility implied by the Principle of Sufficient Reason is not quite valid. Cf. No. 77.

[71] *Ibid.* No. 77.

course of the *Ontology* that to posit these two Principles is to posit the truth of things; to remove them is to destroy the difference between truth and the world of dreams. So much so that "he who admits a difference between truth and dreams must admit the universal application of the Principle of Contradiction and the function of the Principle of Sufficient Reason without any restriction."[72]

While the Principle of Sufficient Reason is a proposition within the system whereby it can function to provide the reason of things, still it is the system itself which provides the meaning of the Principle. Sufficient reason means sufficient coherence; it denotes meaning or understanding in terms of a nexus between concepts formed into definitions and marshalled in logical order for demonstration. The Principle of Sufficient Reason says, then, that everything is in order, everything is connected, everything is deducible. For the details of this order and hence for the context of *ratio* or reason of things as manipulated by Wolff in his Principle, we must start at the beginning of his system, which is to start at the beginning of his textbook series.[73]

The Principle of Sufficient Reason in the Context of Wolff's Metaphysics and Method

In the very first sentence of his "Preliminary Discourse on Philosophy in General," Wolff involves himself in the dualism of a split world already noted in Descartes and Leibniz. He took the dichotomy of the rational and the sensible as the starting point in his analysis of the nature and method of philosophy, and *ratio* was to play an important role in his process of achieving systematic unity in this situation. To sense he gave the power of knowing what things are and become in the world; to mind he attributed a consciousness of the changes which take place in itself.[74]

---

[72] *Loc. Cit.;* Wolff concludes with a reference to Thumming's use of this argument for the principle in order to distinguish reality from dreams; cf. Thumming, *Institutiones,* Ontologia No. 10. The example often appears among Wolff's later successors. For example, Bülffinger, *Dilucidationes,* No. 162; Baumeister, *Institutiones,* No. 196. We may note it as foreshadowing the epistemological use which the Principle was to have among nineteenth-century Scholastics.

[73] Systematic philosophy for Wolff is the generation of concepts by rule; his manuals supply the rule in all of its details amounting to hundreds of paragraphs. The entire series of textbooks is the rule for generating the concepts that constitute philosophical science. Cf. Pichler, *op. cit.,* p. 9, n. 1, and Wundt, *Die deutsche Schulphilosophie, op. cit.,* pp. 163-164.

[74] *"Sensum beneficio cognoscimus, quae in mundo materiali sunt atque fiunt, et mens sibi conscia est mutationum, quae in ipsa accidunt.* Nemo haec ignorat: modo

Sensation and its power to occasion changes in the mind are real.[75] But knowledge of existent reality is formed in a context where existence, to a Thomist, seems systematically meaningless and where essence has the primacy. For Wolff, as long as the actual existent real and possible worlds are rendered intelligible in terms of essential structure, there is no need to analyze or define such an obvious element as existence other than to point out its relation to the essential. The mind, conscious of changes in itself, is also conscious of the intelligibility of the essential order, and it is here, rather than in the unstable flux of the sensible world, that it grasps the real.[76] The order of essence is an order of *rationes* or reasons whereby it can be understood why something is or becomes, and there is nothing which is or becomes that does not have its reason.[77]

Philosophy in general is the knowledge or science of the reasons of those things which are or become.[78] More particularly, it is the science of possibles in so far as they are able to be; philosophy's function then is to render in strict demonstration from certain principles the reason why the possible can be actualized. This is what giving the reason for something means: to show demonstratively why it can be, and thus *ratio* or reason is "that whereby it is understood why something is."[79]

Now since sensation is radically distinct from rational knowledge, at least in its object, and since existence is systematically

semetipsum attendat." *Philosophia rationalis sive logica, Discursus praeliminaris,* No. 1.

[75] *Ibid.,* No. 2.

[76] This dichotomy between matter and spirit, body and soul, physics and metaphysics (or history and philosophy) is the point to which all discussion of the meaning of sufficient reason, and the difference between reason and cause, must recur. In this "duoverse" there is never any escape from rationalism, no getting out of the conceptual and the essential because there is no *unum per se* in our experience of being to sustain a theory of judgment which can combine the operations of intellect and sense in one cognitional operation. Nor are there any principles in being itself, and the difference between "ground" and "cause" will always be reduced to that between possible essence and real existence. There is a cleft between being and thought which forces anyone (like Jacobi, for instance) who is "not satisfied with a subjective system of concepts and demands more than clearness in logical necessity, to leave philosophy and take refuge in *Glauben,* which alone gives access to the real." Norman Wilde, *op. cit.,* p. 8.

[77] *Philosophia rationalis sive logica,* No. 4. Cf. also Nos. 575, 576.

[78] *Ibid.,* No. 6. The evolution by easy steps from this definition to the definition of philosophy as a "science of principles" is significant. Cf. Oswald Kulpe, *Introduction to Philosophy,* trans. W. B. Pillsbury and E. B. Tichener (New York: The Macmillan Co., 1897), pp. 10-11.

[79] *Philosophia rationalis,* No. 31.

meaningless in this conception, then philosophy understood as a science of reasons or *rationes* of things must be a science of essences. But the essence is the possible: the possible ultimately is the non-contradictory, and hence the primacy of essence becomes pretty much the primacy of logic. Systematic philosophy is a manipulated scheme of notions or concepts which represent essences and can be united in subject-predicate relationships that yield *rationes* or reasons whence things are understood. Ultimately, then, understanding is in terms of the system which yields at once the clearest and most distinct notions plus the most rigid inferences and legitimate demonstration.[80]

Further along in the *Logic,* Wolff puts this in terms similar to the subject-predicate analysis already noted in Leibniz. We know truth when we know the reasons for attributing a predicate to a subject.[81] And "those things by which it is determined that the predicate belongs to the subject are the *rationes* why the predicate belongs to the subject; consequently, the individual single requisites for truth are the partial reason why the predicate belongs, and all taken together constitute the sufficient reason."[82]

Wolff did not really change any of the essentials of Leibniz' concept of the universe. The ultimate reason for any predicate belonging to a subject lies within the subject itself, so that the mind, for instance, would know what it does even if body and the world did not exist. More particularly, this means that the ultimate reason or meaning of things which order and system alone can provide must lie within the realm of *a priori* reason.

"Reason is the faculty of discerning the nexus of universal truths."[83] Reason is deductive, and deductive reason is pure when

---

80 "In philosophia reddenda est ratio, cur possibilia actum consequi possint . . . Enimvero qui demonstrat, cur aliquid fieri possit, is rationem reddit, cur id fieri queat: ratio enim id est, unde intelligitur cur alterum sit. In philosophia itaque reddenda est ratio, quomodo ea, quae fieri possunt, actu fiant." *Ibid.,* No. 31.

81 *Ibid.,* No. 573.

82 *Philosophia rationalis,* Nos. 573, 578, 121.

83 Wolff, *Psychologia rationalis methodo scientifica pertractata, qua ea, quae de anima humana indubia experientiae fide innotescunt, per essentiam et naturam animae explicantur, et ad intimiorem naturae ejusque auctoris cognitionem profutura proponuntur* (Editio novissima; Verona: M. Moroni, 1779), Nos. 452-53. Cf. also *Psychologia empirica methodo scientifica pertractata, qua ea, quae de anima humana indubia experientiae fide constant, continentur* (Editio novissima; Verona: M. Moroni, 1779), No. 83. Thus Meyer's observation concerning Leibniz applies here: "The application of the mathematical mode of thought to problems of reality rests upon an acceptance of the subject-object theory of reality. It presupposes that nature

we use "only those definitions and propositions known *a priori*,"[84]
that is, grasped by inference through syllogistic deduction. By
abstracting from existence,[85] that is, not taking it into consideration,
and avoiding (but not denying) any clear-cut division between the
actual and the possible, Wolff sets up a metaphysics which is constituted like mathematics by theorems which are true propositions
even if nothing at all were in existence.[86]

Hence, because the *ratio* or reason of a thing is deduced from
the clear and distinct notions formulating its definition or assign-
ing its predicates, in *Ontology* the first step is to seek out distinct
notions of being, general and particular, and of the predicates per-
taining thereto, "in order that from those *notions* determinate
propositions may be deduced."[87] So also in *General Cosmology*
(which is the science of the *nexus* or *a priori* connection of things
to form a universe), the *rationes* of many things are derived from
the *notions* of body, matter, nature, motion, and elements as they
are elaborated in that science.[88] Likewise in *Rational Psychology*,
we derive *a priori* from one single *concept* of the human soul (*ex
unico animae humanae conceptu a priori omnia*) all those notions
which in *a posteriori* experience are observed to belong to it.[89]
This is why Wolff's *Empirical Psychology* is merely descriptive in
its nature; only in the deductive system of concepts and notions of
Rational Psychology is science, that is, metaphysics, achieved be-

is not existence *per se,* but a phenomenon of the *res cogitans.* As a consequence of
the Cartesian dualism, the material *extensio* was 'intellectualized' and 'functional-
ized.' " R. W. Meyer, *Leibnitz and the Seventeenth Century Revolution,* trans. J. P.
Stern (Cambridge, England: Bower & Bower, 1952), p. 56. Where "is" means "true"
and "true" means "deducible," then reality is established by deduction, not by sense
perception and existential judgment. Hence, everything that is can be deduced from
something else, that is, from some other truth that implies it.

  84 Wolff, *Psychologia empirica,* No. 495.

  85 The beings that we know are God, the human soul and bodies or things of
the material world. Cf. *Philosophia rationalis,* No. 55. But existence itself is a notion
so simple and obvious that it is impossible to define, says Wolff and many of his
followers. *Philosophia prima, No. 139.* Cf. Gaston Grua, *Jurisprudence,* p. 53, for
observations on Leibniz' First Philosophy which apply equally to that of Wolff.

  86 Wolff, *Psychologia empirica,* Nos. 495, 490, 498; *Psychologia rationalis,* No. 453.

  87 Wolff, *Philosophia prima,* 1729 Preface.

  88 Cf. *Cosmologia generalis methodo scientifica pertracta qua ad solidam, inprimis Dei atque naturae via sternitur* (Editio novissima; Verona: M. Moroni, 1779),
No. 119 ff. Also *Philosophia rationalis,* No. 94.

  89 "In psychologia rationali ex unico animae humanae conceptu derivamus a
priori omnia, quae eidem competere a posteriori observantur, & ex quibusdam ob-
servatis deducuntur, quemadmodum decet Philosophum." *Philosophia rationalis,*
No. 112.

cause only there in the realm of the *a priori* does the mind find those *rationes* or reasons of things which constitute philosophical knowledge.

Finally, these first three divisions, *Ontology, Cosmology* and *Psychology,* supply the starting point for the fourth and culminating part of *Metaphysics,* the science of *Natural Theology* "in which knowledge of God is linked up in a series of ratiocinations to produce certitude."[90] Because of this dependence of *Natural Theology* for its principles on the prior development of the system, it is as impossible, says Wolff, to give a popularized demonstration about God to people ignorant of his *Ontology, Cosmology,* and *Psychology* as it would be to teach astronomy to one unacquainted with geometry and trigonometry.[91] And since, from the same nominal definition used in demonstrating God's existence, all of his attributes are to be deduced, then one proof for the existence of God is sufficient. Otherwise you will have as many natural theologies as you have nominal definitions as starting points, each treating of the same object in a different way and requiring further unnecessary expenditure of labor to reduce to systematic unity.[92]

Here again the existential weakness of Wolff's system appears. The demonstration supposes a nominal definition of God already systematically established in terms of previously defined notions and concepts. God is defined as "that being in which is contained the sufficient reason of the existence of this contingent universe,"[93] and then by a manipulation of the *notions* of necessity and *ens a se,* the arrangement purports to show that this being exists.[94]

[90] *Theologia naturalis methodo scientifica pertractata. Pars prior integrum systema complectens, qua existentia et attributa Dei a posteriori demonstrantur* (Editio novissima; Verona: M. Moroni, 1779), Preface. Wolff also wrote a *Theologia naturalis methodo scientifica pertractata. Pars posterior qua exsistentia et attributa Dei ex notione entis perfectissimi et natura animae demonstrantur, et atheismi, deismi, fatalismi, naturalismi, Spinosismi, aliorumque de Deo errorum fundamenta subvertuntur* (Editio novissima; Verona: M. Moroni, 1779).

[91] *Theologia naturalis, pars prior,* Preface.

[92] *Ibid.,* No. 10.

[93] "Ex definitione nominali, qua utimur ad demonstrandam existentiam Dei, deducenda quoque sunt ipsius attributa. Ponamus aliquem in demonstranda existentia Dei hac uti definitione, quod sit ens, in quo continetur ratio sufficiens existentiae contingentis hujus universi, seu quod eodem redit, qui est causa efficiens mundi hujus aspectabilis, aut, si mavis, quod creavit caelum et terram. Ubi demonstraveris Deum existere; non aliud demonstrasti, quam existere aliquod ens, in quo continetur ratio sufficiens existentiae contingentis hujus universi, seu quod caelum et terram creaverit." *Theologia naturalis, pars prior,* No. 6.

[94] Since Wolff defines absolutely necessary being as that, the non-existence of

This, then, is the realm in which the Principle of Sufficient Reason functions as an aid to demonstrating the propositions which depend on definitions fashioned with clear and distinct ideas. It is in this context that the dichotomy between necessary reasons of the essential order and the lack of necessary reasons in the brute facts of the existential world make the question of causality a metaphysical crossroads for modern philosophy. It is perhaps making it too simple to say that in one direction lie Kant and the German Idealists, while in the other we find Locke and the French sensationists.

But it may be useful to think of the Scholastic imitators of Wolff as maintaining a kind of static tension between these tendencies. While making the metaphysics of Wolff pretty much their own, they yet refused any concession to the consequences which Kant found inherent in the position; while cognizant of the reality of the concrete singular and the value of sense knowledge of the real so important to Locke and the Empiricists, they were yet unable to integrate it as an element in their system. In this situation, the Principle of Sufficient Reason was vague and flexible enough to serve both the systematic exigencies of the essential order and the common-sense realities of the existential.

Frederick William I (1688-1740) in 1723 gave Wolff twenty-four hours to leave Halle or be hanged with a halter (*Bei Strafe des Stranges*), a threat which was a reaction to those dangers for freedom of will thought to exist in the context of the Principle of Sufficient Reason. The Jesuits, who also were alert to the moral implications of freedom and the theory of sufficient reason that seemed to them to determine the human will, nevertheless reacted to Wolff in a way more complimentary than a hanging. They were among the first to adopt his systematization for Catholic philosophy, and while criticizing him on some disparities in doctrine, proceeded to adapt their manuals to his methods of development and arrangement of matter and format.

We now turn to the German Jesuits, who produced their textbooks in the years between the death of Wolff and the suppression of the Society of Jesus (1773), and to the Franciscans, who finished out the century as imitators of Wolff. These writers were his

which is impossible (*Theologia naturalis, pars prior*, Nos. 32-34) and the impossible is that for which there is no notion, then this being really is defined in terms of that which is unthinkable (i.e., no notion of it available) by us.

imitators rather than successors.[95] It was through them that many Catholic manual-writers came under that influence of German rationalism which made itself felt even in the nineteenth and twentieth centuries.

[95] A useful distinction can be made between successors of Wolff and his imitators as these terms are used here. Chronologically, the former were both contemporaries with and subsequent to the master, while the imitators—those in whom we are interested at least—published their manuals after the death of Wolff in 1754. Geographically, both groups were chiefly residents of Germany; within Germany some geographical distinction is possible on the basis of Prussia (successors) and Austria (imitators) and then according to individual universities. As to religion, the successors were non-Catholic almost exclusively. His imitators included Catholics and non-Catholics alike.

Chapter III

⮞ Jesuit and Franciscan Use

of the Principle of

Sufficient Reason, 1750-1800

J AMES VENTURA DE RAULICA, ex-Jesuit and a former general of
the Theatines, comments sharply, in his 1861 edition of *La
philosophie chrétienne,* on the part played by the Jesuits in
propagating the philosophy of Wolff. After an acrid commentary
on Wolff's dogmatism and its failure, he says:

> Despite these defects, these warped encomiums and shortcom-
> ings, from its first appearance in the philosophical world, the
> *Logic* of Wolff encountered a crowd of fanatic admirers and
> dedicated satellites. The Jesuit Mako and his confrère, pupil
> and successor in the chair of philosophy at Vienna, Père Storche-
> nau, were of this number. Their *Logic* is only a copy, more or
> less faithful, but always pitiable, of that of Wolff. Nevertheless,
> with the aid of the powerful influence which the order to which
> they belonged exercised in the teaching of science and letters,
> they succeeded in accrediting this logical dogmatism not only
> in Germany but also in Italy and even in France.[1]

1 "Malgré ces défauts, ces fausses lueurs et ces défaillances, dès a sa première
apparition dans le monde philosophique, la Logique de Wolff rencontra une foule
d'admirateurs fanatiques et de satellites dévoués. Le jésuite Mako et son confrère,
son écolier et son successeur dans la chaire de philosophie à Vienne, le P. Storchenau,
furent de ce nombre. Leur *Logique* n'est qu'un calque, plus ou moins fidèle, mais
toujours pitoyable, de celle de Wolff. Cependant, à l'aide de la puissante influence
que la corporation dont ils ètaient membres exerçait dans l'enseignement des sciences
et des lettres, ils parvinrent à accréditer le dogmatisme logique, non-seulement en
Allemagne, mais encore en Italie et même en France." James Ventura de Raulica,
La philosophie chrétienne (Paris: Gaume Frères et J. Duprey, 1861), III, 106-107.
Ventura (1792-1861) was first a Jesuit and then later (1817) entered the Theatines
where he became Superior General in 1830. A Moderate Traditionalist of the Bonald-
Bonnetty school, he espoused the systems of de Lamennais, de Maistre and de Bo-

51

This passage is no exception to a general tendency in Ventura's historical analysis toward facile generalization. Whether or not he credits too much to the power of the Jesuits, he certainly neglects to mention both the extent of Wolff's non-Catholic influence,[2] and of his popularity with non-Jesuit Catholics. Granted there was no lack of Jesuit imitators of Wolff in the second half of the eighteenth century, the fact that the Society of Jesus was suppressed in 1773 certainly restricted the time in which its "powerful influence" could work at imposing Wolffian Logic upon Catholic philosophers. Yet, judging from the number of editions of their works, Mako[3] and Storchenau[4] are well-selected examples to which Ventura might have added the other Jesuit manual-writers it will be our purpose to examine in this first part of chapter three.

German Wolffians and the Jesuits of Austria Before the Suppression

Including a few examples of transition to the new method, the Jesuit manuals of 1750-1800 may be arranged chronologically in two groups for the two decades from mid-century to approximately the time of the Suppression (1773). On the basis of first publication dates and prescinding from any overlapping of later editions, the period from *1750 to 1760* included Erber, Redlhamer, Klaus, Hauser, and Sagner.[5]

nald; he was instrumental in "accrediting" Traditionalism in Italy. There is a brief biography in the *Catholic Encyclopedia.*

2 Wundt, op. cit., p. 74.

3 Paul Mako de Kerck-Gede, S.J. (1723-1793), taught rhetoric, mathematics, philosophy and physics at Vienna until the Suppression in 1773, when he returned to Hungary and received several ecclesiastical dignities, including the title of President of the Faculty of Philosophy at the University of Budapest. His *Compendiaria logicae institutio quam in usum candidatorum philosophiae elucubratus* went into many editions (1759, 1765, 1767, 1772, 1773, 1784, 1796) including an Italian edition at Venice in 1819 by Francis Andreola. His *Compendiaria metaphysicae institutio (1761)* had several reprints (1766, 1769, 1771, 1773, and 1784) but had only a second edition (1797), which appeared as late as 1832-33. He also produced two works on physics, many poems and much writing on mathematics; cf. Carl Sommervogel, S.J., *Bibliothèque de la Compagnie de Jésus* (Nouvelle edition, Brussels, Oscar Schepers, 1890-1900), s.v.

4 Cf. *infra*, n. 49.

5 In addition to Sommervogel, other basic bibliography includes: Joseph Burnichon, S.J., *La Compagnie de Jésus en France. Histoire d'un siècle 1814-1914* (Paris, G. Beauchesne, 1916); Bernard Duhr, S.J., *Geschichte der Jesuiten in den Ländern deutscher Zunge im 18. Jahrhundert* (München-Regensburg, G. J. Manz, 1928), IV, 2; Bernhard Jansen, S.J., *Die Pflege der Philosophie im Jesuitenorden während des 17-18. Jahrhunderts* (Fulda: Parzeller, 1938). (Also his articles in *Philoso-*

The more important, that is, the more totally Wolffian, writers appeared from *1760 to 1773*. Of these, Stattler and Storchenau are classic. They continued, after 1773, to write and publish new editions of their earlier works omitting the designation "S.J." after their names, a practice rendering identification somewhat confusing. Between 1773 and 1800 the works of other ex-Jesuits like Horvath, Monteiro, Unterrichter, and Zallinger were in circulation. Criticism of Kant also began to appear, and Horvath, Stattler and Mutschelle were authors of monographs and essays which discuss and oppose the great German.

Among the Austrian Jesuits, the break with the old "Peripatetic" organization of the philosophy manuals and the introduction of the new format came between 1745 and 1755. The story of this evolution has not yet been written in detail; here we can only indicate some of the straws in the winds of change.

From 1750-1760. The *Philosophia Peripatetica antiquorum principiis et recentiorum experimentis confirmata* (1739) of Anton Mayr, S.J., (1673-1749)[6] indicates by its title that the impact of the new science was being felt in the traditional manuals, although, as Wundt points out, the Aristotelian foundation was still there, and it was only in the order of the subject matter with its strong emphasis on physics and a corresponding reduction of space allotted to metaphysics that the trend appeared.[7] Leibniz and Wolff had not yet become a problem at Ingolstadt, although Mayr refers indignantly in his *Physica particularis,* under "De Coelo," to Wolff's audacity in asserting that giants inhabit the planet Jupiter.

There is no sign of the Principle of Sufficient Reason in Mayr, nor does it appear five years later in the posthumous edition of *Cursus philosophicus methodo scholastica elucubratus* (1750-51) by Antonius Erber, S.J., (1695-1746).[8] His discussion of principles

---

phisches Jahrbuch LI, 1938, pp. 172-215, 344-366, 435-456.) Many of the textbooks mentioned in this section of chapter three are included in the E. A. Cudahy Collection of Jesuitica at Loyola University, Chicago.

[6] Anton Mayr, S.J. (1675-1749), *Philosophia Peripatetica antiquorum principiis et recentiorum experimentis confirmata* (Geneva: Gosse, 1746); (Ingolstadt: Shleig, 1739); (Venice: N. Pezzana, 1745), etc. The four volumes of the single binding are: *Logica, Physica universalis, Physica particularis Pars Prima,* and *Pars Secunda,* this latter "Cum metaphysica." Mayr was primarily a theologian.

[7] Cf. Wundt, op. cit., p. 229.

[8] Antonius Erber, S.J. (1695-1746), *Cursus philosophicus methodo scholastica elucubratus* (Vienna: J. Trattner, 1750-1751). This work is in three parts, *Logic, General,* and *Particular Physics.*

occurs in Logic, where, while rejecting the Cartesian doubt as destructive of science, he did admit that it is difficult to decide which is the first principle: *impossibile est idem simul esse et non esse,* as the Peripatetics held, or *quidquid clare, et distincte percipio, verum est,* as the Cartesians wished.[9]

But no one, he notes, can doubt that the Peripatetic principle is true; and he exempts from application of the clear and distinct test, as a criterion of truth, such propositions as *two and two are four,* or *the whole is greater than its part* because the truth of these is immediate and not dependent on other propositions. Experience, or the internal sense alone as it experiences the truth in forming these propositions, is the rule or criterion persuasive of their truth.[10] In the *Physica generalis,* Erber devotes an article to the quiddity of principle, specifying three genera: composition *(in facto esse)*, generation *(in fieri)*, and cognition *(in cognoscendi)*. He defines the principles of cognition as "certain axioms from which the sciences deduce their conclusions."[11]

In 1755, Joseph Redlhamer, S.J., (1713-1761) did not have Erber's doubt about clear and distinct ideas as a criterion of truth. He states plainly that "the first principle of all science is the following axiom: Whatever I clearly and distinctly know of any thing can be affirmed of it with the greatest certitude."[12] Moreover, his

9 *Ibid.,* I, 472.

10 *Ibid.,* I, 475.

11 *Ibid.,* II, 23. "Principia cognitionis sunt certa axiomata ex quibus scientiae suae conclusiones deducunt: de quibus hic non agitur." Principles are concerned with the composition and generation of *things,* rather than with cognition, as a criterion of truth in these Peripatetic manuals. Also there is nearly always a discussion of the difference between principle and cause in terms of the latter implying an effect and a positive influx while the principle prescinds from these. A favorite example frequently is the relation of Persons in the Trinity. In the *Physica particularis,* Erber has an *Appendix ad metaphysicam Aristotelis* which begins as follows: "Metaphysica est habitus contemplativus entis ut sic per prima, et evidentissima principa, quae est illud: *impossibile est simul esse, et non esse.* Est igitur scientia pure speculativa. Ejus objectum materiale est ens in tota sua latitudine acceptum: formale ratio entis latissime accepti, quae nihil aliud dicit, quam aptum esse quomodocunque, seu realiter, se in intellectu, physice, vel logice, positive, vel negative, proprie denique, vel improprie: attributionis est substantia." p. 459. He demonstrates the existence of God: 1. auctoritate Apostoli ad Romanos; 2. quo Deus demonstratur sub conceptu Entis improducti; 3. sub conceptu Entis necessarii. p. 462. There is no sign of the Principle of Sufficient Reason.

12 "Primum scientiae omnis principium est sequens axioma: Quidquid clare ac distincte alicujus rei cognosco, id de ea re affirmari potest certissime." Joseph Redlhamer, S.J., (1713-1761), *Philosophiae tractatus primus seu philosophia rationalis ad praefixam in scholis nostris normam concinnati. Philosophiae tractatus alter, seu*

work marks a radical departure in format from the old Logic-Physics-Metaphysics sequence, in place of which he presents *Philosophia rationalis* in volume one. A second volume of *Metaphysics* is composed of ontology, cosmology, psychology and natural theology.

But at Augsburg in the same year 1755, Berthold Hauser, S.J., (1713-1762) professor of mathematics in the Episcopal University of Dillingen, printed the first of a series of manuals in which those familiar with Wolff must have experienced a genuine sensation of *déjà vu.* Hauser's *Elementa philosophiae ad rationis et experientiae ductum conscripta atque usibus scholasticis accommodata*[13] is a clear but cautious use of Wolff's system, adapted to tradition and designed as a middle way between the old and the new. The framework is that of Wolff, beginning with the distinction in the title itself between "Reason" and "Experience" and extending to the divisions of the sciences, first as history, mathematics, and philosophy, and then the latter into theoretical and practical. Even when disagreeing with Wolff, as was necessary for Scholastics, Hauser tried to limit its extent or to use Wolff's prestige as a suasive argument for points at issue *(Wolfio ipso fatente et docente).*[14]

metaphysicam, ontologiam, cosmologiam, psychologiam, et theologiam naturalem complectens ad praefixam etc. (Vienna: J. Trattner, 1755), I, 175. After teaching grammar and the humanities for a time, he taught philosophy for eight years at Lintz, Gratz and Vienna; there followed six years of theology at Vienna, where he died of apoplexy during class, July 9, 1761. He also wrote a *Physica generalis* and *Institutiones scholastico-dogmaticae.* His first *dissertatio* in metaphysics comprises three parts. Part one is devoted to the nature, division, notion (univocal) of being and its possibility, existence, relations. Part two concerns attributes. Part three, "De causis rerum," ends with an article on the doctrine of First Truths. They are defined as "axiomata, pronuntiata, propositiones, aut notiones adeo clarae, ut illarum veritas intellectui rite disposito statim innotescat, et unde tanquam ex principiis propositiones aliae minus evidentes rite deduci possunt." *(Philosophiae tractatus,* I, 93). The dichotomy of sense and intellect appears clearly when he says, "In eruenda veritate utimur vel solo sensu, vel ex aliis cognitis ratiocinando eligimus nondum cognita." In a list of axioms on essence and existence, the nearest to a Principle of Sufficient Reason is: "Nam quod contingenter existit, rationem, cur existat, in sua essentia non continet, alioquin necessario existeret." *Ibid.,* I, 97.

¹³ Berthold Hauser, S.J., (1713-1762), *Elementa philosophiae ad rationes et experientiae ductum conscripta atque usibus scholasticis accommodata* (Augsburg: J. Wolff, 1755-1758). Three volumes include *Logic, Ontology,* and *Pneumatology;* one is devoted to *Physica generalis* and *Physica particularis* is spread through four volumes.

¹⁴ Disagreement with Wolff on such points as the body-soul union, for instance, did not mean acceptance of any Aristotelian matter and form theory. So also in rejecting Wolff's criterion of truth ("in determinabilitate praedicati per notionem

Another Jesuit whose textbook appeared in 1755 at Vienna was Michael Klaus, S.J., (1719-1792).[15] He attempted a combination of Wolffian division and method with Buffier's *Traité de Premières veritatés* doctrine.[16] Although less directly concerned with the metaphysical formulations of the Principle of Sufficient Reason, Gaspar Sagner, S.J., (1720-1781), Roger Boscovich, S.J., (1711-1787), and Joseph Mangold, S.J., (1716-1787) may be mentioned in conclusion here.[17] Sagner exemplified the use of the Principle of Sufficient Reason to establish *a priori* the nature of the continuum; Boscovich rejected the principle and such *a priori* deduction in favor of what he considered an empirical induction of the fact of *inextension.* Mangold protested against the abuse of the Principle of Sufficient Reason by Leibniz and Wolff in connection with the perfection of the world and the liberty of God.[18] Also against Wolff he argued for the mortality and the corruptibility of the brute soul, appealing to the Principle of Sufficient Reason for support: there would be no sufficient reason for such a soul existing without a body.[19]

From these authors and this first decade after 1750 we now turn to a more detailed view of two prominent Wolffians.[20]

subjecti") he took Buffier's ("intima notionum convenientia subjecti et attributi"). *Ibid.,* I, 135, 474.

[15] Michael Klaus, S.J., (1719-1792), *Prima ac generalis philosophia, seu metaphysica quinque partibus comprehensa*: *doctrina primarum veritatum, ontologia, cosmologia, psychologia, et theologia naturalis* (Vienna: J. Trattner, 1755).

[16] For Buffier, cf. *infra.* 4, nn. 47 ff. Klaus draws on Wolff for his doctrine on the Principle of Sufficient Reason; it does not appear in Buffier.

[17] Gaspar Sagner, S.J., (1720-1781), *Institutiones philosophicae ex probatis veterum, recentiorumque sententiis adornatae in usum suorum dominorum auditorum. Tractatus III, seu Physica* (Prague: Academy Press, 1758). A later edition (1767) contained the four volumes, *Logica, Metaphysica, Physica generalis, Physica specialis,* with *Metaphysica* composed of *Ontologia, Psychologia empirica, Psychologia rationalis,* and *Theologia naturalis.* Roger Boscovich, S.J., (1711-1787), *De continuitatis lege, et ejus consectariis pertinentibus ad prima materiae elementa, eorumque vires* (Rome: Salomoni, 1754). Joseph Mangold, S.J., (1716-1787), *Philosophia rationalis et experimentalis hodiernis discentium studiis accommodata* (Ingolstadt: Cratz & Summer, 1755-56). Together with Stattler, these three were selected by Fejer in his little study of typical corpuscular theories taught at Jesuit universities in the late eighteenth century. Cf. Joseph Fejer, S.J., *Theoriae corpusculares typicae in universitatibus Societatis Jesus Saec. XVIII Monadologia Kantiana Doctrina J. Mangold, G. Sagner, R. J. Boscovich, B. Stattler* (Rome: Officium Libri Catholici, 1951).

[18] Mangold, *op. cit.,* I, 347; II, 17.

[19] *Ibid.,* III, 64.

[20] Cf. the bibliography of the following authors in Sommervogel, *op. cit.,* for additional insight into this Jesuit Wolffian movement: Antoine Boll, Joachim Zim-

From 1760 to 1773. These mid-century Jesuit textbooks just noted are but blossoms on the Wolffian tree that bears its real fruit in the works of later writers like Stattler and Storchenau. In the *Philosophia methodo scientiis propria explanata* (1769-1772) of Benedict Stattler, S.J., (1728-1797),[21] the use of the Principle of Sufficient Reason reaches almost a saturation point. Here it is granted an eminence that rivals its use in Wolff and is probably not equaled in any subsequent Scholastic work.

Stattler defines philosophy as the "science of the sufficient reason of those things which are or become or are able to be or become," and the very possibility of such a science is proved by recourse to the evident Principle of Sufficient Reason.[22]

In the first section of his *Logica,* Stattler presents the principles which are preliminary to that science; in the first chapter of the section he considers principles supposed from Ontology. He gives a neat twist to the meaning of sufficient reason in terms of cog-

merl, Nicolas Burkhaeuser, Adam Cotzen, Joseph Geiger, Joseph Reebmann, Francis N. Steinacher, and Philip Steinmeyer.

[21] Benedict Stattler, S.J., (1728-1797), *Philosophia methodo scientiis propria explanata* (Augusburg: M. Rieger & Sons, 1769-1772). This work is composed of eight volumes in six: *Logic, Ontology, Cosmology, Psychology, Natural Theology, General Physics,* and *Special Physics* (2 vols.). As a philosophy professor at Innsbruck, and before publishing this result of his philosophy lectures, he wrote: *Tractatio cosmologia de viribus et natura corporum publice proposita* (1763; *Minearologiae et metallurgiae principia physica* (Innsbruck, 1765); *Mineralogia specialis* (1766). In 1762 he won the Prize essay contest of the Bavarian academy of science with a paper on hydrostatics, later published (1775). On November 14, 1772, for the sake of uniformity, the Bavarian Provincial, Erhard, ordered that the *Compendium* of Benedict Stattler be followed as a foundation of philosophy teaching. Already on the press, this appeared as *Compendium philosophiae Benedicti Stattler professoris Theologiae Ingolstadii et soci electoralis Boicae Academiae Nonacensis* (Ingolstadt: A. Attenkover, 1773-1774). (Cf. Duhr, *op. cit.,* pp. 52-53.) It was delivered to the state Censor in 1772 and appeared after the Suppression in two volumes. *Logic, Ontology, Cosmology, Psychology,* and *Natural Theology* were in the first volume with the second volume devoted to *General* and *Special Physics,* including many mathematical and physical demonstrations. He presents the Copernican system as a theory proved with arguments from astronomy. (Copernicus was not removed from the *Index* until 1835.) Stattler was thus a scientist who taught philosophy and was teaching theology when he wrote his textbooks in philosophy. His "Anti-Kantian" writings are listed by Sommervogel.

[22] "Recte itaque *Philosophiam* definimus esse scientiam rationis sufficientis eorum, quae sunt, vel fiunt, aut esse, fierique possunt." *Philosophia methodo scientiis propria explanata,* I-1, 2. "*Philosophica scientia possibilis omino est.* Nihil enim est in rebus, cuius cognitio et intellectio evidens repugnet. Atque rerum omnium, quae sunt, fiuntque, rationes sufficientes reipsa dari, evidens est principium; ut suo loco dicetur. Non ergo earum evidens intellectio, id est, philosophica scientia, repugnat." *Loc. Cit.*

noscibility. Whatever is truly conceivable is *ens,* or something real
and all being is conceivable; if it were not, it would not be distinguished from nothing.[23]

This cognoscibility is the *ratio* of being in general, and that
which individuates or specifies any particular being, i.e., renders
it conceivable in its species or individuality, is the *ratio* of being
in a particular species or individual. If nothing more is required
beyond this *ratio* or cognoscibility to conceive or fully know the
being, then this is called the Sufficient Reason. If further concepts,
however, are necessary, then this is only an insufficient reason and
those insufficient reasons which, when taken all together, constitute the Sufficient Reason, are called the notes of the particular
being or its predicates or real *affects.*[24]

From this follow two basic propositions. 1. *Every being has a
sufficient reason and no being is without one.* In other words,
everything has its notes or predicates by which it can be fully distinguished from everything else as such. 2. *Nothing, or every non-
being whatsoever, has no sufficient reason.*[25] Taken together, these
two statements constitute or are called the *Principle* of Sufficient
Reason, a principle which in ontology is shown to be the First
Principle of all *knowledge.* This primacy appears also in the essential relation between the mind, or the faculty of knowledge,
and its object. For any knowledge to be possible there must be an
object which has cognoscibility or Sufficient Reason; for cognition
actually to exist the mind itself or the knowing faculty is required.[26]

[23] "Quidquid ergo vera sui repraesentatione in mente concipitur, vel quidquid
vere conceptibile est, ens, seu reale quid, est: et omne ens est vere conceptibile; secus
a nihilo non distingueretur." *Ibid.,* I-1, 15.

[24] "Cognoscibilitas haec seu conceptibilitas etiam *ratio entis in genere* dicitur;
et id, per quod ens quodvis in specie vel individuo habet, ut in hac specie vel individuo conceptibile sit, *ratio entis in specie,* vel individuo vocatur: quod si praeter
rationem eiusmodi ad ens plene cognoscendum nihil aliud praeterea mente concipere
opus sit, illa *ratio sufficiens entis* appellatur; *insufficiens* vero, si praeter eam adhuc
aliam concipere ad ens plene cognoscendum opus sit. Porro rationes insufficientes,
quae simul conceptae rationem sufficientem entis conficiunt, etiam vocantur *notae
entis illius,* item *praedicata, affectiones reales* etc." *Ibid.,* pp. 15-16.

[25] "*Omne ens rationem sufficientem habet: nec ens sine ratione sufficiente:* sive:
res omnis notas suas habet, quibus ab omni re alia plene discerni, seu ut talis prorsus,
et non alia, cognosci queat. *Nihilum,* seu non ens quodcunque, *nullam habet rationem
sufficientem; multo vero minus ullius entis ratio sufficiens esse potest.*" *Ibid.* p. 16.

[26] The following under the asterisk appears with the text in n. 25: "*Hoc
utrumque principium simul iunctum vocatur *principium rationis sufficientis.* In
Ontologia ostendam, hoc *primum omnium principium cognoscendi* esse. Quamquam
vel ex sola mentis, seu facultatis cognoscentis, ad obiectum essentiali relatione id

With this Principle of Sufficient Reason established in terms of cognoscibility, Stattler (reversing the order of Wolff) proceeds to the notion of contradiction, which he defines as "the identity of one and the same reality with its negation."[27] From this it follows that a contradiction is truly inconceivable, involving as it does, a reality simultaneously with its negation. Therefore, contradiction does not have the *ratio* of being, nor can it have it. Thus, every impossible is non-being and every being is possible; or, every being from the very fact that it is conceivable must lack contradiction.[28]

Worded somewhat differently, this is called the Principle of Contradiction: *idem non potest simul esse, et non esse.* Truth, therefore, and the possibility of being itself are the same. Because being is immune to contradiction, it is conceivable, i.e., true, and *vice versa.*[29]

Stattler's reversal of Wolff's relation between the Principle of Contradiction and the Principle of Sufficient Reason is strikingly evident in the conspectus of his *Ontology* and elaborated in detail in the first two chapters of Section I.[30] Ontology is divided into three sections: 1. Concerning the highest generic notions of being and proper to any individual being taken singly; 2. Concerning the notions which are derived solely from the multiplication of beings; 3. Concerning the connection and order of a plurality of beings among themselves.

The first two chapters of Section I are concerned with our two first principles; but that of Sufficient Reason comes first. In keeping with the notion of *ratio* as cognoscibility already noted above in

patet. Ut enim *cognito* quaecunque possibilis sit, obiectum esse debet, quod cognoscibilitatem, seu rationem sufficientem habeat; ut *cognitio* actu *existat,* mens ipsa, seu facultas cognoscens, requiritur." *Ibid.*, p. 16.

27 *Ibid.,* I-1, 16.

28 *"Omne impossibile est non ens; et omne ens est possibile.* Contradictio enim hoc ipso, quod realitatem simul cum eiusdem negatione involvat, vere conceptibilis non est (No. 20, n. 1) adeoque rationem entis non habet, nec ens esse potest. (No. 21). Item: *ens omne* hoc ipso, quod conceptibile sit, *contradictione carere* debet." *Ibid.,* 17.

29 *Veritas* ergo et *possibilitas entis reipsa idem sunt.* Per hoc enim quod a contradictione immune est ens, etiam habet, ut sit cognoscibile, ac vicissim." *Ibid.*

30 "Sectio I. 'De notionibus entis summe genericis, et cuivis entis simplici singillatim propriis.' Caput I. 'De veritate entis, et principio rationis sufficientis.' Caput II. 'De possibilitate entis, et principio contradictionis.' " Stattler, *Conspectus Operis Ontologiae.* Wolff, of course, put the Principle of Contradiction first. But, like Wolff, Stattler then moves on from "truth" and "possibility" to "existence": Caput III, "De existentia entis."

the Logic, the chapter is labeled, "Concerning the truth of being
and the Principle of Sufficient Reason."

In this treatment of the Principle, Stattler argues that if sufficient and adequate reason of being be defined as that which once
known leaves nothing further to be cognized in the same being,
then the Principle of Sufficient Reason can be doubted by no one
because it falls within the grasp of an immediate intuition.[31] Neither
is it to be confused with that other principle common in the schools
that *nothing is without a cause* because cause denotes that which
is the Sufficient Reason of some finite thing distinct from itself.

As to its origin, Stattler does not wish to dispute the question
whether it originated with Leibniz or was known to philosophers
before him. He thinks it was at least substantially, if confusedly,
known to traditional philosophers who held that all being is metaphysically true and all metaphysical truth is being.

Applied to God, that which has adequate cognoscibility in
itself, without reference to any other being distinct from it, is said
to be the sufficient reason of itself. Where there is a series of
rationes, they may be distinguished as proximate and immediate
and remote and mediate, with an ultimate reason which must be
its own sufficient reason. Whatever is has an ultimate reason;
otherwise there would be no sufficient proximate or remote reasons, and this would contradict the principle that nothing is without a sufficient reason.[32]

---

[31] "I. *Omne ens rationem sufficientem habet:* nec ens ullum sine ratione sufficiente; Omne ens adaequatam cognoscibilitatem habet. II. *Nihilum, seu non ens,
nullius entis ratio sufficiens esse potest: quod cognoscibilitatem non habet, non ens
est.* III. *Omne ens metaphysice verum est: et omne metaphysice verum est ens.*
IV. *Posita ratione sufficiente ponitur ens, cuius haec ratio sufficiens est,* vel, ut vulgo
dicunt, ponitur *rationatum*: cognita enim tota ratione sufficiente posita, nihil su-
perest, ut ens quoque poni cognoscatur. V. *Sublata, vel non posita, ratione sufficiente tollitur, vel non ponitur, ens,* seu rationatum, per Coroll. I. VI. *Posito ente
aliquo ceu raationate ponitur eius ratio sufficiens.* VII. *Sublato ente rationato
tollitur ratio sufficiens ita, ut saltem non adaequata superesse queat;* per Coroll. IV."
He then continues in comment: "*Sic propositum *rationis sufficientis principium,*
quemadmodum haud paullo clarius in oculos mentis incurrit, ita nemini dubium
esse potest; quia suppositis definitionibus (Nos. 5-6) datis totum sub intuitum *sensus
intimi* cadit. Ceterum confundi id non debet cum alio pridem in scholas recepto,
quod ita habet: *nihil est sine caussa.* Per *caussam* enim, ut suo loco videbimus, de-
notatur id, *quod est ratio sufficiens alicuius rei a se dictinctae et finitae*: quae adeo
solum est species, uti entis, ita et rationis sufficientis. Unde multorum datur ratio
sufficiens, quae caussa non sit. Sic Deus est ratio sufficiens suae existentiae; quae
tamen caussam non habet. *Est* nempe *omnis quidem caussa ratio sufficiens, sed non
omnis ratio sufficiens est caussa.*" Stattler, *Philosophia,* I-2, 7-8.

[32] "Quod adaequatam cognoscibilitam habet in se ipso sine alio distincto ente,

In his discussion of the Principle of Contradiction Stattler turns quickly to the question of its priority. He notes that a principle of knowledge is called a logical truth and that from its intuition, as from a sufficent reason, comes the intuition and knowledge of other truths. Similarly, an ontological principle is that from whose intuition depends the intuition and knowledge of the most general demonstrable truths which are principles of all the others. An absolute first principle is one, the intuition of whose truth does not depend on the intuition of any other principle as from its sufficient reason.[33] Ontological principles are the first fonts and bubbling springs of all human knowledge and these are what we here seek, says Stattler.

But the question is posed: which of the ontological principles is the first of all, and are there more than one of this kind of absolutely first principle? Stattler replies that while it has been customary to assign the Principle of Contradiction to first place,[34] he

dicitur *ratio sufficiens sui ipsius;* quod vero adaequate cognoscibile non est nisi per aliud ens distinctum, quod eius ratio, saltem insufficiens, sic evadit, dicitur *ens sibi insufficiens in eo genere;* in quo adaequate se solo cognoscibili non est. Realitatem utriusque notionis istius tunc ostendam; eum dari entia contingentia iuxta ac necessaria, item substantias & accidentia ostendam . . . Non sequitur ex hac notione Filium Divinum esse ens insufficiens . . ." *Ibid.*, I-2, 8-9.

[33] "Principium absolute primum est, cuius veritatis intuitus non dependet ab intuitu alterius principii tanquam a sua ratione sufficiente: *non absolute primum* principium vero est, quod ab alio dependet, quod prius illo id circo dicitur. *Principia ergo Ontologica aut sunt veritates & principia absolute prima, aut primis proxima;* quia veritatum generalissimarum, quae demonstrabiles adhuc sunt, principia existunt." *Ibid.*, 12.

[34] "*Huiusmodi principia, ceu primos humanae omnis scientiae fontes ac scaturigines hic inquirimus. Quaestio tamen est, quodnam ex principiis Ontologicis sit omnium primum? Aut num plura dentur id genus principia absolute prima? Passim *principium contradictionis* per Corollaria #phi (sic) praec, propositum (Vulgo vero alias hoc modo enuntiatum, *idem non potest simul esse, & simul non esse*) pro omnium primo absolute haberi solet, ita, ut id ex nullo alio se priore cognoscatur, & nullius alterius veritas determinate absque illo cognosci queat. *Probant* ita *apogogice.*

"Pone, principium, contradictionis ex alio principio se priore demonstrari. Poterit ergo principium illud prius adhuc esse verum, & simul non esse verum, adeoque verum simul & falsum; eo quod nondum praestabilitum ante se habeat principium contradictionis. Igitur reipsa determinate verum nec ipsum illud prius principium cognosci poterit, determinate verum nec ipsum illud prius principium cognosci poterit, neque ex eo principium contradictionis demonstrari: quae sequela absurda assumpti falsitatem prodit. At mihi falsa manifesto prima sequela videtur, quae ex assumpta prioritate alicuius principii alterius infertur; scilicet tale principium adhuc & verum simul, & simul falsum esse posse. Aio itaque." *Principium rationis sufficientis per Corollaria No. 7. propositum verum esse cognoscitur independenter a principio contradictionis." Ibid.*, I-2, 10-13.

prefers to assert that the Principle of Sufficient Reason is known to be true independently of the Principle of Contradiction.

> By immediate intimate intuition we experience the logical truth of that judgment which the Principle of Sufficient Reason expresses: *being is cognoscible,* or has a sufficient reason; and at the same time, by immediate intimate intuition we experience the logical falsity of the judgment which says *being is not cognoscible* in the fact that we know it. And so, *sensu intimo,* we know by experience *being is not at the same time cognoscible and non-cognoscible,* but only cognoscible; and therefore only true, and in no way is that principle of sufficient reason at the same time false. Now for neither of these immediate intuitions is there any need for a previous intuition or cognition of the logical truth of that judgment which expresses the universal principle of reason: being cannot at the same time be something and at the same time that same something not be.[35]

Moreover,

> The Principle of Contradiction expressed by the corollary in par. 15 is known *a priori* and depends on the Principle of Sufficient Reason distinctly asserted in par. 5 & 7. The following syllogism is proof of this. What does not have cognoscibility, is not being, but non-being; but a contradiction does not have any cognoscibility. Therefore, it is *non ens,* i.e. (by proper conversion of a negative proposition), therefore not being is at the same time the same and not the same. In this syllogism the major is the Principle of Sufficient Reason; the minor is the experience of *sensu intimo;* the conclusion is the Principle of Contradiction itself. Therefore, through paragraph 16 the Principle of Contradiction is known from the Principle of Sufficient Reason which is prior to it and itself known independently of it.[36]

Stattler then proceeds to a definition of the possible as being in so far as it is free of contradiction, or as it is without negation of itself. Whence it derives, as a consequence, that every possible has a sufficient reason because it is being, and being is without contradiction. Then, after defining determination in terms of sufficient reason and contradiction, he establishes the principles of Excluded Middle and of Individuation. From here, in approved Wolffian

[35] *Ibid.,* I-2, 13-14.
[36] *Ibid.,* I-2, 14.

fashion, that is, "methodo scientiis propria" there follows clear and distinct ideas of *reality, defect,* and *limitation.*

Following the treatment of the First Principles, Stattler then turns in chapter three to the existence of being. Existence is defined as the complement of possibility, and the relation between the actual and possible is in terms of sufficient reason: some reality must be the sufficient reason for the actual existence of a possible. This extra something "we call the complement of possibility or the very reason of existence."[37]

Throughout the rest of the *Ontology* the development of concepts and the demonstration of propositions make constant use of the Principle of Sufficient Reason. One particular point in Section III, "On the Nexus and Order of Multiple Beings among Themselves," should be noted. This connection of beings among themselves is the "ratio" which enables one to understand that the existence of one posits the existence of the other. This is the relation of principle and what flows from it. Here Stattler treats of the notion of cause.[38] "Causality, or the aptitude of cause, is that *ratio* which cause contains and through which is understood the *a priori* connection with the caused result." Rejecting Wolff's definition of *agere* as destructive of action *ad extra,* Stattler makes it the *ratio* of the existence of a different reality which is called the term of action; and "in transient action the term of action has the sufficient reason of its possibility in the patient subject."

[37] *Ibid.,* p. 19.

[38] "*Nexus* nempe rerum est ratio, ex qua intelligitur quod existentia unius posita ponatur existentia alterius, illa autem non posita nec ponatur altera. *Connexum a priori* cum altero dicitur; quo non existente tanquam ratione sufficiente non ponitur existentia alterius tanquam eius rationatum: *connexum a posteriori* vero cum altero, quo existente tanquam rationate ponitur, & quo non existent tanquam rationate non ponitur quoque existentia alterius tanquam rationis sufficientis existentiae eiusdem, *connexa a concomitanti* demum sunt, quorum unius existentia posita tanquam rationate entis tertii, ceu suae rationis sufficientis in existendo, intelligitur etiam existentia alterius tanquam itidem rationati respectu eiusdem plane tertii entis, ceu rationis sufficientis in existendo utrique illorum communis. Quae nullum prorsus in existendo inter se nexum habent, *entia in existendo disparata* vocantur. Ens demum quod absque ullo nexu cum alio quocunque ente existit, vel existere saltem potest, *ens absolutum,* quod vero non nisi cum nexu aliquo cum aliquo ente existere potest, *ens in existendo relativum* appellatur." *Ibid.,* pp. 120-121. "Quod cum altero *a priori* connexum est istius *principium,* quod a posteriori eius *principiatum* dicitur: quodsi principium et principiatum inter se absolute contingenter et mutabiliter (i.e., cum mutatione ex non connexis in connexa) connectantur; illud etiam *caussa,* istud *caussatum* appellatur, *et dependens* in existendo ab altero, seu a sua caussa. *Caussalitas,* seu *aptitudo caussae* vocatur illa ipsa ratio quam continent causa, et per quam a priori connecti posse cum caussato intelligitur." *Ibid.,* I-2, 122.

The division of causes into material and efficient is a division according to the possible and the existent, says Stattler, and the commonly-used formal cause is not really a cause at all.[39]

Although he paid tribute to the great influence and many merits of Wolff, Stattler from the very preface of his Natural Theology criticized the mistakes which vitiate the work of the master. He promised to take them into account when writing his own work. One grave error singled out as having its origin in Wolff's psychology is the concept of liberty, an error which, by the very strength of Wolff's connected reasonings, is brought into natural theology and generates further concepts detrimental to the attributes of God.[40] These errors in turn infect practical philosophy and generate error in moral science, which it is vain to answer without going back to their roots in the definitions established in natural theology and psychology.

This fundamental error on the nature of liberty, which is peculiar to the Leibnizian philosophy so prevalent at the time,[41] also influenced Stattler's arrangement of his *Natural Theology* text. Since the *Leibnitiani* argued that all necessity in this world derives from the very perfection of the divine will itself, the falsity of this contention cannot be demonstrated, and the way is thus left clear

[39] "Caussae divisionem primam maxime genericam supra iam . . . indicavimus, dividendo scilicet in *caussam materialem et eficientem,* quarum illa est solum ratio possibilitatis, haec vero ipsius existentiae. *Materialis* in *substantialem et accidentalem* dividi potest, quarum illa ipsum substantiale subjectum, ista dispositio subiecti accidentalis est . . . *Vulgo in generali caussarum definitione *formalem caussam* addere solent, quae scilicet sit ipse effectus in subiecto productus; quem tamen non aliarum caussarum more priorem natura ad se ipsum esse fatentur. Sed hoc ipso patet, caussam formalem nequaquam notionem caussae genericam participare; quia eius existentia utique secum ipsa a priori non connectitur." *Ibid.,* p. 155. *"Causa finalis est,* cuius actu nondum existentis cognitio, repraesentando eiusdem bonitatem, caussam efficientem intellectu & voluntate praeditam disponit ac ciet (sic) ad agendum et producendum vel ipsammet, vel aliquid cum ipsa a prior connexum." *Loc. Cit.*

Stattler, as the table of contents of his *Ontology* indicates, considers motion, time, and the nature of extension here rather than in *Cosmology.* This latter, already without any doctrine of matter and form to give it substance, is more of an outline of the apologetics of miracles and a remote preparation for "proving" the existence of God from the fact of law in nature. The Austrian government in 1752 forbade the teaching of Aristotelian Matter and Form doctrine, and the same prohibition was also asked for in Germany. Whether or not this was still in force at the time of Stattler's writing, the disrepute of hylomorphism was quite complete. Cf. Duhr, *op. cit.,* I, IV, 46.

[40] Stattler, *Philosophia,* III-5, and Preface (unpaginated).

[41] Cf. section one of the following chapter, "Sufficient Reason and the Accusation of Fatalism."

for a demonstration of God's existence, until the true character of divine liberty can be established.[42]

Hence, immediately after his first chapter on the existence of God, Stattler devotes almost 140 pages, all of the six articles in chapter II, to the liberty of God and the absolute contingency of this visible world. This involves such topics as: the ultimate end of creation, the problem of evil, the question of a best possible world, God's liberty in creation, and creation in time. Stattler seemed to visualize his problem, in general, as a need to rescue the contingency of the existential world from the necessities that keep cropping up in a primacy-of-essence philosophy, where contingency and necessity are involved more in the formalities of logical demonstration than in the analysis of existential being and its limitations. The reason the question of God's liberty is so important, it seemed to him, lies in the fact that ultimately contingency is dependent on free creation. His system cannot show that the existential being of our experience is contingent except by relating its existence to a free act of God.

As for proving the existence of God, Stattler describes in detail Wolff's proof and its relation to an optimum world, the sufficient reason of a composite of inseparable elements, and the contingency demonstrated from composition of elements, none of which is *ens a se*. He is critical of the flaws which he finds in Wolff's conceptions.[43] None the less, he leans heavily on cosmology to support his natural theology and supplements the more general philosophical concepts with applications of Newtonian physics.[44]

By means of the Principle of Sufficient Reason this mathematical order of the world as disclosed by physics (Newtonian) can be made to speak of an intelligent author and absolute source. There is no other sufficient reason for this ordered succession according to mathematical law. Thus, in answering those who wish the world to be eternally self-made or to have arrived by chance at its present state of development, "it is clearly evident that this marvellous order could not have originated from mere confusion without a sufficient reason wholly external to its existence."[45] From the need for an ultimate reason of order and sequence, it is also clear that

[42] Stattler, *Philosophia*, III-5, 26-27.
[43] *Ibid.*, pp. 76-78.
[44] *Ibid.*, pp. 33 ff.
[45] *Ibid.*, pp. 37-39.

this source of order must be intelligent. The emphasis is all on contingent order and contingent (God is free to create) choice; there is no metaphysics of contingent *being*.

In the third chapter of his *Natural Theology*, Stattler makes extensive use of sufficient reason to explain the object and operation of the divine intellect.[46] For instance, the total object proper to God's knowledge of simple intelligence is defined as follows:

> The adequate sufficient reason of the total object of knowledge of simple intelligence, that is, its adequate cognoscibility, is the intrinsic possibility, or immunity from contradiction of the determinate *essentialia* and attributes of any being, both infinite (i.e., God Himself) and finite, and their compossibility with the varied series of modes, and the variability of the same.[47]

So also with the object of the knowledge of vision, its adequate sufficient reason is the very infinitude of possibility of finite being as such.[48] This same infinitude of essence or divine possibilities is also the partial ultimate reason of the existence of God's free decrees, which constitute the object of God's free knowledge of vision. But the total cognoscibility, or adequate formal sufficient reason of this object of knowledge, consists in the free decrees alone.

---

[46] Chapter III, *De intellectu divino,* is composed of three articles: Art. I: De universitati objecti intellectus divini, & scientiarum divinarum diversitate. Art. II: De realitate & ratione sufficiente adaequata, seu cognoscibilitate, obiectorum cuiuslibet scientiae divinae. Art. III: De realitate ipsius cuiuslibet scientiae divinae, seu de ratione sufficiente tam possibilitatis quam existentis, cuiuslibet singillatim. Article II is composed of the following seven parts: 1. De ratione sufficiente, seu cognoscibilitate, obiecti scientiae simplicis intelligentiae. 2. De ratione sufficiente, seu cognoscibilitate, obiecti, scientiae visionis absolutae necessariae. 3. De ratione sufficiente obiecti scientiae visionis absolutae obiectorum absolutorum naturalium. 4. De ratione sufficiente obiecti scientiae visionis absolutae obiectorum creaturis rationalibus liberorum. 5. Ratio sufficiens & realitas obiecti scientiae mediae naturalis ostenditur directe & indirecte. 6. Ratio sufficiens & realitas obiecti scientiae mediae directae, item directe & indirecte ostenditur. 7. Ratio sufficiens & realitas obiecti scientiae mediae reflexae ostenditur.

[47] Ratio sufficiens adaequata totius obiecti Scientiae simplicis intelligentiae, sive eiusdem cognoscibilitas adaequata (No. 5, Ont.) est intrinseca possibilitas (No. 36, Ont.) seu immunitas a contradictione, determinationum essentialium & attributorum cuiuslibet entis, tam infiniti (ipsius nempe Dei) quam finiti, item compossibilitas earumdem cum varia serie modorum, & istorum ipsorum variabilitas. Stattler, *Philosophie,* III-5, 250.

[48] "Ratio sufficiens adaequata obiecti scientiae visionis absolutae necessariae est ipsa infinitudo possibilitas entis infiniti qua talis, seu omnes realitates puras sine defectu complectens." *Ibid.,* p. 251.

Clearly, the details of this divine epistemology, even defining *Scientia Media* in terms of sufficient reason, are not our concern here. But this sketch of Stattler's use of sufficient reason in regard to God's knowledge serves to illustrate how it was taken into a context of freedom and foreknowledge somewhat foreign to the conceptions of Leibniz and Wolff and made to function in a way not widely imitated by subsequent Scholastic tracts on natural theology.

Sigismund Storchenau, S.J. (1731-1797/98). A more usual example of late eighteenth-century use of the Principle of Sufficient Reason is found in the four-part metaphysics text, *Institutionum metaphysicorum libri IV* (1772) of Sigismund Storchenau, S.J.[49] The order of his natural theology proceeds from the essence of God to His existence; in this section only twelve pages were devoted to "De essentia Dei & Atheismo" plus "De existentia Dei Metaphysice demonstrata." God's metaphysical essence consists in His necessity for existing and the metaphysical demonstration of this existence is quite simple, and subject to doubt, says Storchenau, only by those who do not understand the terms: "If contingent being exists, so also does necessary being. But . . . Therefore."[50]

Chapter three presents the physical demonstration of God's existence from the obvious signs of intelligence and wisdom in the visible world. Newton and Cicero and a bibliography of astronomers are drawn upon as corroboration. Storchenau's moral proof rests first on the existence of common sense testimony, confirmed by over a dozen pages of data drawn from history and anthropology. A second moral argument rests on the necessity for God's existence

---

[49] Sigismund Storchenau, S.J., (1731-1797/98), *Institutionum metaphysicarum Libri IV* (editio altera; Venice: J. Trattner, 1772). This edition includes four volumes in two, i.e., *Metaphysics* and *Cosmology* in the first, *Psychology* and *Natural Theology* in the second. His first work was *Institutiones logicae* (Vienna, 1769). Both the *Logic* and the *Metaphysics* appeared together in 1775 and 1784, at Budapest in 1798 and again at Venice in 1833. Single editions of the works were quite numerous. The *Logic*: 1770, 1791, 1794, 1795, 1816, 1817, 1825, 1833; the *Metaphysics*: 1771, 1775, 1791, 1794, 1795, 1798, 1816, 1819, 1823, 1833. His *Die Philosophie der Religion* (Augsburg, 1773) and *Der Glaube der Christen wie er seyn soll* (Augsburg, 1792) were also popular, the latter going into Dutch and French translations after the turn of the century. Storchenau had taught philosophy and metaphysics at Vienna for ten years when the Jesuits were suppressed in 1773, at which time he retired to Klagenfurt where he devoted his time to study and preaching until his death in 1797 or 1798.

[50] *Institutiones metaphysicae*, II-2, 6. For a study of the relationship between both Storchenau and Stattler and Suarez, see Carl Werner, *Franz Suarez und die Scholastik der letzten Jahrhunderte* (2d ed.; Regensburg: E. L. Manz, 1889), *passim*.

if there is to be any morality, any distinction of human actions into good and bad, just and unjust. Moreover, "without opinion of God's existence no society of men can long remain tranquil."[51]

Working through the attributes of God, negative and positive, he comes to a tract on the operation of God and uses Sufficient Reason to prove conservation of creatures.[52] The last section of *Natural Theology* is "De Religione," a not unusual ending for a philosophy series at the time, where an explicit *apologia* for revealed religion and Catholic teaching reveals what is implicit in much of the actual philosophical matter. Particular reference is made to Rousseau's argument in *Emile* and to Locke's position on "natural religion."

Moving backward through the series of principal parts included in metaphysics, we find that Storchenau in his *Psychology,* divided into the two usual Wolffian partitions, uses the Principle of Sufficient Reason to discuss pre-established harmony. He argues that such a system contradicts the Principle by postulating too many states of soul, with no sufficient reason for their reality either in the soul itself or in the body.

But he exhibits the usual caution of the manual-writers in the face of the big names of the time when, after presenting a summary of pre-established harmony and occasionalism, he says of the physical influx theory or system of secondary causality only that it "can be defended by the philosopher with great probability." After all, in view of the primacy given to essence in manuals such as these, little more can be said of it than that it is not impossible, it is not openly false and it has a certain aptitude for explaining the data! In Storchenau's more orthodox Wolffian metaphysics,[53] we find the usual four-fold division. The subject matter of ontology is

[51] Storchenau, *Institutiones Metaphysicae,* II-2, 35.

[52] *Ibid.,* p. 88.

[53] Defined as: "Scientiae, quae notiones maxime universales in examen vocando, & principia demonstrationum generalissima constituendo, accuratissimas de rebus quibusvis ideas animo informare docet." *Ibid.,* I. 1. Although he divides "things known to us" into the three classes of God, soul, and matter, from which originate the ideas proper to ontology, cosmology, psychology, and theology in the approved Wolffian manner, he expresses in a scholion the following reservations: "Wolfii haec est partitio, hodieque ab omnibus fere melioris notae philosophis, si Dariesium demas, retinetur, Mea tamen opinione istud metaphysicae nomen sola sibi ontologia verius vindicat, reliquis partibus totidem separatas disciplinas constituentibus, quae principiis ontologicis proxime nituntur; ipsa enim sola in notiones maxime universales inquirit, generalissimaque ratiociniorum principia subministrat: haud igitur aberrauerit a vero, qui cosmologiam, psychologiam, & theologiam aliud reipsa esse negau-

divided according to, first, the most general principles of demonstration (Contradiction and Sufficient Reason), second, the most universal properties of being,[54] and, finally, the diverse species of being.

These general principles of demonstration are not derived by Storchenau from the notion of being but are used in the demonstrations necessary to evolve the notions which constitute metaphysical science. Since the truths to be demonstrated are either necessary or contingent, there are, as Leibniz said, two first principles, one for each of these realms of truth.[55] In the analysis of any necessary truth, the mind immediately arrives at the Principle of Contradiction.[56] And by converting analysis into synthesis every necessary truth flows legitimately from the Principles of Contradiction. This principle, *impossible est idem simul esse & non esse,* does not have any proposition prior to it from which it flows, and in no way can it be demonstrated. It is not inferred from the Principle of Excluded Middle nor does its negative formulation make it any less a principle.[57]

erit, quam applicationem ontologiae, seu potius metaphysicae ad doctrinam de mundo, anima, & deo, quemadmodum id quoque in aliis omnibus, praecipuis theoreticis scientiis usuvenit. Verum utcumque res sit, ego usitatem hodie metaphysicae explanandae partitionem, ac methodum sequar." *Ibid.,* I-1, 2.

[54] This notion of the object of metaphysics in terms of most general properties and the most general principles involved in the concept of being guides the construction of his manual. Because ontology contemplates the notions common to God, souls and matter, chief of which is that of being, then it must consider the properties and species of being, together with the indubitable principles necessary to evolve these notions. "Ex his perspicuum est, ea, de quibus ontologia agit, ad tria suprema genera revocari." *Ibid.,* p. 9. As to the question of the origin and progress of metaphysics he says: "Ad extremum quaeret fortasse aliquis, quae origo, quae progressio fuerit metaphysicae? Primum quidem communem cum reliqua philosophia fortunam experta fuit metaphysica; cum ea exorta, lentisque passibus progressa; cum ea collapsa, cum ea denique post generalem in Europa literarum instaurationem restituta brevissimumque intra tempus maximis accessionibus acuta est (Prol. in Phil.). Deinde restituae amplifiicataeque gloriam praecipue sibi vindicant Cartesius, Gassendus, Leibnitius, quos Wolfius, aliique complures praestantissimi viri in hunc usque diem secuti sunt, & ut spes est, sequenter porro: horum ego nomina, doctissimosque labores, ut occasio tulerit, abunde laudabo." *Ibid.,* I-1, 6

[55] He differed from Stattler on this.

[56] "In analysi cujuscumque veritatis necessariae statim pervenitur ad principium contradictionis. Cum in quavis veritate necessaria praedicatum ita subiecto conveniat, vel repugnet, ut non convenire, aut non repugnare, sine contradictione nequeat." *Ibid.,* p. 14. As a corollary, therefore, "omnis veritas necessaria reducitur ad principium contradictionis."

[57] *Ibid.,* p. 16. He also denies that as a model proposition it must be subsequent to pure proposition. Evidence is a font of principles, not principles themselves. It is

The section on the Principle of Contradiction closes with a long passage showing its relation to and primacy over the famous "clear and distinct" principle of the Cartesians. As for the Principle of Sufficient Reason, Storchenau states it as follows: *There is nothing without a sufficient reason.*[58] This he proceeds to amplify so that it means that:

> Whenever any predicate is truly attributed to a subject over and beyond its essence, there must be a sufficient reason which effects that this predicate belongs to this subject.[59]

This is so clear and *per se evidens* that it has all the clarity of an axiom; but since there are some who nevertheless ask for a demonstration, it can be shown by reduction to the Principle of Contradiction that the Principle of Sufficient Reason is true.[60] This is exactly opposite to Stattler's procedure, as Stattler was to Wolff.

Consequently, when the sufficient reason is postulated, then its *rationatum* also, and *vice versa.* Hence, in the analysis of any contingent truth whatever, the reduction comes immediately to the Principle of Sufficient Reason because it is the nature of contingent

not the Principle of Contradiction's evidence but its use in demonstration that makes it prime. *Ibid.,* I-1, 18-19.

[58] "*Principium rationis sufficientis* haec compellatur enunciatio: *nihil est sine ratione sufficiente.*" *Ibid.,* p. 22.

[59] "Ex his facile patet legitimam huius eunciati: *Nihil est sine ratione sufficiente:* significationem aliam esse non posse, atque hanc: *Quotiescumque praedicatum quoddam alicui subiecto praeter essentiam vere tribuitur, adesse debet ratio sufficiens, quae efficiat, ut hoc praedicatum huic subiecto conveniat.* Sensus hic videtur ad mentem Leibnitii maxime accommodatus esse; cur enim is principium hoc saepius vocat principium convenientiae? Nonne, quia rationem reddit, cur hoc, vel illud subiecto cuidam conveniat, vel non conveniat? Iam vero enuntiatio haec ita intellecta non potest non esse verissima, per se evidens, atque adeo verum axioma: possum igitur Leibnitii exemplo illius demonstratione omnino supersedere, atque ad casus duntaxat singulares, ac experientiam provocare; quia tamen sunt nonnulli, qui eiusdem claritate se perstringi inficiantur, eamque ob caussam, ut sibi demonstretur, postulant, petitioni huic aequae, an iniquae satisfaciam." *Ibid.,* I-1, 22-23.

[60] "*Nihil est sine ratione sufficiente,* id est, *cum praedicatum subiecto praeter essentiam vero tribuitur, debet esse aliquid, quod efficit, ut hoc praedicatum huic subiecto conveniat.* Si nihil esset, quod efficeret, ut posita in hypothesi praedicatum *a* conveniat subiecto *b,* etiam nihil esset, quod efficeret, ut in eadem hypothesi contradictiorium praedicati *a* nempe *non-a* non conveniat subiecto *b;* sed si nihil esset, quod efficeret, ut in dicta hypothesi contradictorium praedicati *a* non conveniat subiecto *b,* tum posset contradictorium praedicati *a,* seu *non-a* in eadem hypothesi subiecto *b* convenire, quod cum principio contradictionis pugnat: ergo cum praedicatum *a* subiecto *b* praeter essentiam vere tribuitur, debet esse aliquid, quod efficit, ut praedicatum *a* subiecto *b* conveniat, sive nihil est sine ratione sufficiente." *Ibid.,* I-1, 23.

truth that the predicate belongs to the subject over and above the essence of the thing. Analysis reveals immediately there must be something present which brings about this union of subject and predicate; this is to arrive at the Principle of Sufficient Reason.[61]

As with the Principle of Contradiction, here, again by converting analysis into synthesis, every contingent truth legitimately proceeds from the Principle of Sufficient Reason, and what so proceeds is demonstrated by that principle.[62] The Principle of Sufficient Reason is then the first principle of all contingent truth.

The chapter closes with five objections answered at some length,[63] and Chapter III institutes a short discussion of the relation between the Principle of Contradiction and that of Sufficient Reason. As with Wolff, Storchenau reduces the latter to the former because its analysis depends on the impossibility of anything both being and not being at the same time.[64] Hence also it follows that all contingent truths are mediately reduced to the Principle of Contradiction since they are reduced to the Principle of Sufficient Reason, which in turn reduces to Contradiction.[65]

Applied to ontology then, it is clear, says Storchenau, that the two principles, as Leibniz pointed out, are *required* because that science must set forth both the essence of being and those elements which actually or possibly pertain to or adhere to that essence. The Principle of Contradiction is the "principle of essences." Other

[61] "Posita ratione sufficiente ponitur rationatum, & vicissim; item sublata ratione sufficiente tolitur rationatum, & vicissim." *Ibid.*, p. 24. "In analysi cuiuscumque veritatis contingentis statim pervenitur ad principium rationis sufficientis. Cum in omni veritati contingente praedicatum praeter essentiam subiecto conveniat, ut ex natura harum veritatum patet, in illius analysi progrediens statim deprehendo aliquid, quod efficit, ut hoc praedicatum huius subiecto conveniat; sed hoc est pervenire ad principium rationis sufficientis." *Ibid.,* I-1, 25.

[62] "*Omnis veritas contingens per principium rationis sufficientis demonstratur.* Omnis veritas contingens analytice reducitur ad principium rationis sufficientis; ergo etiam analysis convertendo in synthesin omnis veritas contingens ex principio rationis sufficientis legitime profluit; sed veritas, quae ex altera legitime profluit, per eam demonstratur; ergo omnis veritas contingens per principium rationis sufficientis demonstratur." *Ibid.,* p. 26. "*Principium rationis sufficientis est primum omnium veritatum contingentium principium.*" *Loc. Cit.*

[63] *Ibid.,* I-1, 26-31.

[64] "*Principium rationis sufficientis reducitur ad principium contradictionis.* Omnis ea veritas reducitur ad principium contradictionis, in cuius analysi eo pervenio, ut deprehendam, aliquid, si ita non esset, simul fore, & non fore; sed in analysi principii rationis sufficientis deprehendo aliquid, si illud falsum esset, fore simul, & non fore; ergo principium rationis sufficientis reducitur ad principium contradictionis." *Ibid.,* I-1, 31.

[65] *Loc. Cit.*

aspects of being pertain to the Principle of Sufficient Reason since it governs the predicates of contingent things and can be called the "principle of existence." These principles also *suffice* for the science of ontology because they fully satisfy the question: why anything is or why any given enunciation is true—a question we spontaneously ask out of a natural propensity of the mind as soon as we observe anything to be.[66]

The Principle of Sufficient Reason Among Certain Franciscans

Franciscan manual-writers also reflected the current of the times in the second half of the eighteenth century. As with the Jesuits, an effort was made at the mid-point of the century to defend the old Peripatetic tradition; unlike the Jesuits, the defense was particularly committed to the principles of Scotus. In 1743 Joseph Ferrar, O.F.M.Conv., produced a *Philosophica Peripatetica adversus veteres, et recentiores praesertim philosophos firmioribus principiis propugnata.*[67] Ten years later (1754) an enlarged edition was printed at Venice and included responses and objections by Fortunatus of Brescia.[68]

[66] "Schol. 1. Atque haec sunt duo illa omnium nostrorum ratiociniorum, ac demonstrationum principia, de quibus ita Leibnitius . . . Haec porro duo principia & requiruntur, & sufficiunt; requiruntur: quia in ontologia exponi debet tam essentia entis, quam ea, quae in eadem praeter essentiam vel insunt, vel inesse possunt; essentia vero ad principium contradictionis, quod propterea *principium essentiarum;* reliqua ad principium rationis sufficientis, quod ab existentia, velut primario ex contingentibus praedicato, *principium exsistentiarum* dici consuevit, pertinent; sufficiunt: quia plene satisfaciunt questioni. *cur aliquid sit,* vel *cur data quaevis enunciatio vera sit?* quam ex naturali mentis propensione ponimus, quamprimum aliquid esse observamus. Restat ut nonnullis dubiis occuram." *Ibid.,* pp. 32-33. These doubts concern necessity and are answered by the distinction between mediate and immediate demonstration by the principle of contradiction.

[67] Joseph Anthony Ferrar, O.F.M.Conv., *Philosophica Peripatetica adversus veteres, et recentiores praesertim philosophos firmioribus propugnata rationibus Joannis Dunsii Scoti Subtilium principiis* (2nd ed.; Venice: T. Bettinelli, 1754). Volume one contains a Prolegomena to philosophy, *Logic* and *Metaphysics,* together with *Ethics. General Physics* and *Special Physics* make up the last two volumes, although he calls volume two the first part of physics and volume three the second and third parts, not using the term Special Physics. Both of these volumes are provided with the usual diagrams of machines, figures, etc.

[68] Fortunatus a Brixia, O.F.M. (1701-1754), *Dissertatio Physico-Theologica, de qualitatibus corporum sensibilibus* (Brescia: J. Rizzardi, 1741). Fortunatus is also the author of *Philosophia mentis methodice tractata atque ad usus academicos accommodata* (Brescia: J. Rizzardi, 1741-42) in which the Principle of Sufficient Reason figures as an axiom under his discussion in ontology in "De rerum essentia & exsistentia." *Ibid.,* II, 33. He thinks it was known to the Scholastics as "nihil gratis, sive

In his preface, Ferrar promises to espouse the whole of philosophy and not merely the old Peripatetic subject matter, although this latter must be made firm by evidence submitted from recent experimental philosophy. Volume one, he promises, will present the new opinions as well as the old questions, leaving aside the minutiae which are only disputes about words. To the usual Aristotelian list *(Nichomachaean Ethics* vi, 6) of virtues Ferrar adds a sixth, "the virtue of opinion" by which our minds so assent to a proposition in such a way as not to rest in evident certitude. This is necessary because in Ferrar's philosophy (which also includes his physics) there are many things which we know only as bare conjecture.

There is no trace of the "new method" in his division of philosophy; he includes himself among those who use the Peripatetic method and he ascribes its source to Peter Lombard, the parent of Scholasticism. It is not surprising then that there is no trace of the Principle of Sufficient Reason in this work of the Italian Franciscan. But it is useful to note the context in which his early reference to First Principles occurs.

With an eye to the skeptics of the time, Ferrar says there are three great certitudes on which we can depend: First Principles, the existence of bodies and the existence of the acts of our own minds.

> Indeed there are first principles which are certain and clearly established; such as *Impossible est idem simul esse, & non esse; omne totum esse majus sua parte,* and similar ones as the Teacher [Scotus] shows. Those terms from which First Principles arise [coalescunt] are such that one includes the other and the knowledge of one also embraces knowledge of the other. When our intellect perceives those terms, it must also perceive their mutual connection or repugnance . . .[69]

sine causa." *Loc Cit.* In part two of his *Metaphysics,* Fortunatus devotes a long section (pp. 306-309) to the refutation of pre-established harmony, with detailed reference to Wolff's *Psychology* and at one point arguing that the harmony system violates the Principle of Sufficient Reason.

[69] "Et quidem prima principia certa prorsus esse & explorata: qualia sunt, *Impossibile est idem simul esse, & non esse: Omne totum est majus sua parte;* atque his similia; sic ostendit Doctor. Termini illi, ex quibus Prima Principia coalescunt, sic se habent, ut unus alterum includat, atque unius notitia notitiam quoque imbibat alterius. Quoties ergo intellectus noster terminos illos percipiat, oportet etiam attingat eorum invicem connexionem, aut repugnantiam . . . Atque adeo cum mens nostra non possit simul explicite duobus assentiri contradictoris: hoc est, nequeat

In his Metaphysics,[70] Ferrar returns to the Principle of Contradiction where, after a first disputation "Concerning Being and its properties," he devotes the whole of disputation six to the single question: "What ought to constitute the First Principles of certain knowledge?" It belongs to metaphysics to answer this question; and, while according to Scotus there are no principles of being in so far as it is being, being nevertheless does have principles of knowing, "which can be manifested in certain general axioms and can guide those demonstrations which we undertake concerning Being itself."[71]

The Cartesian *Cogito ergo sum* and its systematic function are explained at length only to be rejected in favor of what the Peripatetics set up as alone constituting the First Principle: *Impossible est idem simul esse & non esse.*[72]

---

simul affirmare, & negare: idcirco necessario primorum principiorum veritati assentitur: nec nisi voce tenus eadem valet abjicere." Ferrar, *Philosophica Peripatetica*, I, 13.

[70] His metaphysics is composed of two parts: *Ontologia* and *Pneumatologia*. This latter includes *Theologia naturalis* (First disputation is "De Deo, & Illius Perfectionibus") and part of *Psychology*. God's existence is demonstrated from sensible things, which are contingent and could not exist unless God, "ens videlicet summe necessarium" did also; the unity of God is gathered from his government of the world. "Sed & illae omnis generis perfectiones, quas Deo attribuimus, eae omnes ducuntur ex rebus, quas vulgo miramur in nobis, detractis earum imperfectionibus quibuscumque." *Ibid.*, I, 105.

[71] "Entis, in quantum Ens, nulla esse principiis essendi. Nihilominus, ita idem Doctor affirmat, habet ens principia cognoscendi; quippe generalibus quibusdam axiomatibus patefieri possunt, & dirigi demonstrationes illae, quas circa Ens ipsum instituimus." *Ibid.*, I, 156.

[72] "Peripatetici hoc unicum constituunt Principium Primum: *Impossibile est idem simul esse* & non *esse.*" *Ibid.*, p. 158. "Dicimus tertio, propositionem illam: Impossibile est . . . habere rationem Primi Principii in genere demonstrationis redarguitivae: ut scribit Aristoteles quarto Metaphysicae, & Scotus assentitur in primo, distinctione tertia, quaestione quarta. Verum in altero ordine Demonstrationis ostensivae, nec illud: impossibile est &c., nec aliud quidpiam constitui potest *a priori* principium. Tantumodo nobis fas est, *a posteriori* intima rerum praedicata colligere: ut, quemadmodum diximus in loco citato Logicae, cognita ex effectis intimiore proprietate rei, hinc essentiam illius utcumque describamus, eandemque ab aliis secernamus . . . Principium illud: Impossible est &c. essentiis rerum explicandis non est aptum. Non ergo spectat ad genus demonstrationis ostensivae, cujus proprium est, rerum naturas explanare. Antecedens probatur. Eo principio cognito, adhuc rerum essentias ignoramus, quae in sese sint, & quales,; atque principium illud non evincit, quid sit res, sed solum quid non sit; & solummodo probat, non posse rem non esse, si est." *Ibid.*, p. 162. "Inter cetera Metaphysici munera illud merito recensetur, quod in primo certae cognitionis principio assignando versatur. Porro Primum Principium illud est, quod praestat omnibus aliis, tum certitudine, & firmitate, tum evidentia, tum officio; adeo ut ex eo cetera profluant, illud ex nullo." *Ibid.*, I, 157.

Whether it was due to the passage of time or to the circumstances of location in Germany, there appeared, less than ten years later, at Augsburg, a Franciscan textbook which combined basic Scotistic notions with the Wolffian order of ontology. The Principle of Sufficient Reason now has its accustomed place after the Principle of Contradiction, at the very beginning of the dissertation "Concerning the Concept of Being and its Attributes in General." This is the *Metaphysica vetus & nova* (1761) of Herman Osterrieder, O.F.M.Conv., (1719-1783).[73]

Written in sequence to a *Logica* by the same author, the work is designed for those beginners in philosophy who do not have the time for physics and yet who want to study theology or law (but not medicine) without difficulty. This is a practical purpose which has several theoretical implications in any division of the sciences and in the question of the object of metaphysics.

Briefly indicated in the title, this pedagogical end-in-view receives some elaboration in the author's preface. From the body of matter assigned to the old physics, Osterrieder transferred to metaphysics certain tracts such as those on causes and on the rational soul, left aside those subjects which are more subtle than useful, and resigned himself and his readers to the fact that not everyone has time for the vast amount of matter involved in the experimental physics of the current scene.

Since metaphysics has a strict connection with logic and supplies solid principles for the other sciences, it is rightly treated in modern schools immediately after logic; it is good procedure to take up the universal nature of being and the most general principles before coming to the particular sciences. Of the greatest utility to beginners aspiring to the study of theology, this science treats of the ideas of the mind and the first principles.[74] It is a speculative science which concerns being in general and its conditions as abstracted by the mind, and more particularly deals with immaterial substances within the range of natural knowledge.

---

[73] Herman Osterrieder, O.F.M.Conv., (1719-1783), *Metaphysica vetus & nova, logicae criticae nuper editae tanquam pars altera adjuncta, usibusque philosophiae tyronum sic accommodata, ut hi, solis istis duabus partibus mediantibus, etiam sine physica ad SS theologiam aut jurisprudentiam absque difficultate ascendere valeant* (Augsburg: M. Rieger, 1761). Osterrieder taught philosophy to Franciscan students in Ratisbonn.

[74] Osterrieder, *op. cit.*, Prolegomena metaphysicae (unpaginated).

Because abstraction from matter is either universal or particular, metaphysics has a two-fold generic division, each distributed further into the four parts characteristic of Wolff. Osterrieder, for the sake of brevity, reserved cosmology for treatment in general and particular physics, where its matter is particularly congruous. Like Ferrar, he quotes Aristotle to justify ontology as "the knowledge of first principles or common axioms, which are forged from the most obvious ideas."[75]

The most obvious idea, of course, is that of Being and the first dissertation concerns *being in general* and its common attributes. There is a preliminary section on the first principles of human cognition organized on the basis of necessary and contingent truths, which results in two articles: one on the Principle of Contradiction, the other on the Principle of Sufficient Reason. He defines a First Principle as "that kind of proposition which occupies first place in a series of truths in such a way that all the following truths are deduced from it and ultimately can be reduced to it."[76] The Principle of Contradiction is that proposition formulated by Aristotle as: *Impossible est idem simul esse, & non esse.* Osterrieder gives it a logical interpretation and an orientation to essence[77] and proves by the priority of its position in all demonstration that it is absolutely first of all first principles of truth. Thus the Principle of Sufficient Reason can be only relatively first in respect to contingent

---

[75] Aristotle, *Nic. Eth.* vi, 6. "Cognitio primorum principiorum, seu Axiomatum communium, quae ex ideis notissimis sunt conflata; male vero, nec sine gravi injuria praeclarissimam utilissimamque hanc scientiam aliis praesumunt nominare Lexicon Philosophicum, aut faraginem terminorum barbarorum, vel sulvam spinosarum subtilitatum." *Ibid.,* pp. 11-12.

[76] "Est autem Principium primum talis propositio, quae in serie veritatum prima existit, adeo ut ex illa veritates reliquae omnes deduci, atque in eam ultimato resolvi queant. Sic e.g. est haec propositio: anima est ens simplex, a plerisque Philosophis assignatur pro principio hujus propositionis: anima est immortalis, eo quod omnis de animae immortalitate demonstratio in eam recidat. Quia porro omnes, quas cognoscimus veritates, vel necessariae sunt, vel contingentes (Log.), duplicis quoque generis Principia pro hac duplici veritatum classe vulgo assignantur, nempe pro necessariis Principium contradictionis, pro contingentibus vero rationis sufficientis principium, agamus de singulis!" *Ibid.,* pp. 16-17.

[77] "Nempe quia sublata hujus propositionis veritate aperta sequeretur contradictio, hinc merito contradictionis principium ab omnibus indigitatur. Et quia insuper rerum essentiae aeque ac necessitas ex eodem principio determinatur, ut sit haec potius quam alia, Principium quoque necessitatis, et essentiarum ab aliis audit. Propositio: Principium Contradictionis est omnis omnino veritatis principium absolute primum." *Ibid.,* pp. 17-18.

truths, and it flows from and derives its force from the Principle of Contradiction.[78]

Osterrieder begins his article on this relatively first Principle with a definition of Sufficient Reason as "that motive or end from which it is known why some other thing exists."[79] He then distinguishes six species of Sufficient Reason: possibility, actuality, extrinsic, intrinsic, simple, composite—distinctions which seem designed especially for discussing the theological problems of free will and grace.[80]

In differentiating Sufficient Reason from physical efficient causality, the notion of finality again appears. A man is the physical cause of his own walking because he really and effectively contains the reason of the walking in himself; he effects it. But the motive for walking, that is, to visit a friend, has not a physical but only a moral influx or influence on the actual walking.[81]

This distinction is noteworthy. Among the subtitles judged to be useless and dropped from metaphysics by many of the Scholastics of the eighteenth century is the "physical reality" of any causality other than efficient.[82] Nonetheless, as Osterrieder continues, "The following proposition always remains and will remain true: Nothing becomes or happens without a sufficient reason."[83]

This statement of the Principle of Sufficient Reason and its proof[84] lead to certain corollaries which we note briefly only as an

---

[78] *Ibid.*, 25-26.

[79] "Ratio sufficiens vocatur illud vel motivum vel finis, ex quo cognoscitur, cur alterum existat. e.g. aeterna beatitudo est homini probo ratio sufficiens, ut in hoc mundo abneget semetipsum, et sequatur Christum." *Ibid.*, pp. 22-23.

[80] For some of the literature on this subject see part one of chapter four, *infra*.

[81] "Ratio sufficiens a causa efficiente physica per hoc distinguitur, quia haec rationem alterius in se vere realiter & effective continet, non autem semper illa, e.g., Sempronius est causa physica efficiens deambulationis, quam facit; ratio vero sufficiens, ob quam deambulat, potest esse vel repraesentatio tempestatis amaenae, vel visitatio amici, vel devotio in templo persolvenda &c. quarum nulla in deambulationem physice influit, sed solum moraliter, ut consideranti liquet." Osterrieder, *Metaphysica vetus & nova*, p. 24.

[82] Thus the Principle of Sufficient Reason seems to do service for the unpopular Principle of Finality.

[83] "Interea tamen vera semper manet atque manebit sequens Propositio: Nihil fit, sive contingit, absque ratione sufficientie." *Ibid.*, p. 24.

[84] "Probatur. Si aliquid fieret absque ratione sufficiente, sequeretur, quod TO nihilum illam rem produxisset, adeoque etiam TO nihilum existeret, (nam non existens nil agere vel producere potest) & simul non existeret, (quia alias non esset nihilum) atqui hoc fieri nequit: ergo &c." *Ibid.*, p. 24. After adding the proof of the minor, Osterrieder provides an argument from Holy Scripture: "Accedit Authoritas S. Scripturae dicentis Job. 5. v. 6 nihil in terra sine causa fit." *Ibid.*, p. 25.

example of how much of the writing on the subject in manuals previous to his has been gathered in as grist for Osterrieder's mill, without delaying on the controversies and assumptions involved.

I. The Principle is relatively prior to the Principle of Contradiction in virtue of the distinction between necessary and contingent truths. II. It is universal and applies throughout the range of all contingent being, whether corporeal or spiritual. In the latter segment however it is only suasive, not necessitating, and in moral action the exercise of free will itself is a Sufficient Reason. III. Whatever has a Sufficient Reason has it in itself or in another; only God has the Sufficient Reason for His existence in Himself. IV. Whatever exists is conceivable in itself.[85]

Hence, as a Scholion, and in final focus on the theological *finis* of the manual, the author points out that the Principle of Sufficient Reason is not accurately employed in matters dealing with the Supernatural order and in necessary things, unless careful distinction is made between the external and internal Sufficient Reason; for example, the external Sufficient Reason of a Mystery is the authority of revelation; its internal Reason may be assent. The failures in Wolff and the Leibnizian doctrine of First Principles of things, says Osterrieder, are rooted in their neglect to make this important distinction.[86]

Another ten year interval in this survey of Franciscan manuals returns us to Italy and *Elementa philosophica in adolescentium usum ex probatis auctoribus adornata* by Laurentius Altieri, O.F.M.Conv.[87] The third edition of this work (1779) was printed in the same city, Venice, by the same printer, Bettinelli, who pro-

85 *Ibid.,* pp. 25-26.

86 "Scholion. Principium rationis sufficientis in rebus supernaturalibus, & ad fidem immediate pertinentibus, sicut & in rebus necessariis, (hoc est primas rerum essentias, concernentibus) universaliter non procedit, nisi accurate fiat divisio rationis sufficientis in externam & internam, primam hic voco authoritatem revelationis, in qua sola circa ejusdem Mysteria habetur ratio sufficiens, etsi altera seu interna desit valetque hic illa S. Prosperi sententia de vocat. gent. Lauda & venerare, quod agitur, quia tum est nescire, quod agitur. Ex hac ignorata, vel insuperhabita divisione rationis sufficientis in intrinsecam & extrinsecam non unum est, (ut ait Cl. P. Fort. A Brix. Phy. Gen. p. 1, No. 531) tam in Wolfiana, quam Leibnitiana de primis rerum principiis doctrina, quod plane corruat, nempe in illis determinandis ratio tota producti est voluntas producentis, Dei scilicet, qui teste Psalmista, omnia quaecunque voluit, fecit, Ps. 113 v. 11. Huic etiam supposito innititur decantatum illud Axioma: id quod omne ratione sufficiente (tam interna, quam externa) destituitur, nec est, nec esse potest." Osterrieder, *Metaphysica vetus & nova,* pp. 26-27.

87 Laurentius Altieri, O.F.M.Conv., *Elementa philosophiae in adolescentium usum ex probatis auctoribus adornata* (Editio tertia; Venice: T. Bettinelli, 1779).

duced the 1754 second edition of Ferrar noted at the beginning of this section.

As in Ferrar, the work comprises three volumes, the first including a prolegomena to metaphysics and the elements of logic; the second, the elements of metaphysics and general physics; and the third, the elements of special physics. Unlike Ferrar, Altieri eliminated ethics for the sake of brevity; unlike Osterrieder, he included physics and sought to present beginners destined for theology the aspects of recent philosophy of which they should not be ignorant, yet without presuming that they have much time for difficult and prolonged study. Useless loquacity avoided, he wished to make full use of the mathematical method without, however, minimizing the syllogistic form.

From a brief survey of the elements of arithmetic as a beginning, he proceeds then to logic and metaphysics. His use of both old and new is professedly eclectic and free of detailed commitment to any system. An important aspect of his logic format, which presages future arrangements of philosophy manuals is seen in the emphasis given to *critica*. Logic is defined as that part of philosophy which directs the mind in finding truth, "or which lays down the rules by which the trained mind is able to distinguish the true from the false."[88] Logic is divided into two parts, the second of which, "Exercitationes Scholasticae," concerns itself with the existence of truth and its criterions.[89]

Metaphysics or "scientia ultra naturam" has immaterial things for its object: God, angels, human mind, and the material objects of physics, in so far as they are abstracted from matter to furnish immaterial concepts common to both material and immaterial being, such as the notions of being, possibility, and future.[90]

In his *Ontology* Altieri was more inclusive than earlier writers in his listing of candidates for the position of First Principle. Although, he says, the Peripatetics and some moderns take Aristotle's Principle of Contradiction as first, others suggest *ex nihilo nihil fit,* concerning the truth of which all philosophers agree; or that of the Scotists, *ens est ens;* or that of Locke, *whatever is, is;* or even that of Descartes, *ego cogito, ergo sum.*[91]

---

[88] *Ibid.,* I, 184.
[89] *Loc. Cit.*
[90] *Ibid.,* II, 1.
[91] *Ibid.,* pp. 8-9.

But there is no need to decide definitely which of these is to be preferred to the others since the truth of all of them depends on rational evidence, and the Principle of Contradiction can be used with the greatest utility for finding out necessary truth. The process of discovering necessary truths proceeds by showing the impossibility of some attributes because of their repugnance to the essential determinations of a thing, or their possibility from the lack of repugnance in their notes.[92]

Since, however, to determine the possibility of something from the Principle of Contradiction is not to establish its existence, a further principle is necessary. This, as Leibniz said, is the Principle of Sufficient Reason.[93] Concerning this Principle, Altieri makes three further precisions: (1) Sufficient reason is not to be confused with cause. (2) Nothing is more opportune than the Principle of Sufficient Reason for seeking the cause of things. (3) The distinction between external and internal, as made in Osterrieder, is to be observed.[94]

---

[92] *Ibid.,* p. 9.

[93] "Demonstrata tamen ex principio contradictionis rei possibilitate, non inde sequitur ejusdem existentia: sic ex quo aliquis demonstraret non repugnare bruta operari, ut videmus, absque anima, non inde sequeretur revera bruta esse puras machinas quacunque anima destitutas. Hinc pro rerum contingentium existentia comprobanda aliud assignant principium Metaphysici cum Leibnitio, nempe principium *rationis sufficientis*: nomine autem *rationis sufficientis* intelligunt id unde colligimus cur aliquid sit, vel fiat, curque hoc potius modo sit, vel fiat, quam alio: sic video duo corpora in aequilibrio posita quiescere, licet deorsum utrumque nitatur: hujusce quietis ratio est virium aequalitas, ac contrarietas, haec proinde erit *ratio sufficiens,* cur illa corpora aequilibrium servent. Hoc principio usi sunt etiam veteres; uti observat Brukerius (in Hist. Crit. Phil. 7. 5.)." *Ibid.,* II, 9-10.

[94] "Sedulo tamen advertendum est ne ratio sufficiens alicujus rei cum ejus caussa confundatur. Nam datur quidem ratio sufficiens cur existat Deus, quae in ejus perfectissima essentia includitur, non tamen datur caussa ejus non existentiae. Similiter voluntatis divinae potest aliqua sufficiens ratio assignari, non tamen ulla caussa. Caussa itaque, cum est completa, debet sui effectus sufficientem rationem continere, non tamen debet cum ipsa confundi: id est data caussa explicari ex ipsa debent ejus effectus intelligibili modo, sive per rationem sufficientem in ipsa caussa comprehensam. Hinc Peripatetici qui multorum effectuum caussas assignabant occultas qualitates, nec illorum effectum sufficientem rationem nec veram propterea caussam assignabant: sed inanem terminum pro caussa habebant. Igitur principium rationis sufficientis diversum plane est ab illo Scholasticorum *nihil est sine caussa*: cum hoc secundum pendeat a primo; si enim aliquid fieri potest sine ratione sufficienti, cur fiat, poterit etiam aliquid fieri sine caussa.

"Nihil porro principio rationis sufficientis opportunius ad inquirendas veras rerum caussas, quas investigare tenetur Philosophus, atque ad seponenda animi praejudicia. Cum enim nihil existere possit absque sufficienti ratione, alias mundus fortuito existeret, quod absurdum est, profecto ubi rerum sufficientem inquiimus

Chapter three ends the first part of Altieri's *Metaphysics* with the promise that the use of the Principle of Sufficient Reason will become clearer as the course of philosophy progresses.[95] With this in mind, we might expect to find the Principle at work in his demonstration of God's existence. But he argues from contingent being back to the demand for necessary being as a cause of everything, without reference to Sufficient Reason.[96]

In the *General Physics* he gives three rules from Newton and one from Leibniz as rules of philosophy. This latter rule is the Principle of Sufficient Reason. At the beginning of the *Special Physics* he touches the problem of an eternal world and, before answering objections on creation, laying it down to be held as certain that God operates freely and out of His infinite wisdom and in such a way that, even in God, there is place for a sufficient reason. In answering objections based on a supposed conflict between sufficient reason and free will in God, he makes use of the distinction between moral and physical necessity; there is no reference to any metaphysics of God's knowledge or to a doctrine of exemplarity.[97]

One final and quite prominent example of Franciscan manuals using the Principle of Sufficient Reason is the text of Joseph Tamagna, O.F.M.Conv.[98] Printed at Rome in 1778, with a second edition in 1780 under the patronage of the Minister General of the Franciscans, this *Institutiones philosophicae* is composed of

---

rationem fallax imaginatio temperatur, ac veritates in naturae gremio delitescentes feliciter inveniuntur." *Ibid.*, II, 10-11.

[95] "Sed rationis sufficientis usus in Philosophiae progressu clarius innotescet." *Ibid.*, p. 11. Of two and a half pages devoted to principles, a page and a half are given to the Principle of Sufficient Reason. One is tempted to state a law of inverse proportions in this regard: as the metaphysical content of a manual goes down, the importance of the Principle of Sufficient Reason expands.

[96] There is no use bothering, he notes, with the doubtful *a priori* Anselmian argument which would have no weight with Atheists; three evident *a posteriori* arguments are enough: the metaphysical, which depends on consideration of the human mind; the physical, which is from contemplation of the physical world; and the moral, which is based on the customs of men. *Ibid.*, II, 12-13. He takes for granted the existence of the human soul in his *Psychology*, which immediately follows the forty-five pages devoted to natural theology. "Animae itaque humanae supposita existentia, de qua nemo sanae mentis potest ambigere, de ejus natura, origine, dependentia a corpore, atque potentiis disputabimus." *Ibid.*, p. 46. This extends to about 100 pages.

[97] *Ibid.*, II-2, pp. 14-15.

[98] Joseph Tamagna, O.F.M.Conv., (1747-1798), *Institutiones philosophiae* (Editio secunda; Rome: P. Junchius, 1780). First a professor of philosophy and mathematics, he later taught dogmatic theology at the "Sapienza" in Rome.

four volumes, the first of which includes logic, ontology, cosmology, natural theology and psychology. Apparently, from the approbations, the title of this work when first issued in 1778 was *Institutiones logicae, & metaphysicae, in quibus divinitas religionis Christianae naturali ratione contra incredulos demonstrantur etc.* The Minister General, John C. Viper, had previously decreed that his ecclesiastical students merely learn *about* physics through the history of the science rather than engage in the study of the subject formally in itself. But on the occasion of this new edition he positively encouraged the study of mathematics and physics, without giving them the importance accorded to logic and metaphysics.

Tamagna begins with a "Protheoria in Universam Philosophiam," in which he discourses briefly on the vicissitudes of philosophy in history, taking his nominal and real definitions from Pythagoras and Cicero, respectively. He considers the question of Adam's philosophical knowledge as a subject belonging to theology and revelation.[99]

In his *Logic*, Tamagna shows concern for the practical aspects of *Critica*: there are four rules for clear and distinct ideas, three rules against error, eight rules for directing judgment in general. The art of *critica* is focused on the three sources of truth man has in the use of his reason, testimony of his senses, and the witness of authority. The remainder of the *Logic* is devoted to the syllogism and to method; the question of principles is not discussed in this part of philosophy.

Metaphysics likewise has a practical application. Since the metaphysics of the age tends to the irreligious result of godlessness, Tamagna plans his *Institutiones* not only to present the usual fare found in such texts but especially to provide demonstration of the fact that the Christian religion is the only one worthy of God, has God as its author, and alone can lead man to his end.[100]

Following the customary order noted so often before in these pages, the first section of his *Ontology* presents the First Principles

[99] *Ibid.,* I, 2 ff.

[100] "Saeculum metaphysicum, saeculum dici potest irreligiosum . . . Scilicet scopus epidemicae hujus metaphysicae non alius est, quam Numen quodlibet de medio tollere: hominem jumentis comparare insipientibus illisque similem efficere . . . Metaphysica igitur non aliud nobis significat, quam facultatem, quae de entibus sensui non subjectis pertractat . . . Quoniam ergo entia vel tanquam indeterminata possunt considerari, vel prout sunt determinata, ideo statim duplex occurrit metaphysicae partitio, in Ontologiam scilicet, & Pneumatologiam." *Ibid.,* I, 93-94.

of the science. But the color of the whole presentation has been changed by insertion into the context of the Critical Problem. The First Principles of ontology are the base and foundation of all natural knowledge, and since metaphysics sheds its light on, and is as a fountain to the other sciences, then the question of principles has a place at the very threshold. This is a familiar theme. But Tamagna adds a new note: "Unless," he says, "it is first demonstrated that man is capable of undoubting cognition and truth, . . . then it is vain to undertake inquiry as to the first principle."[101]

Therefore, he shows first, against the skeptics *(Pyrrhonicos)*, that man is so constituted as to be capable of knowing many things without fear of error; secondly, he presents the means which can be used safely in the pursuit of truth. Hence, Article One is devoted to destroying the insane theories of Pyrrohists and Skeptics. As to the means of attaining truth, five propositions on the nature of evidence and the criterion of truth are noteworthy for their epistemological context and the distinction made between evidence and experience, sense and intellect.[102]

After some forty pages given to these epistemological considerations, Tamagna then presents the Principle of Contradiction as the first principle of our knowledge and its basic foundation.[103] In contrast to the three pages alloted to this Principle, his discussion of the Principle of Sufficient Reason in article five extends through almost ten pages. As in Altieri, but at greater length, it sums up a long era of discussion, and, on the basis of the Principle's history, establishes some careful distinctions.

---

[101] *Ibid.,* p. 95.

[102] "Propositio I: Rei evidentia est optimum, indubiumque criterium pro dignoscendis veritatibus intelligibilibus: illis tamen dutaxat . . . quae ratiocinatione non indigent. II: Ut autem certi simus, nos ea tamquam evidentia non percipere, quae reipsa talia non sunt, confugiamus oportet vel ad intimae conscientiae testimonium, vel ad universalem perspicuitatem. III: Regulae logicales sunt optimum veritatis criterium ad detegendas eas veritates, quae primo intuitu perspicuae non sunt. Probatio istam ad literam fere excerpsimus ex Logica Wolfii edit. Veronae Ann. 1735. IV: Pro veritatibus sensibilibus evidentia sensuum est certum veritatis criterium. V: In rebus facti testimonium Historicorum non potest nos in errorem perducere." *Ibid.,* I, 113-130.

[103] "Principium contradictionis est primum cognitionum nostrarum principium, eorumque velut fundamentum, & basis." *Ibid.,* p. 131. "Demonstratione itaque ostensiva probamus, certissimum esse hoc contradictionis principium, quia in idea existentiae &c. relucet pugna non existentiae &c. demonstratione vero redargutiva, seu apogogica probamus per principium contradictionis, id esse certissimum, quod relucet in idea clara, & distincta, ut diximus n. 478." *Ibid.,* I, 132.

Tamagna blurs somewhat in the following definition the distinction between Sufficient Reason and the Principle of Sufficient Reason when he says, "The Principle of Sufficient Reason is that through which it is understood why anything is and is such."[104] This is immediately given a problem focus on the question as to whether or not anything can be admitted to be or to be possible without any sufficient reason of its existence.

Tamagna insists that Leibniz was the restorer rather than the inventor of the Principle of Sufficient Reason and differs sharply with an observation of Genuensis which makes Wolff say the opposite.[105] Since the Peripatetic Scholastics used the principle, *nihil esse sine propria causa,* which is found also in Leibniz along with the Principle of Sufficient Reason, and is always distinguished from it, there is a Leibnizian and an anti-Leibnizian meaning of this latter. The anti-Leibnizian philosophers, unidentified here by name, granted that *nothing is without a sufficient reason* but spoke only of causality. Tamagna therefore wishes to speak of Sufficient Reason as distinct from Cause, and then ask whether the Principle means that *nothing is to be admitted by us* without a Sufficient Reason or that *nothing is* without a Sufficient Reason. It is one thing to assert that there is some Sufficient Reason for clearly and distinctly explaining a thing, even when this reason is unknown to us; and another thing to contend that the Sufficient Reason ought to be so known to us that, as long as it is unknown, we ought not to admit the existence of that thing whose reason is sought. Wolff certainly meant the former interpretation.

Putting aside the question of Sufficient Reason and free will until notions of liberty have been developed, the author limits

---

[104] "Principium rationis sufficientis est illud, *per quod intelligitur, cur aliquid sit, & tale sit." Ibid.,* p. 133.

[105] Although used by Archimedes, "primus tamen Leibnitius aperte de eodem loquutus est, eodemque tanquam principio in rectificandis notionibus, & demonstrandis propositionibus usus est in egregio Theodiceae opere . . . Num istis luculentiora tradere ipse Wolfius potuerit, ut nobis innueret, restauratorem quidem principii istius Leybnitium fuisse, non autem inventorem, ego non video, nec alius, ut puto qui Wolfium perlegerit, videre valebit unquam: & tamen Cl. Genuensis *Metaph. part.* i. *Sch. prop.* 49. ita ex tripode definit. 'At quod hujus axiomatis primus usum fecisse Leybnitius Wolfio dicitur, id vero est, in quo aut affectu decipitur, aut veterum Philosophorum, Platonis potissimum, & Aristotelis monumentorum imperitiam patefacit': potius ipse patefacit imperitiam Wolfii monumentorum. Ideo autem ista retuli, ut intelligatis, quanta fides sit Genuensi praebenda, licet viro non infimo praedito acumine, dum aliorum opera carpit libere fortasse nimis." *Ibid.,* I, 133-134.

discussion to natural, i.e., non-human, actions and effects. For the purpose of clarifying the question at issue, there are four points to be established:

> 1. Whether in natural things sufficient reason is distinct from cause? 2. Whether the sufficient reason is a certain criterion of truth where it is discovered? 3. Whether anything is to be admitted although the sufficient reason is unknown to us? 4. Finally, whether there is anything without a sufficient reason?[106]

The following four propositions answer these questions and establish the basic outline of Tamagna's understanding of the Principle of Sufficient Reason. I. *Sufficient reason in those things which do not depend on the exercise of liberty is the same as cause and cannot be discovered elsewhere than in a cause.* This is demonstrated by the fact that *to understand is to know through causes,* and when we know the cause of something we know thereby that in which the sufficient reason consists. To look for a sufficient reason over and above cause in the physical order is to run after hallucination and to multiply distinctions without foundations. The very examples, says Tamagna, which Wolff and Genuensis used prove this. The cold rock becomes warm under causal influence; the three lines of the triangle cause the three angles.[107]

II. *If anything clearly existing is perceived, its existence is not to be denied because the sufficient reason is unknown.* The denial of this proposition leads to skepticism or to a kind of imaginative idealism in which we know the cause of all things. Magnetism, for instance, and the relation between body and soul, are not explained by the philosopher, yet they are evident facts of experience and cannot be denied. Wolff's mistake, comments Tamagna, was to confuse the *existence of sufficient reason* and the *ability to assign* a sufficient reason when he argued that the existence of any being must be founded in another and, therefore, unless we know that other we do not know its existence because we do not know the sufficient reason.[108]

What Tamagna, of course, is doing here is to break out of a logic of essences into the assertion of existential reality independent of deduction, and as such it is a useful example of the causal mean-

---

106 *Ibid.,* I, 135.
107 *Ibid.,* I, 136-37.
108 *Ibid.,* p. 138.

ing given to Sufficient Reason when in an existential framework. The third proposition is more epistemological in its conception but is also founded in existential assertion.

III. *Where the sufficient reason of any being is discovered, there is not to be entertained any doubt whatever concerning its existence, possibility etc., according as the sufficient reason indicates.*[109] IV. *If we do not refuse to take sufficient reason as meaning cause, then nothing occurs in the material world without sufficient reason.* Otherwise, we must say that something comes from nothing.[110]

To the objection that once it is admitted that everything has a Sufficient Reason, then it must also follow that everything is necessary, Tamagna answers with a distinction between what belongs to essence and what is outside essence. Only those things are necessary whose Sufficient Reason of existence is contained in their very essence, as in the case of God. But since the Sufficient Reason of things other than God is in the cause producing them, then they are not essentially necessitated. The Sufficient Reason of the *logical* possibility of a being makes that being necessarily possible. But the Sufficient Reason of existential possibility is only accidental; it is founded in both the essence of the possible being and in the cause by which the possible can be led forth into act.[111] Whatever may be said of the concept here of possibility in relation to existence, the distinction between essential reason and existential cause is an advance over the logical ontology of rationalism.

After this long treatment of Sufficient Reason, Tamagna proceeds to the notion of being, its states and conditions and follows through with the Wolffian conceptions, neatly sidestepping at the very beginning the controversy on univocity to which Scotistic metaphysics is usually determined. He will not, he says, attempt, as Altieri did, to loosen that Gordian knot.[112] It is enough to say that:

> Being, whether you mean that participle derived from the verb, *sum, es, est,* or some verbal term concerning which the old Metaphysicians did not agree, is all that which does not involve

109 *Ibid.,* p. 140.
110 *Ibid.,* I, pp. 140-141.
111 *Ibid.,* pp. 141-142.
112 "Cordium igitur hunc nodum modo solvamus . . . o miram jurgiorum generandi aviditatem!" *Ibid,* p. 144; cf. also p. 167.

contradiction and therefore is not repugnant to existence, whether actually in act or only able to be.[113]

As for the various states of being, the most simple, and the first which can be considered in being, is that called possibility, which belongs to any and all being whatsoever. The second is that of potentiality, found only in finite being. The third is the state of existence in which, by virtue of his nature, God is.[114]

Existence itself is the placing of a thing outside the possible, drawing it from nothing; the notion of existence is one of the concepts which is better understood than explained. Something is in act when existence is given, which is also called act because it actuates the essence or constitutes it beyond nothing.[115]

After the treatment of the primary conditions of being as one, true and good, the further notions of identity and distinction, necessity and contingency are explained. Tamagna devotes a long article to the principle of indiscernibles. He says that Leibniz argued to that principle from the Principle of Sufficient Reason and was opposed by Samuel Clarke, whom many philosophers, and especially Catholics, followed, although Sagner and Genuensis can be listed with Wolff, Bülffinger, Holman, Baumeister, Cantzius, and Gotscheid as embracing the principle.[116] Tamagna saw the whole question reduced to the distinction between similitude and identity and rejected the *a priori* repugnance of two absolutely similar beings, although he stated it only as quite probable that two such beings actually exist.[117]

As to the objection that in the case of two absolutely similar possible beings, God would have no Sufficient Reason for creating both, i.e., one in preference to the other, since both are the same,

---

[113] "Ens, sive illud participium dicas derivatum a verbo sum es est, sive nomen aliqod verbale, qua de re veteres Metaphysici non conveniunt, ets id omne, quod contradictionem non involvit, & idcirco non repugnat esse, sive actu sit, sive tantum esse possit." *Ibid.*, p. 143.

[114] "Simplicissimus, & omnium primus, qui in ente considerari potest status, est ille, qui dicitur possibilitatis; hic convenit cuilibet enti. etc." *Ibid.*, p. 147. There is a reference here to Mako's *Ontologia*. "Ratio ergo sufficiens potentialitatis in possibilitate intrinseca reperitur entis, & in causa, a qua potest produci; per haec duo enim ille status clare, & distincte intelligitur, ac per consequens haec duo rationem illius sufficientem constituuntur." *Ibid.*, I, 152.

[115] "Existentia est positio rei extra possibilitatem, seu extra nihilum. At existentiae notio ex illis est notionibus, quae melius intelliguntur, quam valeant explicari." *Ibid.*, I, 152.

[116] *Ibid.*, p. 190.

[117] *Ibid.*, pp. 190-191 ff.

he rejected the kind of Sufficient Reason which Leibniz placed in dissimilitude in favor of Sufficient Reason constituted in distinct numerical entity. Or, if that answer does not satisfy, then, Tamagna suggested that the whole Sufficient Reason for the creation of this rather than that is the free will of God.[118]

In his Natural Theology, Tamagna understands by the word "God," a being *a se*, that is, one whose Sufficient Reason of existence is not found outside his very essence. But his primary proof for the existence of God makes no special use of the Principle of Sufficient Reason.[119]

This concludes the survey of manuals produced in Scholastic circles from 1750 to 1800, manuals which definitely were tied into the rationalism of Christian Wolff and clearly imitated the new style he inaugurated in textbooks.[120]

Based on the examination made thus far, rationalism as concretized in the methodology of textbook philosophy has the following two characteristics: *First,* at the level of *format,* the external structure of the textbook is designed to concatenate link after link of definitions and demonstrations derived from clear and distinct concepts, bringing the chain into focus by numbering in arithmetical succession the paragraphs and the divisions, and even setting off parts and whole with indentations of the page margin and by a variety of print forms; *Second, a theory of method* which is committed to geometry as to an ideal, and views metaphysics, for instance, as a geometry-of-being wherein deductive intelligibility reigns supreme. The use of "Ontology" as a title for metaphysics (the philosophy of being) is often a sign of this theory of method.

[118] *Ibid.,* p. 196.

[119] "Dei nomine intelligimus modo ens aliquod a se: cujus videlicet existentiae ratio sufficiens extra ipsius essentiam non valeat reperiri." *Ibid.,* 249. Tamagna's Cosmology is quite short; he sees it, like ontology, as a foundation for philosophy and science and it not only is of service, but of absolute necessity for demonstrating natural theology and a right idea of the universe. When the nature of material beings, their nexus and order are rightly considered and proposed, then we can scarcely err when treating of the existence, attributes, and providence of God. *Ibid.,* p. 215. He objects to the assertion that before Wolff the name of General Cosmology was unheard of by the Scholastics; such a statement is true only by restricting it to the name which Wolff gave it, "Cosmology." But as to the matter treated, it is certainly in St. Thomas, Scotus and recent physicists, perhaps scattered, but certainly profoundly grasped. *Ibid.,* p. 216.

[120] Cf. John E. Gurr, S.J., "Some Historical Origins of Rationalism in Catholic Philosophy Manuals," *Proceedings of the American Catholic Philosophical Association,* XXIX (1955), pp. 121-133.

Later, some authors attempt by definition to clear away the Wolffian vestiges from "Ontology"; but it is strongly impregnated with the implications of a genus and species relation between the parts of philosophy, implications hard to dispel.

The relevance of these textbooks for us today lies in their connection with the manuals which appeared in Europe a century later. This connection is evident from an analysis of the references in these later manuals of 1850 to 1900 and a comparison of format, arrangement and doctrine, all of which indicate that it was mainly through these late eighteenth-century Jesuit and Franciscan authors that our recent and current manuals come under the influence of German rationalism. In other words, twentieth-century textbooks still draw from the manuals of the late nineteenth-century Thomistic revival, many of whose authors, in reacting against the predominant Cartesianism of the first half of their century, 1800 to 1850, and, according to usual policy, left free by the Church as to how they carried out the directives of Leo XIII on returning to St. Thomas, found themselves either by accident or by design depending on the manuals of 1750 to 1800 for considerable blocks of doctrine and numerous points of orientation.

This is not surprising when we recall that the rationalistic manuals written by Wolff and the Austrian Jesuits had made a distinct break with the old Peripatetic philosophy of the sixteenth and early seventeenth centuries.[121] Hence, in the absence of historical studies such as we enjoy today, and lacking an unbroken tradition of Scholastic philosophy between the high Middle Ages and their own time, philosophy textbook authors of the middle and late nineteenth century easily missed, at first, many of the consequences of a return to St. Thomas, and, while faced with the prac-

---

[121] Cf. *Infra*, Ch. 2, nx. 34. This break was not purely arbitrary. In no way was it malicious, and, indeed, in many ways, it was quite necessary. The world had moved on, not only beyond St. Thomas and the Middle Ages, but also beyond decadent Scholasticism and the hodge-podge of sense and nonsense which had collected under the label "Peripatetic." This put the nineteenth-century manuals at least three stages removed from the source to which they sought return: immediately preceding them were the Cartesian textbooks as the immediate cause of reaction, and beyond these lay the manuals of rationalism viewed as already having been a reaction for the better against the decadence which in turn had preceded them in "Peripateticism." A further first stage point of difficulty in reaching St. Thomas might be indicated in the wide-spread acceptance of Capreolus, Cajetan, and John of St. Thomas by some nineteenth-century Thomists and of Suarez by others as the authentic voice of Aquinas. Cf. George Klubertanz, S.J., "Being and God According to Contemporary Scholastics," *The Modern Schoolman*, XXXII (1954), pp. 1-17.

tical problem of speaking the language of their own generation, they tried not to speak in an historical vacuum.

Thus it was inevitable that many of the authors of the Thomistic revival, in their lack of contact with a tradition really stemming from St. Thomas himself, credited the rationalistic manuals of the late eighteenth century with a Thomistic content and meaning. This credit *de facto* was an historical error, but it led some philosophy manual authors so to identify rationalism with Scholasticism that their revival of Scholastic philosophy inevitably involved a revival of rationalism. They decided that the Wolffian manuals such as we have examined in this chapter were reliable guides in the perennial task of Scholastic philosophy itself—that of being ever ancient yet ever new. In thus reading St. Thomas into a framework furnished by rationalism the hand seemed to be the hand of Aquinas but the voice was that of Wolff, and for many years this synthetic product received the blessing intended for the great original.

But attention now must be given in the next chapter to the manuals which were in popular demand during the first half of the nineteenth century. A brief survey of their origin and quality is essential for an assessment of the reaction which later in the century diminished Cartesian and Ontologist influence and produced the philosophy textbooks which ushered in the twentieth century. Here again, the method of presenting the evidence in chronological sequence and with a minimum of analysis and comment may make for tedious reading. But this material is needed groundwork, for lack of which the final conclusions of this study would be less well founded.

ɞ❧ The Transition
to Neo-Scholasticism

B Y THE END of the eighteenth century, the popularity of the Wolffian-style philosophy manual was on the wane. Under the impact of the French Revolution and the turmoil it spread through colleges and seminaries, and in view of the varied mixture of "schools," doctrine, format, and general purpose of the textbooks themselves, various attempts were made to get clear of confusion and above controversy in the teaching of philosophy. Rationalism was under fire in a reaction to *a priori* methods and starting points; empiricism, quite right in its insistence on experiential starting points for knowledge, was wrong in its characteristic devotion to sensism.

Some of the attempts at solution resulted in a more intense "Cartesianism," which seemed to find a workable combination of experience and principle in the data of the mind itself. Others led the way into a complete reaction against all reasoned philosophy and tried to establish religious and social sources of starting points and data. By 1850, some of this philosophical chaos had been ordered one way or another, and a new era for Scholastic philosophy and its textbooks had begun.

This period of transition from the clearly defined format and style of the late eighteenth-century manuals, in which we have seen the Principle of Sufficient Reason at work, to the Neo-Scholasticism of the middle nineteenth century is worth examination on three points. 1. There is an important body of Catholic and non-Catholic writing devoted to the Principle of Sufficient Reason and the accusation of Fatalism which enveloped it in the eighteenth century. 2. Then comes a "Cartesian" group of manuals belonging to the Catholic tradition distinct from, yet chronologically both parallel and subsequent to, the textbooks we have just examined in chapter two. We will also note both the earlier influence of men like Buffier on these textbooks and some late offshoots and modifications. 3. This will indicate the textbook situation in the first half of the nineteenth century and provide added example of the tendency of the Principle of Sufficient Reason to appear on the fringe of movements that are a blend of several traditions.

Sufficient Reason and the Accusation of Fatalism

The work of a discalced Augustinian, Mansuetus of St. Felice, O.S.A., will serve doubly as an example of Scholastic writing on the Principle of Sufficient Reason outside the formal context of a philosophy manual and as an occasion for sketching in outline the perennial controversy over Fatalism, which was in the background of many a textbook presentation of the Principle.[1] Opposition to Wolff's Principle of Sufficient Reason became widespread and highly vocal at Halle among Protestant theologians as well as among members of the Berlin Academy, of whom Prémontval is a classic example. But Catholic writers likewise dealt with the subject in manuals, monographs, and special studies.

Thus Mansuetus wrote several philosophico-theological dissertations on the Principle of Sufficient Reason in connection with liberty, a best possible world and the various aspects of grace and pre-destination (involved in any discussion of freedom and necessity, especially by theologians). These dissertations were printed at Cremona in 1775 under the title: *Concerning the Discord of the System of Sufficient Reason with Human Liberty, with Divine Liberty, Omnipotence and Wisdom, and with the Mysteries of Grace and Predestination.*

In his preface Mansuetus disavows any motives of passionate dispute or hatred of new opinions impelling the writing of this work. Love of truth, the dangers which novelty has for morals and theology, and the peace and tranquility of Catholic schools as threat-

---

[1] Mansuetus a S. Felice, O.S.A., *De discordia systematis rationis sufficientis cum libertate humana cum libertate, omnipotentia, & sapientia divina cum mysteriis gratia, & praedestinationis. Dissertationes VII Philosophico-Theologicae* (Cremona: L. Manini, 1775). In addition to the points made in this title, Mansuetus also includes in his subject matter the knowledge of future conditionals, grace in the state of both natural innocence and after the Fall, and the mind of St. Augustine concerning the state of innocence. Mansuetus was a professor of moral theology.

ened by the new and varied theories then current, constitute his reasons for taking up the pen. Despite the title, he says:

> . . . it is not my plan to reject and overthrow the general Principle of Sufficient Reason if it is taken for cause or reason of some effect and action. No prudent philosopher or theologian can impugn or call in doubt the principle understood in this sense; and rightly has it had among writers of both past and present an eminent and renowned use.[2]

The precise sense in which he wishes to examine and confute the use of Sufficient Reason is that which is given it in the systems of those commonly referred to as "Sufficientists," "Optimists," "Meliorists." The seeds or principles of this systematic use of Sufficent Reason are found in several ancient philosophers, especially Plato, Aristotle, Proclus, Lucretius, and others of the Platonist and Stoic sects. These principles, says Mansuetus, were first given prominence by Leibniz and then developed into a systematic philosophy by Christian Wolff, "so that these two are more the authors and architects of the system than restorers or mere propagators." From them the system gets its name, commonly called Leibnizian or Wolffian.[3] Although many philosophers and theologians have opposed this new system, none of them has done so systematically; no one *ex professo* has combatted it in its entire amplitude of philosophical and theological import.

Mansuetus, in his first dissertation "On Human Liberty," began by listing twelve fundamental principles of the Sufficient-Reason tradition as culled from Leibniz *(Theodicy),* Wolff *(Natural Theology),* and others.[4] They amount to a definition of free will and

---

2 "Consilium mihi non fuit rejiciendi, confutandique generale princîpium rationis sufficientis, si pro caussa seu ratione cujuscumque effectus, & actionis accipiatur. Principium enim hoc sensu intellectum nullus cordatus Philosophus, aut Theologus inficiari, aut in dubium vertere potest: atque jure merito tum apud veteres, tum apud recentes Scriptores usum insignem habuit, & illustrem." *Ibid.,* Preface (unpaginated).

3 ". . . ita ut hi duo potius quam instauratores, aut professores, veluti auctores, & architecti hujus systematis habeantur: ab hisce enim systema etiam nomen accepti, quod vulgo Leibnitianum, & Wolphianum appellatur." *Loc. Cit.*

4 In his introduction he lists "Hanschius, Thummigius, Bulfingerus, Daries, Kanzius" as followers of Leibniz and Wolff, together with "nonnulli Itali Philosophi." Then he continues, "Hos secuti sunt recentissime alii Itali Philosophi, & Theologi, qui hujusmodi systema tum ad cognoscendam, explicandamque humanae, & divinae Libertatis indolem, ac naturam; tum ad evolvenda, & explananda difficilora Theologiae mysteria; tum denique ad varia scholarum dissidia componenda, & concilianda plurimum valere existimarunt." *Loc. Cit.*

of liberty, in which the part played by a sufficient or determining reason or motive is so strong and infallible that freedom is defined as "the faculty of choosing from many possibles that which is most pleasing and suitable to the motive presented by an indifferent judgment of reason."[5]

After listing the principal errors on the subject of human liberty, the author turned to St. Thomas and Cardinal Berti for his doctrine on the essence, definition and extent of human liberty. He then proceeded to show how the Sufficient-Reason schools sin against it.

There are two things necessary for freedom of choice: (1) The judgment must be free and the mind open to opposites. (2) The will must not be determined to one particular but must be able to choose freely. But these two requisites are not present in the systems of Sufficient Reason, and Mansuetus shows how neither the will nor the judgment therein are free as to act, object, or end.[6]

With this precise and competent anlysis of error, together with the presentation of practical doctrine completed in the first dissertation, Manseutus laid the ground work of his further discussion. He advances to the subject of liberty in God and the questions of an *optimum* world,[7] God's knowledge of conditional futures and the subject of grace, its efficacy and God's distribution of it.[8]

As a point of departure for high-lighting some fifty years of controversy on the apologetical aspect of the Principle of Sufficient

[5] "Et libertas dicitur facultas eligendi ex pluribus possibilibus, quod magis placet convenienter ad motiva per indifferens judicium rationis proposita." *Ibid.*, p. 2.

[6] *Ibid.*, pp. 3-4. References to St. Thomas: *Sum. Theol*, II-II, q. 17, a. 1, ad 2; *De veritate* q. 22, a. 6 in corp.; and to Cardinal John Laurence Berti, *De theologicis disciplinis* (Rome-Venice: Recurti, 1750), I, Lib. 12, cap. 10. The following articles of this first dissertation eliminate various attempts to escape the weakness of the Sufficiency argument, such as an appeal to the power of attending or not attending to motives, with only a moral necessity in the prevailing one. The moral necessity is not superable, hence freedom is not present. And this system, by taking the heart out of any notions of merit and demerit, destroys the fundamentals of moral theology; it does not square with an explanation of the connection between the ultimate practical judgment and the choice of the will, nor can it be ranged under the patronage of St. Thomas and his authority used for the position.

[7] Dissertationes II, "De Libertate, Omnipotentia, & Sapientia divina," and III, "De Optimismo cui additur Appendix de Systemate Leibnitiano Melioris & Optimi."

[8] Dissertationes IV, "De Scientia futurorum conditionatorum"; V, "De Gratia status utriusque naturae Innocentis, & Lapsae"; VI, "De Mysterio Praedestinationis," and VII, "De mente D. Augustini circa Gratiam Status Innocentiae."

Reason, we may note in Mansuetus a recurrent theme of appeal for peaceful discussion rather than acrid polemic, an appeal which awakens echoes from the early writings of Wolff and his successors. In 1775 this Italian Augustinian pleaded for kindness and objectivity rather than the impulsive, prejudiced and uncritical carping characteristic of many writers.[9]

Similarly, fifty years earlier, in 1724, Christian Wolff had also begged for openness and objectivity in the conflict over fatalism (and Sufficient Reason) which had engulfed him at Halle, a plea seconded also by Bülffinger and Baumeister.[10] Wolff, in passing, ironically lamented the kind of logic which he found twisting reasoned conclusions around to sit in judgment on premises.[11] In 1724, defending himself against the accusation of atheism, he wrote a short treatise entitled, *Concerning the Difference Between the Concatenation of Things According to a Theory of Divine Wisdom and a Theory of Fatal Necessity, Along with that between the System of Pre-Established Harmony and the Hypothesis of Spinoza*

[9] "Rogo interea, obtestorque Leibnitiani systematis Professores, ut nihil adversi de me suspicentur; ac pro certo habeant me nihil ipsorum doctrinae, eruditioni, sapientiae, & splendori velle detrahere; sed tantum, quod propius ad verum accedit, inquirere, & si fieri potest, invenire: & sicuti refellere sine pertinacia; ita & refelli sine iracundia paratus sum." Mansuetus, De Discordia, *op. cit.*, Preface.

[10] Opposition to Wolff stemmed from the theological faculty at Halle, from John Lange (1670-1744) in particular, and centered on Wolff's famous discourse on morality among the Chinese. (Bartholmèss noted the similarity between this Protestant tempest and the happenings twenty years before at the Sorbonne between Boileau and the Jesuits who eulogized the Chinese.) Another source of friction between Wolff and Lange lay in the appointment of the former's pupil, Thumming, to a position Lange expected for his own son. Eventually Wolff was branded as an atheist in disguise and the Emperor was finally persuaded to order his banishment (November 8, 1723). Ten years later he was invited to return, an invitation politely declined, and in 1738 Frederick, by edict, made the teaching of Wolffianism obligatory in all the Prussian universities and particularly at Halle. Cf. Christian Bartholmèss, *Histoire philosophique de l'Académie de Prusse depuis Leibniz jusqu' à Schelling particulièrement sous Frédéric Le Grand* (Paris: Marc Ducloux, 1850), I, 92-96, 135.

[11] "Quae e conclusionibus, quae per evidentem consequentiam e praemissis deductae sunt, praemissas ipsas seu principia dijudicari & evidentiam consequentiae ex multitudine consentientium aestimari jubet." Christian Wolff, *De differentia nexus rerum sapientis et fatalis necessitatis, nec non systematis harmoniae praestabilitae ab hypothesium Spinosae. Luculenta commentatio in qua simul genuina Dei existentiam demonstrandi ratio expenditur et multa religionis naturalis capita illustrantur* (Halle: Rengeriana, 1724), p. 60. Thus Wolff's enemies, through Paul Gundling, pointing out to the Emperor that under a theory of pre-established harmony and sufficient reason nothing was more natural or more necessary than desertion, aroused fears that led to Wolff's banishment, lest such a philosophy, sown among the students at Halle, should spread to the army.

*in which also the Genuine Method of Demonstrating the Existence
of God and Many Topics of Natural Religion are Explained.*[12]
Wolff contended that in demonstrating the existence of God he
had used an argument already well established by St. Thomas,
whom even the Lutherans honored, and by Protestant theologians
—the argument from contingency. Moreover, anyone who had read
his metaphysical meditations, he challenged, knew that he had im-
proved and strengthened this old argument, giving it a new form
especially by advertence to strict method and to the Principle of
Sufficient Reason, which before Leibniz was not sufficiently valued.[13]

This was also part of the purpose envisaged for Wolff's new
science of Cosmology, to emphasize the *connectedness* and *harmony* of things in the world and thus to establish their contingency.
It is from contingency and not from order and harmony as such,
says Wolff, that we argue best to divine existence.[14] Wolff also
points out his use of the notion of possibility, and how this concept
and his ideas of the necessary and contingent differ from Spinoza.
Moving then to the order of causes in the universe and the impossibility of an infinite series presenting a sufficient reason for its
existence, Wolff concludes to God as the "being in which is contained the sufficient reason of the existence of the universe."[15] He
then points out how his conception of God is wrongly identified
with that of Spinoza and that the accusation leveled against him of
holding an eternal world is also a *non sequitur;* even if it were eternal, it would remain eternally distinct from God, and there is no
need to contend over it with atheists.[16]

In this same year Bülffinger took up the question of Sufficient
Reason and moral evil in his *Philosophical Comment on the Origin
and Permission of Evil, Especially Moral Evil.*[17] By 1741, Baumeister had written a summary of the controversy over Wolff's
fatalism and made the attempt to reduce it all to a dispute over

---

[12] Cf. *supra*, n. 11.   [13] *Ibid.*, pp. 4-5.   [14] *Ibid.*, p. 6.

[15] "Dixi Deum esse ens, in quo continetur ratio sufficiens existentiae universi,
& hanc definitionem ejus nominalem dedi in meditationibus meis metaphysicis, quoniam a contingentia universi ad existentiam Dei argumentior." *Ibid.*, p. 53.

[16] *Ibid.*, pp. 54-56.

[17] George B. Bülffinger, *De Origine et permissione mali, praecipue moralis,
commentatio philosophica. Sectio Prima cautelas dijudicandae rei necessarias; Secunda definitiones fundamenta systematis, & objectionum occupationes; Tertia expositionem originis & permissionis ipsam; Quarta usus doctrinae morales; Epilogus
universam in compendio tractationem exhibet* (Frankfurt: T. Mezlerum, 1724).

words and their definition.[18] This work was structured in a series of logical and ontological definitions, brief and clear, of Wolffian concepts. Definition No. 189 says that "the Principle of Sufficient Reason is the proposition: Nothing is without a sufficient reason why it is rather than is not."[19]

After proceeding through the definitions fundamental to logic, ontology, psychology and moral philosophy, Baumeister then established what he called *Positiones*. Under metaphysical positions for ontology, this Principle of Sufficient Reason is again presented, this time in a series of propositions amplifying its meaning. He held that it is demonstrated from the Principle of Contradiction and that, while it is not an absolutely first principle, it is absolutely necessary.[20]

Despite the influence of Wolff and the loyalty and prominence of his followers, by 1745 the opposition to his rationalism began to reduce the extent of his popularity, and he was subjected to criticism on more than one score from a variety of sources. The famous mathematician and member of the Berlin Academy, Leonard Euler, was particularly vocal in his ridicule of the "disciples of Leibniz" and made known to all of Europe his grievances against Wolff in the famous *Letters to a German Princess*.[21]

André Pierre Le Guay de Prémontval, another mathematician and academician, rivaled Euler in the vehemence of his ridicule and passionate opposition to Leibniz and Wolff. As a Frenchman and as a member of the Berlin Academy he sought renown both as a metaphysician and as an incorruptible French-language purist.[22]

---

[18] Frederick C. Baumeister, *Philosophia recens controversa complexa. Definitiones theoremata et quaestiones nostra aetate in controversiam vocatas* (Leipzig: Marcheana, 1741).

[19] "CCCXXXIX. Principium rationis sufficientis est propositio: Nihil est sine ratione sufficiente, cur potius sit, quam non sit." *Ibid.*, p. 61. For further information on the subject, he says: "De hoc principio, recentiori aetate a permultis in controversiam vocat, videantur *Burfingerus* dilucid. Sect. I, c. 3. item *Straehlerus* in tr. de sensu atque usu Principii rationis suff. *Hagmeieri* disser. de Princ. Rat. suff. & *Carpov* in disp. de Principio Rat. suff & *Hagen* in Commentat. de Methodo Mathematica p. 13 ubi novam huius principii demonstrationem concinnare voluit, quam tamen uberius examinare, non est huius loci. Quae Langius, aliique contra hoc principium monuerunt, dudum confutata sunt." *Ibid.*, p. 61.

[20] *Ibid.*, pp. 229 ff.

[21] Leonard Euler (1707-1783), *Lettres à une princesse d'Allemagne sur quelque sujets de physique et de philosophie* (St. Petersburg, 1768-1772).

[22] André Pierre Le Guay de Prémontval (1716-1764), *Du Hazard sous l'Empire de la Providence, pour servir de préservatif contre la doctrine du Fatalisme moderne* (Berlin: J. C. Kluter, 1755). He fled his father's house to avoid studying theology

Taking aim at both the Principle of Sufficient Reason and the Law of Continuity, he hurled the stock charge of "fatalism" at the reeling Wolffians. The first of these laws did not appear to him as absolutely false, yet he none the less argued that as a consequence of these two principles the actual state of the universe always depends on those states that precede it. Fatal necessity leaves no room in the world for either chance or Providence. Moreover, he wished to replace the theodicy of Leibniz and the natural theology of Wolff with what he called the "theology of being," a combination of "atheism refuted" and a new attempt to demonstrate the existence of a supreme being.[23]

Although Prémontval's attack on the Leibnizian-Wolffian position was neither adroit nor measured, his treatise of 1754 on *Chance under the Reign of Providence* is, says Bartholmèss, "an estimable work; and the numerous contradictions which Béguelin pointed out therein did not prevent other mathematicians from citing it with praise."[24]

In an introduction to this work addressed to the German people (in which he included Swiss and Hollanders), Prémontval declared the enemy to be all those philosophical sects which have only a very imperfect idea of chance and fatalism and, consequently, of human morality. But it was especially against Leibniz, as against a source of infection, that the attack was leveled, and although Leibniz was the light and glory of Germany, "your master and mine," wrote the author, "I must declare that I hold the fundamental principles of his philosophy to be false and intolerable."[25]

---

or law and in order to take up the exact sciences. Disinherited by his father, he took refuge at Geneva in 1743. Later at Bâle, where the Benedictine Lacroze had embraced the Evangelical faith, he became a Protestant. In 1752 he came to Berlin where he and his wife were teachers at the court. He was received into the Prussian Academy and began his criticism of Wolffian philosophy and his campaign for the purity of French. Bartholmèss says his *Préservatif contre la corruption de la langue française an Allemagne* was expressive of his self-love and irritable vanity; his *Pensées sur la liberté* (1750) was especially directed against the school of Leibniz. Moses Mendelssohn pointed out its sophisms and paradoxes. He singled out two kinds of enemies: pious disciples of Wolff and atheists of all kinds. Cf. Bartholmèss, *op. cit.,* I, 212-213.

23 Bartholmèss, *op. cit.,* I, 214-216.

24 "Son traité *Du hasard* . . . dont le titre ingénieux annonce le dessein souvent formé de concilier des opinions extrêmes sur le gouvernement du monde, est un travail estimable; et les contradictiones nombreuses que Béguelin y a relevées; n'ont pas empêché d'autres mathématiciens de le citer avec éloge." *Ibid.,* p. 209.

25 "Fidele, dis-je, à la véracité de mon caractere, j'ose déclarer que je tiens le

Meaning by the words chance or hazard, "any cause whose action, contingent in nature, is not directed by design (purpose), or at least by a purpose related to its effect,"[26] Prémontval, after a brief general classification of philosophies involved, concentrates on the Leibnizian school. Their entire system depends on the Principle of Sufficient Reason being true in all of its generality. But Prémontval wishes careful distinction of its application in the case of God, where it is generally true, from the case of creatures with an infinity of happenings, where it is very false.[27]

The assertion by Leibniz and Wolff that the Principle of Sufficient Reason is axiomatic is just one of those examples where an absurd opinion is lodged in minds otherwise highly admirable. Despite his high esteem for their system, and an attempt to grasp in a totality its connections and relations, Prémontval still could not accept the Principle of Sufficient Reason as an axiom. To their assertion that it is the same as the old axiom, "no effect without a cause," Prémontval retorts: yes, it is similar, but, of all the empty phrases on the lips of men, what is more frivolous than that hackneyed axiom, "There is no effect without a cause?"[28]

Not only of the Leibnizians but also of the world he asks: What do you understand by this word, "effect?" What else are you saying than that there is nothing which has a cause which does not have a cause. You wish, he continues, to show that there is a God and you argue that since there is no effect without a cause then the world ought to have its cause. Yes, *when you have shown that the world is an effect!* If the world has a cause, it has one. But the precise point of the question is here: *if the world has a cause.* There are some who try to say that "Everything has its cause; nothing is without a particular cause." But to say "Everything has its cause" is false. *The First Cause has no cause!*[29]

principe fondamental de sa philosophie pour faux & insoutenable." Prémontval, *Du Hazard, op. cit.,* p. v.

26 "J'entens par ce mot *hazard,* ce que tout le monde entend, *une cause quelconque, dont l'action, contingente de sa nature, n'est point dirigée par un dessein, ou du moins, par undessein relatif à son effet.*" *Ibid.,* p. 5.

27 *Ibid.,* p. 78.

28 *Ibid.,* pp. 80-81; "Ce principe, *rien n'est sans un raison sufisante,* n'est pas la même chose, dit l'école leibnitienne, que l'ancien axiôme, *il n'y a point d'effet sans cause;* mais l'un vaut bien l'autre en certitude. Ah! j'accepte la parité. Que sera-ce, si je fais voir qu'entre toutes les phrases vuides de sens qui volent sur les levres des hommes, il n'est pas de plus frivoles, que cet axiôme rebatu, ce grand & universel axiôme, il n'y a point d'effet sans cause?" Prémontval, *Du Hazard,* p. 83.

29 "D'autres expriment l'axiôme d'une autre façon, qui le rend plus semblable

Finally, however legitimate this axiom might be, this very subject, the idea of cause itself, is obscure and problematical for our minds. We see an ordered sequence of *causes* and *effects*. But would there be anything contradictory in reversing the order so that effects become causes and causes effects? Prémontval worked out of this difficulty, which was created by his own mathematical concept of the relation of cause and effect (his examples indicate this), by a rhetorical reflection on man's endowment by God with a living inner sense which testifies to the reality of causality and rescues us from interminable discussion of the metaphysical problem involved. He continues then to deny the self-evidence of the Principle of Sufficient Reason. The very attempt made by Wolff, for instance, to prove it, to demonstrate what he holds as a principle, is itself a manifest *petitio principii*.

The famous argument in paragraph No. 70 of Wolff's *Ontology* is a pure equivocation on the meaning of *nihil*, and the French language, boasts Prémontval, has a clarity and a precision which brings this out better than the Latin.[30] Two of Wolff's illustrious disciples, Baumgarten and Bohm, tried to substitute other proofs, but all the genius in the world can say nothing reasonable about a principle which is both simple and false. Falsity induces error, and simplicity, a palpable error.

au principe léibnitien, sans que ni l'un ni l'autre y gagne. *Tout a sa cause; rien n'est sans une cause particuliere.* Sous ce tour la proposition n'a plus l'espece de vérité puérile qu'elle avoit auparavant; ou plûtôt ce n'est plus la même proposition. Celle-ci n'est point vrai dans cette généralité, ou bien il y faut mettre des restrictions qui la rendent de nul usage. *Tout a sa cause;* cela est faux. La première causa n'a point de cause. La possibilité qu'il y ait des causes, & une première cause entr'elles, n'a point de cause. Les essences des choses n'ont point de causes. Il faut donc dire: *Tout a sa cause, excepté ce qui n'en a point*: proposition des plus ineptes. *Tout a sa cause, excepté Dieu,* par exemple: proposition qui ne poura servir à quoi que ce soit pour démonstrer l'existence de Dieu, puis qu'elle la supose tout net, ni que le monde a une cause, puisqu'elle comence par suposer qu'il en a une." *Ibid.,* pp. 85-86.

[30] "J'ateste le bon foi des disciples de ce grand Homme, en particulier de ceux de ses disciples que je vois ici présens, que toute la force de sa preuve se trouve concentrée en ce peu de paroles. (No. 70, de L'Ontologie) "Si quelque chose, si A par exemple, est sans une raison sufisante pourquoi il est plûtôt que de n'être pas, c'est donc *le rien* qu'il faut poser pour concevoir pourquoi est A. On admet donc l'être de A, parcequ'on pose l'être de *rien'* . . . Equivoque toute pure, Messieurs; équivoque dont il est étrange que tant de gens à reflexions profondes ayent été si longtemps la dupe. Quoi? dire que *rien* ne sert à faire concevoir une chose, est-ce dire que *le rien* ce qui sert à faire concevoir cette chose? 'S'il n'y a point de raison pourquoi un arbre est là plûtôt qu'autre part,' ajoute-t-il dans un éclaircissement qui vient ensuite, 'il faut donc suposer, ou que *le rien* s'est changé en cet arbre, ou que *le rien* a produit là cet arbre, ou qu'il l'a transporté d'ailleurs.' . . . Est-il possible d'abuser

Prémontval's analysis of these Wolffian proofs of Sufficient Reason, while too long for detailed presentation here, is sharp and quite pertinent, although his own metaphysical position does not sustain a very profound positive doctrine in the matter. He distinguishes between the Leibnizians, who apparently restricted the Principle of Sufficient Reason to contingent things, and the Wolffians, who extended it to necessities such as attributes, possibility and essence. Thus, Wolff's first example in explanation of the Principle of Sufficient Reason, notes Prémontval, is drawn from the necessary relations of the angles and sides in a triangle.[31]

Actually, the *pourquoi* is a puerile kind of reason and the priority on which it rests is an arbitrary one. Prémontval contends that the whole argument is a purely verbal way of providing a *because* for the question men ask from childhood, *Why?* Existential explanation is not there.

Far from being a digression, this analysis of Wolffian "proofs" of the Principle of Sufficient Reason brings Prémontval to the precise subject of his dissertation, the contingency of human moral actions, which is over and done with if:

> . . . for the existence of an action, for example, it were always required that there be something by which one could fully conceive why the existence of this action took place rather than not.[32]

du langage à ce point là? Est-ce la même chose de dire, par exemple, *que rien n'a doné à Dieu ses perfections*, ou de dire *que c'est le rien qui a doné à Dieu ses perfectiones?* Coment donc peut-il venir à l'esprit d'un homme, que dire *que rien ne rend raison de l'existence de A*, c'est prétendre *que le rien est ce qui rend raison de l'existence de A;* c'est prétendre le rien à cet usage; que c'est réaliser le rien? *Nihil esse sumitur.* Mais ne voit-on pas au contraire que celui qui assure *que A est sans raison quelconque de son existence*, bien loin de réaliser le rien pour en faire la raison de A, exclud le rien même réalisé, de ce qui pouroit être la raison de A; come il n'y a personne qui en disant *que rien n'a doné à Dieu ses perfections*, n'xclude le rien, réalisé même par impossibile, de ce qu'on voudroit suposer avoir doné à Dieu ses perfections? Et de même en une infinité de phrases pareilles. Oh! tres certainement; dire *que rien n'a ébranlé* cet arbre, n'est pas dire *que le rien l'a ébranlé.* Dire *que rien n'a servi à Dieu de matière pour créer le monde*, ce n'est pas dire *que le rien est une matière dont Dieu s'est servi pour créer le monde.* Notre langue françoise a ici une clarte & une netteté que n'a point de tout la langue latine." *Du Hazard*, pp. 92-94.

31 *Ibid.*, pp. 96-99, 103-105.

32 "Tout est dit, tout est fait, s'il est faux qu'il soit toujours requis pour l'existence, d'une action par exemple, quelque chose, par où l'on puisse *pleinement* concevoir, pourquoi l'existence de cette action a lieu plûtôt que de n'avoir pas lieu." *Ibid.*, p. 111.

A man is capable of nothing, if actions supposedly belonging to him depend entirely on essential dispositions he has not created or on accidental situations beyond his control.

Our French author becomes quite rhetorical here,[33] and from the manifest absurdities for Christian life which fatal necessity entails, he proceeds to justify the intention guiding this work in favor of chance or contingency under the Providence of God. It is not true that there is always a *pourquoi* for each action; rather, there is always an element of chance, of the fortuitous. There is a free and indeterminate possibility in human powers which can best be stated in vivid terms by imagining that the world is annihilated an infinity of times and each time restored as it was for five or six thousand years. We must then realize in such a supposition that it is not only possible, not only probable, but absolutely infallible that the sequence of human events would not be always exactly the same. "The majority of free beings, in the same situations, would determine themselves now one way, now another." This is chance—*Voilà bien le hazard*.[34]

Twelve years later, in 1768, in his collected edition of Leibniz' works, Dutens published Christian Kortholt's disputation denying that any danger to the Christian religion lurked in the philosophy of Leibniz.[35] Kortholt even noted that Leibnizian philosophy might not have been dragged into so much controversy had it not been for the disputes occasioned by the philosophy of the famous Christian Wolff. Unlike Prémontval, he maintained that anyone who thinks Leibniz' defense of the Principle of Sufficient Reason makes his philosophy dangerous to liberty, simply declares he does not understand Leibniz. The Principle, *nothing happens without a cause,* held by innumerable philosophers, is no less inimical than

---

[33] *Ibid.,* pp. 113-116.

[34] Il est donc faux qu'il y ait toujours un *pourquoi* de chaque action. Il se trouve donc toujours dans chaque action quelque chose de *fortuit.* Donc il y a un HAZARD." *Ibid.,* p. 121. "Alors nous ne pouvons que concevoir, qu'il seroit, non seulement possible non seulement probable, mais infaillible, que la suite des événemens ne se retrouveroit pas toujours la même; le plûpart des êtres libres, *dans les mêmes conjonctures,* venant à se déterminer, *tantôt d'une façon, tantôt d'une autre.* O si le même être, dans le même confoncture, se détermine, tantôt d'une façon, tantôt d'une autre; voilà bien le hazard. Donc il'y a un HAZARD. *S'il y a une Dieu, il y a un hazard; s'il n'y a point de hazard, il n'y a point de Dieu."* *Ibid.,* p. 128.

[35] Christian Kortholt, *Disputatio de philosophia Leibnitii Christianae Religioni haud perniciosa, Gothofredi Guillelmi Leibnitii Opera Omnia,* ed. William Dutens, (Geneva: Frartres de Tournes, 1768), I, ccix-ccxxix.

nothing happens without a sufficient reason. To understand Leibniz rightly, one must take into account the different kinds of Sufficient Reason. For instance, in material bodies, it is a necessitating reason; in spiritual substances it is merely moving or inclining; in God it is contained in Himself.[36]

Brucker, whose outline of the philosophy of Leibniz is also published in Dutens, presents the Principle of Sufficient Reason as that according to which we say that "no fact can be found to be true or any true enunciation exist unless there is a sufficient reason why it is so rather than something else, although those reasons most often remain unknown to us."[37] He goes into some detail on the history of the Principle, with references to Epicurus, Seneca, Democritus, Cicero, Lucretius; he observes, tantalizingly, that he will pass over in silence the more recent users of the Principle, *especially among the Scholastics.*[38] After the death of Leibniz put an end to the Clarke Correspondence and the discussion there of the Principle of Sufficient Reason, its validity was sharply and quite vehemently disputed, notes Brucker, when Wolff classed it among the primary truths of metaphysics.[39]

But in the course of apologetical controversy and in the gradual change of metaphysical context of the Principle of Sufficient Reason due to the influx of Newtonian science, Lockian Empiricism and a general disgust with the endless precisions of Wolff's rationalism the relation of Sufficient Reason to causality, and the causal problem which Kant called the crux of metaphysics, became more and more a central point of discussion and difference. As Urban ob-

---

36 *Ibid.,* p. ccxvii.

37 James Brucker, "G. G. Leibnitii Vita" Ex tom. v deprompta, Vol. I of *Leibnitii Opera Omnia,* ejusdem philosophiae historia, cxlii-clxvi. "Alterum est principium rationis sufficientis, vi cujus consideramus, nullum factum reperiri posse verum, cur vero existere aliquam enuntiationem, nisi adsit ratio sufficiens, cur potius ita fit, quam aliter, quamvis rationes istae saepissime nobis incognitae esse queant. Celeberrimum hoc principium rationis sufficientis factum est in orbe philosophico, quam primum resuscitatum & quasi vita donatum ex ingenio Leibnitiano prodiit." James Brucker, "G. G. Leibnitii Vita" Ex Tom. V deprompta, *Leibnitii Opera Omnia,* op. cit., I, clvi-clvii.

38 "Tacemus recentiores alios, praecipue inter Scholasticos, qui passim ex hoc principio ratiocinantur." *Ibid.,* p. clviii; cf. pp. clvii-clvii.

39 Et haec quidem vivo *Leibnitio* disputata sunt; acriter vero & satis vehementer de veritate principii hujus Logici & Metaphysici disputatum est, cum celeberrimus *Wolfius* illud inter veritates metaphysicae primarias referret (c. 2, par. 29, & T. II, p. 26 Metaph. Germ.) ostensoque discrimine inter caussam & rationem sufficientem, hoc axiomate in demonstrando, quod sibi conceperat, aedificio metaphysico uteretur." *Ibid.,* pp. clx-clxi.

serves, "The problem of 'determinism' in the moral order thus forces the metaphysical side of the problem into the foreground."[40]

Under the limits designated for this study of the Scholastic use of the Principle of Sufficient Reason, it is impossible even to sketch, as part of the wider background of the Principle's textbook history, a considerable body of literature down to the end of the nineteenth century in which it functions for non-Scholastic writers along lines stemming directly from Kant and the German Idealists. This is a context decidedly unscholastic in any sense, yet it must have been familiar to the erudite authors of manuals at the time. But in the absence of references and citations in the textbooks themselves, writers such as Crusius, Kant (on this subject of Sufficient Reason), and Schopenhauer, for instance, apparently were not considered pertinent by these authors. Toward the end of the century and after 1900 cognizance was taken, at least in passing reference, of such writers as Drobisch, Herbart, Sigwart, Trendelenburg, and Wundt.

But one non-Scholastic who deserves passing mention here is Nicolas Béguelin (1714-1789), the first Swiss after Euler to become a member of the Royal Academy of Prussia (1747). He authored several memoirs in the annals of the academy, one of which, on the Principle of Sufficient Reason, drew forth a reply from Cardinal Gerdil. Frequently referred to in later manual-footnotes, this caused Béguelin himself for a time to be singled out by some authors (Liberatore, for example) as an important opponent of the Principle of Causality.

Cardinal Gerdil in his "Reflections on a Memoir of Monsieur Béguelin Concerning the Principle of Sufficient Reason and the Possibility of a System of Chance,"[41] presses home the deficiency in Béguelin's concept of Causality. Although he enters into a discussion of the nature of the object of mathematics, in order to deny Béguelin's contention that this science has, as an advantage over metaphysics, the capacity of creating its objects, Gerdil sees as the

[40] Wilbur Urban, "The History of the Principle of Sufficient Reason: Its Metaphysical and Logical Formulations," *Princeton Contributions to Philosophy*, I, 3 (1900), 1-87.

[41] Cardinal Hyacinthus Sigismond Gerdil, Della Congregazione de' Cher. Reg. Di S. Paolo (Barnabites) (1718-1802), "Reflexions sur un mémoir de Monsieur Béguelin concernant le principe de la raison suffisante de la possibilité du système du hazard," *Opera Edite ed Inedite Del Cardinale Giacinto Sigismondo Gerdil* (Florence: G. Celli, 1844-1851), I, 435-471.

fundamental point of the *Memoir*, the author's distinction between the Principle of Contradiction and the Principle of Sufficient Reason in terms of existential reference.[42] Béguelin wanted the Principle of Contradiction as a purely mathematical principle, self-evident because dealing with ideal existence and the mutual repugnance, as ideas, of existing and simultaneously not existing.[43] The Principle of Sufficient Reason, on the other hand, deals with actual existence; it supposes the real existence of a being or of completed change. At this level of reference there is not the clarity and self-evident nature of pure thought; the idea of existence simply does not contain the idea of a Sufficient Reason and hence cannot be the source of a self-evident principle, according to Gerdil.

He goes along with the fact of difference in the nature of the evidence of the two principles and admits that since the definition of existence cannot be arbitrary, depending as it does on the reality of real things, I must be able to assert something of existence which is seized primarily in my knowledge of what it is to exist; the mere concept of existence is not enough to verify the Principle of Sufficent Reason.

In other words, there are, independently of the Principle of Contradiction, truths at the very threshold of human understanding which the slightest attention will suffice to reveal as evident, with no other aid than that of a purely intuitive knowledge. Among these truths he instances, as a refutation of Béguelin, the age-old axiom that *nothingness produces nothing*.[44] This axiom does not

---

[42] *Ibid.*, I, 438-440.

[43] L'Auteur convient, qu'on pourrait concevoir ce principe plus idéalement, en l'énonçant ainsi. Si quelque chose existe, cette chose a une raison suffisante de cette existence: alors, dit-il, on affirmerait simplement que l'idée de l'existence d'un être en lui même, que l'idée de l'existence exclut l'idée d'une d'une non-existence simul-referme ou suppose l'idée d'un suffisant pourquoi. Il soutient néanmoins que 'de quelque manière qu'on l'envisage, la différence entre l'évidence de ce principe et de celui de contradiction, est manifest. Dans l'un il est incontéstable par l'énoncé en lui même, que l'idée de l'existence exclut l'idée d'une non-existence simul-tanée; mais dans l'autre, on ne voit pas par le simple énoncé, que l'idée de l'existence renferme l'idée d'un suffisant-pourquoi. La vérité de cette énoncé dépend de la défi-nition de l'existence, et cette définition n'est par arbitraire, puisqu'il s'agit non d'un être idéal, mais d'un réalité. If faut donc, pour que je puisse affirmer quelque chose de l'existence, que je sache premièrement ce que c'est qu'exister.' " *Ibid.*, I, 443.

[44] "Il faut donc convenir, qu'indépendement du principe de contradiction, il est des vérités que sont tellement à la portée de l'entendement humain, que la plus légère attention suffit pour en découvrir pleinement l'évidence, sans autre secours que celui d'une connaissance purement intuitive. Or entre les principes, dont la

suppose a more exact knowledge of the nature of existence than the Principle of Contradiction; its evidence is likewise founded on the opposition, immediately perceived by the mind, between being and non-being. Without considering Béguelin's questionable wall of separation between ideal and real existence, it is enough thus to show that the mind can apprehend directly an incompatibility which is found among real existents, as objects outside the mind.[45]

The Principle of Sufficient Reason, concludes Gerdil, is nothing else than the application of this axiom that *nothingness produces nothing* and is, therefore, as real and genuine as the Principle of Contradiction. As a crowning argument, he attempts to use the very premises and principles which Béguelin himself adopted to amplify the truth of this conclusion, an attempt whose details we need not follow here.[46]

"Cartesian" Manuals, The New Theodicy and Ontologism

This brings us to our early nineteenth-century survey of what may be termed in general as Cartesian philosophy manuals. Written under Catholic auspices, but related also to certain non-Catholic efforts in the field, these textbooks are representative of the kind from which the initiators of Neo-Scholasticism had to extricate themselves, and which Leo XIII's Encyclical on Scholastic philosophy, *Aeterni Patris* (1879), rendered obsolete.

vérité se fait apercévoir par une évidence immédiate, on n'a jamais fait difficulté de reconnaître cet ancien axiome, que le rien ne peut rien produire." *Ibid.*, I, 445.

[45] "Mais quand ce principe serait applicable au principe de la raison suffisante, tel qu'on a coutume de l'énoncer, il ne paraît pas qu'il ait lieu rélativement à l'axiome, que le rien ne produit rien. L'évidence de cet axiome n'exige pas un autre idée de l'existence, que celle qui entre dans l'énoncé du principe de contradiction. Quoique l'Auteur semble ici élever comme un mur de séparation entre l'existence idéale, et l'existence réelle, il faut pourtant bien qu'il convienne que l'incompatibilité que l'esprit aperçoit entre l'idée de l'existence, et l'idée de la non-éxistence simultanée, se retrouve réellement entre l'existence réelle, et la non-existence simultanée des objets qui sont hors de l'esprit. . . . L'axiome, *ex nihilo nihil fit,* dans le sens exclusif de toute cause, non seulement matérielle, mais encore efficiente, ne suppose pas un connaissance plus exacte de la nature de l'existence, que le principe de contradiction: son evidence est également fondée sur l'opposition, que l'esprit aperçoit immédiament, entre l'être et le non-être." *Ibid.*, I, 446-447.

[46] "Nous pourrons montrer plus particuliérement dans la suite, que le principe de la raison suffisante n'est autre que l'application de ce principe que nous venons de rapporter, savoir, que *le rien ne fait rien.* Mais pour le faire plus efficacement, il faut attendre que l'Auteur nous fournisse lui-même les principes, dont nous devons nous servir contre lui." *Loc. Cit.*

The history of Cartesianism among Catholic philosophers and seminary teachers is long and complex and lies outside the limits of this study. So also does any attempt to label individual manuals as strictly Cartesian and to identify the details of their origin and propagation. But it is possible, by noting their emphasis on psychology and their establishment of the starting point of philosophy in mental experience itself, to classify the following textbooks roughly as of Cartesian orientation.

Although the Principle of Sufficient Reason did not appear until this textbook group had already been influenced by the current Wolffian vogue for method and terminology, there is some profit to be gained from a passing glance at some of these authors. Besides indicating again the relation between starting points and metaphysical content with use of the Principle of Sufficient Reason, this résumé is also useful, at least by contrast, for a partial sketch of the background pertinent to the Revival of Scholasticism which, from mid-century onward, produced the philosophy and the textbooks in which the Principle of Sufficient Reason became an important and quite peculiar stock ingredient. Finally, a further dimension can be added to the chapter on the eighteenth-century history of the Principle by noting the earlier predecessors of the Cartesian texts current from 1800 to 1850. Among these authors, one of the most prominent was the French Jesuit, Claude Buffier.

Buffier's works were many and varied, but the two most important philosophically were: *The Principles of Reasoning Explained in Two New Logics. With Remarks on the Best Known Logic Now Current* (1714), and *A Treatise on First Truths and of the Source of Our Judgments, or An Examination of the Current Philosophical Opinions on the First Notions of Things* (1724).[47] Buffier advocated a simplicity in method and style that avoided the inclusion of frivolous and intricate questions which were either

---

[47] Claude Buffier, S.J. (1661-1737), *Les principes du raisonement exposez en deux logiques nouvelles. Avec des remarques sur les logiques qui ont eu le plus de réputation de notre temps* (Paris: Pierre Witte, 1714); *Traité des premières veritéz et de la source de nos jugements, ou l'on examine le sentiment des philosophes sur les premières notions des choses* (Paris: V. Monge, 1724). Lamennais edited an edition of this work in 1822 to serve as an appendix to the second volume of his *L'Essai sur l'indifference en matière de religion* and suppressed the passage where Buffier limits the extent to which common sense is a rule of certitude. In 1843 Francisque Bouillier edited the *Oeuvres philosophiques du Pére Buffier de la Compagnie de Jésus* (Paris: A. Delahays, 1843), with notes and introduction. An English translation of *First Truths* appeared in London in 1780.

chimerical or useless, or so simple that they could be comprehended
with no difficulty if only presented with clearness and precision.[48]

In his view the only proper end of logic is to direct the second
operation of the mind, judgment. Now the truth of judgment is
in its object, but the mistake made by so many philosophers has
been to miss the precise nature of this object. The true object of
logic is internal truth or inference and not external truth or truth
of principle.[49] The essence of logic consists in the connection, or
unity, of two ideas, and the author indicates the unique means of
making this connection: it lies in the assembly of ideas which themselves are clear. He rejects Locke's explanation of clarity of ideas
as derived from their simplicity and purports to show that it comes
from the inner experience we have of our perceptions.

In stressing the importance of judgment, Buffier reduces the
syllogism to a means of assuring the mind that it has arrived at a
true judgment. Although the syllogism merely analyzes one judgment into two or three other judgments, now seen in detail, this
added verification is not necessary, since each judgment verifies
itself and "it is necessary only to observe the one essential rule of
logic to make a proposition true: to know that the idea of the subject is contained in the idea of the attribute."[50]

The vain and frivolous nature of syllogistic proof is especially
apparent in the case of that truth most essential to man, the existence of God.

> All the syllogisms in the world do not convince the mind as effi-
> caciously as the following consistent and single sequence of
> propositions:
>   1. The universe has parts.
>   2. The parts are ordered.
>   3. This order is established and conserved by some principle.
>   4. The principle which establishes and conserves order in
>   anything whatsoever is intelligent.
>   5. This intelligence which establishes and conserves order
>   in all the parts of the universe is superior to the indi-
>   vidual intelligence which put order only into a part of the
>   universe.
>   6. This intelligence superior to all the others is called God.[51]

[48] Buffier, *Les principes,* I, Preface.
[49] *Ibid.,* I, 367, 172.
[50] *Ibid.,* II, 161, 162.
[51] *Ibid.,* II, 163, 164. Needless to say, Buffier's sequence does not conclude to
anything more than a super-designer of this universe who needs not be infinite since

This method, adds Buffier, was in use long before the invention of the syllogism.

Just as in the *Logic* there is no trace of (nor, at that time, precedent for) the Principle of Sufficient Reason, so also in the more mature *Treatise on First Truths* there is no mention of it. First Truths are "those propositions which are so clear they cannot be proved nor disputed by propositions more clear than they are."[52] The axioms of metaphysics—by which Buffier understands such things as *two and two are four; the whole is greater than its parts; it is impossible that a thing be at the same time and not be*—are not understood in the sense that they are the first to present themselves to the mind. Nor are they principles of all truth, "since they do not serve to prove any external truth, that is to say, the real and veritable existence of anything outside ourselves."[53]

These axioms are merely internal truth, truth of pure harmony or internal fitness of ideas founded on the principle that *this thing is this thing,* or *this idea is this idea and not another.* The Principle of Sufficient Reason is not listed among these axioms of metaphysics nor among those First Truths discovered in relation to the nature and perfection of being.

Buffier, in his introduction to the *First Truths,* says that in the course of his work he speaks of the opinions of Descartes, Malebranche, Locke, and M. Le Clerc, only because without searching for them he has encountered them on the route of his investigations.[54]

Thirty years later Jean Cochet (d. 1771), who also was interested in reducing things to their First Principles, presented a *Metaphysics* which indicated that besides Descartes and Malebranche he had also encountered Wolff.[55] In so doing he searched out a combination of the Cartesian *Cogito*-approach with the Wolffian division and method. He begins his ontology with a division of being into real and rational, to be studied according to its principles, properties, and kinds. Principles are of three kinds: knowl-

---

the universe, though wonderously ordered, is finite in its order and thus demands only a highly intelligent but not an infinitely intelligent designer.

[52] Buffier, *Traité des premières veritéz*, p. 7.

[53] *Ibid.*, p. 71.

[54] *Ibid.*, p. ix.

[55] Jean Cochet (d. 1771), *La métaphysique qui continent l'ontologie, la theologie naturelle et la pneumatologie* (Paris: J. Desaint & C., 1753).

edge, generation, and composition. Axioms are principles of knowledge and these are:

> . . . all the propositions of which in considering with average attention the predicate and subject, it is clearly seen that the idea of one belongs or does not belong with the idea of the other. There are axioms which need to be explained but none which require demonstration.[56]

This definition is followed by a list of twelve axioms ranging from the first, which says that *Everything which is perceived as evident is true,* to the last: *an effect cannot have more perfection than it has received from its total cause.* The Principle of Contradiction is listed second: *It is impossible that a thing be and not be at the same time,* and is followed by the axiom that *whoever thinks, exists.* Equality of equals, whole and part, relative magnitude are also subjects of axioms. There is no Principle of Sufficient Reason.

Skepticism is overthrown, thinks Cochet, by the proposition that *evidence is the first rule of all philosophical truth.*[57] Atheism is confronted with the fact that we have a clear and distinct idea of God, and from this His existence is demonstrated.

In a work which appeared two years later (1756) by Claude Mey (1712-1796), metaphysics is given a more pronounced psychological orientation. In this *Metaphysical Essay or Principles on the Nature and Operations of the Mind,*[58] metaphysics is itself conceived as a study of the principal operations of the mind; the first step therefore, after being assured of its existence, is the conviction that it is a substance essentially different from the body. Experience rather than the construction of systems is the great source of progress in this science because, just as in physics, facts rather than reasonings insure progress, so also the best method of studying the soul is to watch its operations and movements. In the certitude that "I doubt" lies the principle of the certitude of my existence. Here also is the knowledge that *nothingness* is opposed to this doubting existent. Nothingness and existence exclude each other, and thus I know the difference between truth and error, which in turn gives me knowledge of the fact that I am guided by the ideas which the mind has. Their evidence is the light of truth.[59]

56 *Ibid.,* pp. 6-7.

57 *Ibid.,* p. 14.

58 Claude Mey (1712-1796), *Essai sur métaphysique; ou, principes sur le nature et le opérations de l'esprit* (Paris: Desaint & Saillant, 1753).

59 *Ibid.,* pp. 12-15.

Mey wrote a long section to refute Locke, drawing on the doctrine of Original Sin to prove innate ideas. If they do not exist, then how can the effects of Original Sin mean anything? How can there be darkness and weakness in a *tabula rasa?* Moreover, the senses are unworthy of the elevated nature of ideas which the mind itself must form.

A more advanced example of Wolffian method combined with Cartesian doctrine is found in the ex-Jesuit, Para. Writing under the name of L'Abbe Para du Phanjas, he produced in 1779 his *Theory of Non-Sensuous Beings, or Complete Course of Metaphysics, Sacred and Profane, Made Available to the General Public.*[60]

Three characteristics of this work justify its classification as "Cartesian." First, the title itself betrays the orientation toward subjective knowledge. Immaterial being is defined as "insensible," in terms of the knowledge process rather than its constituent nature. Secondly, the historical orientation of the introduction makes Descartes the savior of philosophy after its Peripatetic decadence which extends through the age of Barbarism, from the end of the fourth into the seventeenth century.[61] Thirdly, to establish fixed points of luminous certitude in the midst of a vast amount of speculation and experience, he selects the knowing Ego, the *Moi* of intellect and sense knowledge. By meditating on the "perceptions" which the mind has, one observes that general ideas of things are included therein. This leads to the whole scope and course of the sciences: theories of being, of dialectic, of certitude, of God, of soul, of material substance.[62]

Certain axioms are the general foundation of our knowledge, but Para does not explicitly list any Principle of Sufficient Reason among them. As to the proof for the existence of God, he feels one need only put experience and speculation to work simultaneously. It is evident that something exists from all eternity. In refuting the Optimism of Leibniz, "the most sublime and philosophical dream perhaps ever conceived by the human mind," and his theory of monads, Para makes passing mention of the Principle

---

[60] L'Abbé Para du Phanjas, *Théorie des êtres, insensibles, ou cours complet de métaphysique, sacrée et profane, mise à la portée de tout monde. Avec une table alphabétique des matières, qui fait de tout cet ouvrage, un vrai dictionaire de métaphysique ou de philosophie* (Paris: L. Cellot & A. Jombert, 1779).

[61] *Ibid.,* I, xvii.

[62] *Ibid.,* I, xli.

of Sufficient Reason.[63] Hence, this principle is mentioned only in explaining Leibniz; it is not used by Para himself.

In 1784 a manuscript course of studies dictated by Antoine Migeot, priest and professor of philosophy at the University of Reims, was published by an editor who judged it to be a happy medium between the barbarous rubbish of the Schools and the impious atheism of his contemporaries. From the title, *Philosophical Elements divided into Five Parts*,[64] the work might seem to be another Wolffian text of logic and the four parts of metaphysics. But this is not so; it is composed of logic, moral philosophy, and metaphysics (written in Latin), mathematics and physics (written in French).

Philosophical method is conceived in terms of principles, and for a proposition to be a principle it should lead us by a reasoning process to the knowledge of some other thing or show the movement by which we are impelled to assent to truth. Something different from the usual way of presentation in textbooks appeared when this author, for the sake of his talented and urbane students who are above the barbarity of the Schools, developed the argumentation for each *concertatio* or section in the form of a dialogue. "Theodorus" took the part of Sophistry and "Eugene" refuted the arguments. As a slight concession to the inelegant style of the past, Migeot points out that the first proposition of a reasoned process of argumentation is commonly called the major, and the second and third, the minor and consequence respectively![65]

As a corollary to a Cartesian-like position on the sinfulness of error, Migeot presented a good Cartesian procedure: whoever really studies philosophy ought to doubt all his judgments except those in which no reasoning process is involved.[66] The full Malebranchian flavor of the work appears in the *concertatio* of the second chapter: The senses are useful in attaining truth but they are not the source of ideas; sensible qualities are not in external objects, which "can do nothing more than present the occasion for God to excite sensible qualities in the soul."[67]

[63] *Ibid.*, II, 553; III, 306.
[64] Antoine Migeot, *Philosophiae elementa quinque distincta partibus, studiosae juventuti in collegio bonorum puerorum universi studii Remensis tradita* (Paris: Le Clerc, 1784).
[65] *Ibid.*, I, 29.
[66] *Ibid.*, I, 38.
[67] *Ibid.*, I, 83, 109-117.

Migeot was also a good witness to a wide-spread conception that *Scholastic method* was identical with that of Wolff, and the geometrical ideal in general. To prove his statement that the method previously used in the Schools was worthy of praise in part and partly to be retained, while at the same time possessing defects to be amended, he wrote as follows:

> The first part of the proposition I prove thusly: The Geometric method of demonstration is the best of all . . . *Atqui*: the method established in the schools is like this method . . . *ergo* . . . According to the Scholastic method certain notions and axioms are first laid down; then theorems are set up . . . and finally from an applied principle . . . comes a conclusion which itself is a principle, and so on through the process.[68]

Finally, one of the masterpieces of Cartesian manual writing, which Ventura calls "le cours classique du cartesianisme" and the model for almost all the others,[69] is the famous *Institutiones philosophicae, auctoritate D.D. Archiepiscopi Lugdunensis*.[70] Written by a Father Joseph Valla (whose name does not always appear on the title page of later editions), it was first used in the Diocese of Lyons and became generally known as *Philosophie de Lyon*.

Valla, as well as Ubaghs later on, drew considerable inspiration from Malebranche, but this does not seem to have been counted a defect at the time. Thus, the Mandatum of the Most Illustrious and most Reverend Archbishop of Lyons, Antonius De Malvin de Montazet, to his clergy printed at the beginning of the 1817 edition urged this same orientation toward a conception of man as a soul which for some reason not quite explicable is confined in a body, with which it must have no commerce involving dependence.

Emphasizing the importance of this type of philosophy, Valla warns that in metaphysics, where we study both the existence of

---

[68] *Ibid.,* I, 161.

[69] James Ventura de Raulica, *La philosophie chrétienne* (Paris: Gaume Frères et J. Duprey, 1861), III, 3. According to Ventura, Antonio Genovesi (1712-1769) is a Cartesian "dont la Philosophe, toute cartésienne, est, en Italie, ce que la PHILO-SOPHIE DE LYON est en France." *Ibid.,* III, 79. But usually he is called the Wolff of Italy. He uses the Principle of Sufficient Reason and was quoted by nineteenth-century manuals.

[70] Joseph Valla, *Institutiones philosophicae auctoritate D.D. Archiepiscopi Lugdunensis ad usum scholarum suae diocesis editae* (Bassani: Remondin, 1817). The identification of the author as Valla is written in on the title page of Yale University Library's copy. Earlier editions go back to 1792.

God and His attributes and the reality of the human mind and its dignity, there must be none of those philosophical theories which detract from the excellence and spirituality of the mind of man.[71]

> Let it be presented as a noble substance which has no truck with corporeal impurity, whose life is constituted by thought and love and which does not so depend on the organs of the senses as to derive its ideas therefrom, but rather, coming forth from the hand of its creator, is already in possession of many of its innate ideas.[72]

It is not surprising then that in this work we have "principle-philosophy" with a vengeance. First Principles are "those general and evident propositions the truth of which depends and follows the truth of many other propositions."[73] Philosophy is defined as "knowledge evidently deduced from First Principles," although these latter are merely the foundation of the science and do not constitute it.[74] All men are imbued with First Principles; discussion and controversy among philosophers arises only from the differences in the conclusions which are drawn therefrom.

The Principle of Sufficient Reason is not mentioned among these First Principles, but it appears in Special Metaphysics. Special Metaphysics is *Pneumatologia,* part one of which treats of God. The moral arguments for His existence are given first place.[75] Physical arguments are those "which are deduced from the contemplation of the corporeal world."[76] The three metaphysical arguments depend on the things of which metaphysics treats: 1. from necessary being; 2. from the creation of our minds and their conjunction with the body; 3. from the idea of God.[77] The "no effect without a cause" principle is used.[78]

To establish the repugnance of conceiving a universe consisting entirely of contingent beings, the Principle of Sufficient Reason is brought into play; it is also applied to answer an objection based on the infinity of a series of contingent beings. The infinity of the series would not be the Sufficient Reason for contingent beings because there would be no Sufficient Reason for such an infinity.[79]

In the section on the attributes of God, the Principle of Sufficient Reason appears in the discussion of Leibniz' theory that God

71 *Ibid.,* I, viii.   74 *Ibid.,* I, 14.   77 *Ibid.,* pp. 90-99.
72 *Ibid.,* I, viii.   75 *Ibid.,* I, part 2, 56-75.   78 *Ibid.,* p. 92.
73 *Ibid.,* I, 11.   76 *Ibid.,* I, part 2, 79-88.   79 *Ibid.,* I, part 2, 99.

could not act without being moved by a Sufficient Reason. The proof that this proposition is to be rejected is two-fold: it destroys both divine and human liberty, and it rests on a false principle. This is the Principle of Sufficient Reason *as understood by Leibniz,* who makes Sufficient Reason some particular *ratio* drawn from the nature of objects and efficaciously moving the will. Such a conception misses the fact that in free acts the will itself is the reason for the movement.[80]

During the first half of the nineteenth century the stream of Cartesian textbook philosophy continued to flow through Catholic seminaries and schools.[81] One of the last of these manuals to enjoy prominence was the *Cours élémentaire de philosophie* (1850) by J. V. De Decker, S.J.[82] This too combined a Cartesian starting point in the cognoscitive faculties with Wolffian methods and terminology. Sensation is a psychological fact, not an impression.[83]

The Principle of Sufficient Reason is a more general formula for the Principle of Causality. "In virtue of [this latter] we affirm a strict, intimate, and proper connection between phenomena and the being which is its principal producer."[84] But the Principle of Sufficient Reason applies also to knowledge of the subjective order; the word "reason" indicates not only cause properly speaking but also every *principle* whose act or effect does not have a distinct existence.[85] These principles and others are all reducible to that of Identity and hence are analytic. But of themselves they are abstract, general forms, sterile until experience gives them a content to which they apply.[86]

---

[80] *Ibid.,* II, 68-71.

[81] There is also a considerable body of non-Catholic Cartesian textbook philosophy which cannot be considered here.

[82] J. V. De Decker, S.J., *Cours élémentaire de philosophie* (Namur: F. J. Douxfils, 1850).

[83] *Ibid.,* I, 129.

[84] *Ibid.,* II, 10.

[85] *Ibid.,* II, II.

[86] *Ibid.,* II, 15. Cf. infra, chapter six, n. 4. Two examples of further variations in the context of the Principle of Sufficient Reason are found in the following: Joseph Delboeuf, *Essai de logique scientifique. Prolégomènes suivis d'une étude sur la question du mouvement considérée dans ses rapports avec le principe de contradiction* (Liége: J. Desor, 1865). This author treats of the question of certitude and its criterion in terms of scientific (and mathematical logic). He says that such statements as *all phenomena have a cause, all truth has a sufficient reason* are not principles but consequences deduced from a long series of experiences and absolutized by a process of particular abstraction. p. 52. Delboeuf's background would lead us into

The New Theodicy and Ontologism. From the upheaval and horror of the French Revolution (1789) had come a reaction which was crystallized among Catholic philosophers in France by Joseph de Maistre (1753-1821), Louis Vicomte de Bonald (1754-1840), and Robert de Lamennais (1782-1854) in the doctrine of Traditionalism.[87] At first this movement tended to dethrone reason in all of its forms—*sens, sentiment intérieur, raison*—on the principle that the upheaval of 1789 was only the result of Cartesian reliance on reason and First Principles.

Since the sovereignty of reason proclaimed by Descartes had produced the philosophy of atheistic materialism which led to the Revolution, then in place of the spirit of examination, critique and analysis associated with the enemy, the Traditionalists wanted to substitute authority, tradition, and theology as a kind of universal reason embodied in the universal church and taking the place of all systems of philosophy. Reason and its First Principles were reduced to dependence on language, society, and the intervention of God.[88]

the stream of Condillac's influence on such writers as M. Laromiguière (1756-1837), *Leçons de philosophie sur les principes de l'intelligence, ou sur les causes et sur les origines des idées* (4th ed.; Paris: Brunot-Labbe, 1826) and another variation in the context of principles. Cf. J. Ferreol Perrard, *Introduction à la philosophie, ou nouvelle logique Francaise, pour préparer les jeunes gens à subir l'exâmin de Bachelier ès-Lettres* (Paris: T. Berquet, 1822), and L'Abbé Jules Fabre, *Cours de philosophie ou nouvelle exposition des principes de cette science* (Paris: Durand, 1863). "C'est également dans le sens platonicien ou augustinien que nous devons interpreter les paroles de Leibniz, lorsqu'il définit la philosophie: 'La science des raisons suffisantes.' " *Ibid.*, I, 45.

87 Cf. M. Ferraz, *Histoire de la philosophie en France au XIXe siécle,* Vol. II: *Traditionalisme et Ultramontanisme* (Paris: Didier, 1880).

88 A good example of a philosophy manual in this tradition is that of the Abbé Doney, *Nouveaux élémens de philosophie, d'après la méthode d'observation et ¹a règle du sens commun* (Brusseles: Demengeot et Goodman, 1830). An earlier example is the anonymous *Philosophiae Turonensis institutiones ad usum collegiorum atque seminariorum* (Paris: Le Clerc, 1823). These two are more semi-rationalistic than the anonymous *Elementa ontologiae ad usum alumnorum seminarii Sylvae-Ducensis* (Gestel St. Michaelis: e Prelo Surdo-Mutorum, 1846) or the work of Abbé Combalot, *Élémens de philosophie Catholique* (Louvain: Vanlinthout and Vandenzande, 1833). This latter attempts to show how Catholicism is the principal generator of science, liberty, fine arts, civilization, agriculture, industry and commerce. Theology and the order of faith are the basis of all philosophy, *Ibid.*, p. 100. The use of "Theodicy" in place of "natural theology" among the nineteenth-century philosophy manuals seems to have originated in this Traditionalist movement. Cf. Joseph Owens, C.SS.R., "Theodicy, Natural Theology and Metaphysics," *The Modern Schoolman,* XXVIII (1951), 126-137.

Beyond the borders of France, Traditionalism found its way into Belgium, Spain, and Italy.[89] Belgian Traditionalism prided itself on maintaining a half-way position between pure Traditionalism and pure Rationalism. To the thesis that some exterior teaching was necessary, as a condition *sine qua non* of the use of reason and that there was a distinct knowledge of "innate" metaphysics and moral truths, was added other positions such as that metaphysical truths could not be proved and that the existence of God was not demonstrable.

About 1843, the principal representatives of Belgium Traditionalism, Gerard Ubaghs (1800-1875)[90] was called upon by ecclesiastical authority to correct several propositions in his *Logic* and *Theodicy*. In 1866, after considerable ferment and discussion, he and his Louvain colleagues, Laforet, Lefeboure, and Beelen, were condemned not only as Traditionalists but also as Ontologists.

This mixture of Cartesianism and Catholic theology need not delay us at any length. It will suffice to note that Ubaghs' 1863 edition of his manuals contains the Principle of Sufficient Reason and that it functions in the underlying context of the author's Ontologism.[91]

Although the Jesuits were against Ubaghs and the Ontologism of the time,[92] two of their writers were not far removed on some points from the essentials of this tendency. These were Francis Rothenflue, S.J., *Institutiones philosophiae theoreticae in usum praelectionum*[93] and Joseph A. Dmowski, S.J., *Institutiones philosophicae*.[94] Both of these authors, but especially Rothenflue, used

---

[89] James Ventura was one of its principal representatives in Italy; Donoso Cortes (1805-1853) represented Traditionalism in Spain. Cf. George F. J. Lamountain, "A Note on the Traditionalism of Father Ventura de Raulica (1792-1861)," *The Modern Schoolman*, XXXIII (1956), 190-196.

[90] Gerard Ubaghs, *Ontologiae seu Metaphysicae generalis elementa* (5th ed.; Louvain: Vanlinthout, 1863); *Theodiceae seu theologiae naturalis elementa ad usum discentium accomodata* (Louvain: Vanlinthout, 1863); *Logicae seu philosophiae rationalis elementa* (Louvain: Vanlinthout, 1860) (bound with the Theodicy).

[91] *Ibid.*, p. 127.

[92] Cf. Joseph Burnichon, S.J., *La Compagnie de Jésus en France; histoire d'un siècle 1814- 1915.* Tome Quatrième: *1860- 1880* (Paris: Gabriel Beauchesne, 1922), pp. 25-51.

[93] Francis Rothenflue, S.J., *Institutiones philosophiae theoreticae in usum praelectionum* (Freiburg i S.: L. Piller, 1842 [1st ed. 1840]).

[94] Joseph A. Dmowski, S.J., *Institutiones philosophicae* (Uden: P. Verholven, 1840).

the Principle of Sufficient Reason and are quoted by subsequent Scholastic manual-writers.

Among the Sulpicians, the Abbé Branchereau did not use the Principle of Sufficient Reason in his *Praelectiones philosophicae in majori seminario Claromontensi primum habitae.*[95] Influential in clerical philosophy, this manual was later withdrawn by the author six years after its publication when the Holy Office condemned fifteen propositions taken from its pages, two of them basic theses of ontologism. Somewhat earlier, J. Blatairou, familiar with Storchenau, Dmowski, and Ubaghs, found a place in his writings for the Principle of Sufficient Reason.[96] The popular *Compendium philosophiae ad usum seminariorum* (first issued in 1847 and enjoying a ninth edition in 1871), written by a priest of St. Sulpice who modestly signed himself "Author M . . .,"[97] gave the Principle a familiar place and treatment under causes.

This author also discusses induction, noting that there is a choice between using the Principle of Causality or Sufficient Reason to explain the certitude which we have by innate persuasion of the existence of natural laws and a constant order of things, or calling upon the goodness and providence of God as a foundation. In either case our persuasion of the existence of laws of nature is primitive, immediate and exists in our mind before we are capable of any experience or reasoning. The recourse to further principles is only for purposes of defense against those who question it.[98] He very briefly touches upon and rejects Leibniz' optimism.

Finally, contemporary with Liberatore in the first decade of his writings (1840-1850) are two authors worthy of further study; one, Dionysius of S. John in Galdo, O.F.M., because of his Franciscan blend of the many currents of the age, the other, Aloysius Bonelli, because of his particularly long and intelligent discussion of principles. Here we can only mention them to indicate that our selection of Liberatore in the next chapter does not mean that he was the only author of value at work. In face of the chaotic conditions

---

[95] Louis Branchereau, S.S., *Praelectiones philosophicae in majori seminario Claromontensi primum habitae* (Paris: J. Leroux et Jouby, 1855).

[96] J. Blatairou, *Institutiones philosophicae ad usum seminariorum* (Bordeaux: J. Dupy, 1848).

[97] Manier, S.S., *Compendium philosophiae ad usum seminariorum* (Paris: Lecoffre, 1867). Columbia University Library identifies "Auctor M . . ." as Manier.

[98] *Ibid.*, I, 144.

of textbooks about 1840, the Minister General of the Franciscan Friars Minor proposed for uniform adoption a *Philosophiae universae institutiones* which appeared anonymously in 1843 or 1844 but with the author's name, Dionysius of St. John in Galdo, displayed on the second edition of 1846.[99]

In this manual the meaning and role of the Principle of Sufficient Reason are about the same as in Liberatore, to whom there are several references. There is less concern with Kant, who is mentioned without details as to his theory of judgment.

Much more "modern" was the *Institutiones logico-metaphysicae* of the Roman priest, Aloysius Bonelli.[100] He points out that care must be taken not to step into the skeptics' position in such a way as never to be able to extricate oneself, and that Kant's procedure of first questioning the possibility of science is such a trap.[101] Bonelli prefers to stay with the many facts we know even if we do not know the reasons for them. Hence, he makes psychology the first part of metaphysics with a first section on the existence of a spiritual soul. He has Kant in reference concerning the substantial nature of the soul and Laromiguière in regard to its faculties.[102] In concluding the section on the faculties of the soul, Bonelli takes up the question of liberty and the old difficulty over the Principle of Sufficient Reason. Leibniz' principle may be admitted if the distinction is kept between intrinsic and extrinsic reasons. Free acts have their own sufficient reason. I wish because I wish.[103]

This chapter completes our survey of "the first hundred years" of Wolffian rationalism in Scholastic manuals, including some insight into traditions that escaped at least the direct influence of German rationalism, and noting some wider dimensions of the Principle of Sufficient Reason as involved in the controversy over Fatalism. There are further perspectives to the history and culture of this period from which, unfortunately, our study must necessarily prescind. The growth of Romanticism, reactions to rationalism in literature, history and morals, the growing commitment to realism and naturalism—all this might well be viewed as an at-

[99] Dionysius a S. Joanne in Galdo, O.F.M., *Philosophiae universae institutiones* (2nd ed.; Rome: C. Puccinelli, 1846-1847).

[100] Aloysius Bonelli, *Institutiones logico-metaphysicae* (4th ed.; Rome: Ex Typographia Bonarum Artium, 1846).

[101] *Ibid.*, II, 85-87.

[102] Bonelli, *Institutiones*, II, 104, 120 ff.

[103] *Ibid.*, p. 135.

tempt to return to history, to life, to experience, to *existence,* and the manuals of the next chapter, as well as those already examined belong to this wider framework.[104] But the limits of this work can hardly be extended to include those additional considerations. Rather, we must now proceed to the final inductive examination of evidence from the years 1850 to 1900.

[104] Along these lines in reference to contemporary textbook teaching today, Kenneth L. Schmitz offers some stimulating insights. Considering rationalism as *"an attitude toward reality* whose principal characteristic is a segregation and exaltation of an abstract and speculative human reason and the depreciation of man's other powers," he suggests means for increasing the student's "sensitivity to the integrity of being" so that progress in philosophy is toward vision rather than definition, wisdom rather than abstraction. Cf. Kenneth L. Schmidt, "Natural Wisdom and Some Recent Philosophy Manuals," *Proceedings of the American Catholic Philosophical Association,* XXX (1956), 181, 190.

Chapter V

৯~ The Principle of Sufficient Reason, 1850-1900

W HAT Van Riet remarks of Scholastic treatments of epistem-ology during the last half of the nineteenth century may also be applied to the Principle of Sufficient Reason: "The uniformity of the treatises [*traités*] is disconcerting, although one or the other author may shade the traditional elements with a more personal nuance."[1] There is no essential change in the formulation and meaning we have seen ascribed to the Principle before 1800 or between 1800 and 1840. Nor, as we shall see, is there any radical difference in the remote context of underlying metaphysical assumptions. What does change noticeably in many cases is its relative position in the format of the manuals, as well as its immediate context or application to current problems, of which the chief for many authors is the question, brought on by Kant, of analytic and synthetic judgments.

This chapter, therefore, falls naturally into three parts. First, a brief consideration of the basic metaphysical context in which the Principle's nineteenth-century history develops; then the presentation of a representative example of its use and application in the format of the seminary philosophy manual; and, finally, in the light of this classic example, a brief sampling of the textbooks grouped both chronologically and in some instances according to "schools" in order to indicate the general conformity which marks the century's product in this matter as a whole.

The Nineteenth-Century Metaphysical
Context of the Principle's Use

One purpose for the attention given Leibniz at the beginning of this study was to high-light that basic metaphysical position ad-

[1] George Van Riet, *L'Épistémologie Thomiste* (Louvain: éditions de l'institut supérieur de philosophie, 1946), p. 125.

hered to by Scholastic (and other) manuals from 1750 to 1800—*the primacy of essence.* If care is taken not to over-simplify matter that in many instances is highly complex, this same position may serve now as a kind of touchstone for presenting the context of the manuals in which the Principle of Sufficient Reason functions during this final period under study.

One of the most common and widespread uses of the Principle in these years centers around the problem of explaining universality and intelligibility in "synthetic *a posteriori*" judgments of experience, a problem with ramifications in the further questions of the *nature of induction,* the *objectivity of causality* and the *proofs for the existence of God.* But these questions, ultimately, are rooted in the problem of essence and existence, the problem of relating the two, the problem of the object of metaphysics. Regardless of how little attention was paid to this, especially at first, it almost always can be shown upon analysis that the most involved and detailed presentation of the Critical Problem by Scholastics, that is, the nature of certitude and the ability of the mind to know the real, is at bottom but an aspect of this more fundamental question of the starting-point of metaphysics and the difference between judgment as an assent to existential act and as a combiner of essence-concepts.

In the swirling currents of early nineteenth-century Fideism, Traditionalism, and Ontologism, this problem had lost its focus and even its place. One motive behind that whole movement away from philosophy toward Faith and Tradition was to by-pass what many thinkers realized had no answer in the traditional manuals; the rationalistic dichotomy between reason and experience was unreal and yielded only pseudo-solutions to real problems. One characteristic of Ontologism was its desire to elevate human knowledge from a level essentially abstract and dependent on sensation to a region of pure intuition of object where the primacy of essence created no problem because essence and existence were identical.

Hence, at a more profound level of significance than that of merely chronological or genetic data, it may be said that the initiators or restorers of Scholasticism in the nineteenth century, even when they were falling short of its formal solution, were first of all restoring to its central position the basic problem of relating essence to existence in a unified theory of metaphysical knowledge.

This meant that they brought back into seminary philosophy and once more made respectable such "subtleties" as matter and form, abstraction and universals, potency and act, and an analysis of causality which an over-zealous devotion to the new physics, together with the failures of rationalism, had caused many of their predecessors to dismiss as dusty remnants of a dead past.

More particularly it may be suggested, as a guide for presenting the nineteenth-century manual-writers, that the contribution of Balmes and Kleutgen consisted especially in bringing the fundamental problem back into a focus and sketching the outline of its solution in terms of a more adequate theory of knowledge. Liberatore can be credited with presenting "in form" a solution to the problem which became the classic textbook version for years and may be taken as a type of much of the manual-writing of the century.

Since neither Balmes nor Kleutgen wrote textbooks properly speaking, their appearance in these pages will be only for the purpose of providing some insight into the influence they had on the general *context* of the Principle of Sufficient Reason as used in formal manuals. With this accomplished, then Liberatore's classical exposition of the Principle itself will receive attention. These three, together with Sanseverino,[2] are the generally recognized precursors and originators of the revival of Thomism, and they dominated the period from 1850 to 1879 *(Aeterni Patris)*, after which further groupings of textbook authors appeared. These later writers contributed further to the revival of Scholasticism by producing manuals which were partly a combination and partly an advance over or change from the presentation of doctrine made by the four classic expositors.

Since the basic works of this period from Balmes to Gredt are much more readily accessible than some of the writings we have used heretofore in these pages, it will not be necessary to present such elaborate textual evidence at each point, and this final chapter of findings can be more summary in its outline.[3] Moreover, as mentioned above, there is a kind of common denominator in their treatment of our Principle which makes repetition of examples unnecessary.

2 Cf. *Infra*, part three of this chapter.

3 For a handy survey of the period and its pertinent bibliography, cf. Bernardino Bonansea, O.F.M., "Pioneers of the Nineteenth-Century Scholastic Revival in Italy," *The New Scholasticism*, XXVII (1954), 1-37.

James Balmes, Precursor of Thomism

Except for passing reference, the Principle of Sufficient Reason
is not found formally in Balmes' *Fundamental Philosophy*.[4] This
is in sharp contrast to the writings of Liberatore, Sanseverino, and
Kleutgen, where it appears for the first time, since 1750, in a
Thomistic context, at least by association.[5] Balmes' own philosophical antecedents as well as his orientation to current adversaries of his position may have influenced this omission. The origins
of his philosophy are found in the Scholastic background of the
Spanish tradition, itself relatively unaffected by the eighteenth-
century rationalism of Germany but in the early nineteenth century
directly confronted both with the rise of a sensist school of philosophy among Catholics[6] and also with the general European popularity of German Idealism as represented by Kant and Fichte.

Balmes, therefore, faced extremes: one, sensism, a radical reaction to Wolffian rationalism; the other, Idealism, a kind of ultimate and logical consequence of the same. Balmes was significant
for pointing to St. Thomas as a "datur tertium" in a theory of
knowledge where escape could be made from the error common
to both these extremes: a false reduction to unity, in the one case
to a unity of sensation, in the other to the unity of idea.

Hence, rationalism and the desire to reduce everything to a
fundamental principle had no formal temptation for him. Any

[4] James Balmes (1810-1848), *Obras Completas,* ed. P. Casanovas, S.J., (Madrid:
Biblioteca De Autores Cristianos, 1948). His most important work appeared in four
volumes at Barcelona in 1846, titled *Filosofia fundamental.* A year later he reduced
this to a *Cursio de filosofia elemental* which was then translated into Latin: *Cursus
philosophiae elementaris,* first edition at Barcelona in 1849 and a third edition in
1859. E. Manec translated *Filosofia fundamental* into French: *Philosophie fonda-
mentale* (Liége, 1852), a fifth edition appearing in 1874. References in these pages
will be to James Balmes, *Fundamental Philosophy,* trans. Henry F. Brownson (New
York: D. & J. Sadlier & Co., 1856).

[5] One example of Balmes' infrequent use of the Principle of Sufficient Reason
is at the heart of his famous distinction between subjective and objective evidence.
Prescinding from whether the relation is real or ideal, there must be some relation
or link between "the thing representing and that represented": "Two things, having
absolutely no relation, one of which nevertheless represents the other, are a mon-
trosity. There is nothing without a sufficient reason; and there being no relation
between the thing representing, and that represented, there is no sufficient reason
of the representation." Balmes, *Fundamental Philosophy,* I, 72.

[6] Cf. Gonzalez, *Histoire de la philosophie,* IV, 459 ff. Gonzalez singles out the
Jesuits Monteiro (a Portuguese), Eximeno and Andres as ardent defenders of the
theories of Locke and Condillac, and as preferring the latter while repeating the
strictures of Genovesi and Verney against Aristotelian philosophy.

resort to "principle-philosophy" was fraught with the danger of resolving everything to that monism of idea, such as Fichte espoused, but which did not fit the facts of man's cognitional experience any more than the monism of sensation associated with Condillac and popular in Spain at the time.

Thus we find in Balmes' major and most influential work all the elements of the primacy-of-essence problem. But we do not find its systematic solution nor a statement of the problem at a metaphysical level of being and existential judgment. Balmes was a controversialist and primarily a student of religion and culture. His solution is the *solvitur ambulando* type and is very simple. By taking as his starting point the *fact of certitude* and dividing it sharply into that natural or "man-in-the-street" kind, about which doubt is impossible, and the philosophical or speculative kind about which dispute is endless, he side-steps at the very beginning of his treatise the whole problem of relating essence and existence. He makes a vigorous assertion of the reality of existential reference in knowledge, but at the same time solidifies the primacy of essence. With this distinction between the realm of fact and the real of specification, he steps into the whole Kantian difficulty.

How badly Balmes is caught in this dichotomy and how completely committed he is to the primacy of essence appears more clearly in his further explicit and methodological separation of real truths, facts, or whatever exists, from ideal truths or the necessary connection of ideas where abstraction is made from all orders of existence.[7] For Balmes, this wall of separation is to insure the practical conduct of social and personal life against the descent of error and doubt from the realm of abstraction; it unites philosophy and common sense in a kind of non-aggression pact.[8] But actually it divides the realm of knowledge so radically that his theory is highly vulnerable to Kant's basic criticism of all primacy-of-essence philosophy, namely, that conceptions without intuitions are empty and ultimately purely subjective.[9]

---

[7] "Truths are of two kinds, real and ideal. We call facts or whatever exists, real truths; we call the necessary connection of ideas ideal truths . . . Take any real truth whatever, the plainest and most certain fact, and yet we can derive nothing from it if ideal truth comes not to fecundate it." Balmes, *Fundamental Philosophy*, I, 38-39.

[8] *Ibid.*, I, 236.

[9] *Ibid.*, I, 185-186; II, 68. Cf. also the Introduction by O. A. Brownson, *ibid.*, I, ix. Brownson's solution to the difficulty, of course, is in Ontologism.

Balmes, therefore, by background Scholastic, by intention Thomistic, and by orientation committed to the old rationalistic dichotomy of experience and reason, brought the primacy-of-essence problem back into focus. While making no use of the Principle of Sufficient Reason himself, he did contribute to the circulation of the context in which it most naturally functions: the primacy of essence. Moreover, he added to this a new viewpoint, that of relating a knowledge of essence, which he called subjective certitude, to its existential reference, the objectivity of ideas.[10]

Joseph Kleutgen, German Initiator of Thomism

Joseph Kleutgen's famous philosophical work, *Die Philosophie der Vorzeit*, variously translated as *Scholastic Philosophy Exposed and Defended* or simply *Scholastic Philosophy*,[11] is not itself a textbook. Later by almost twenty years than Balmes' *Fundamental Philosophy* and, like the Spaniard's, of considerable influence on the context and composition of manuals, it is more a series of studies on points of Scholastic doctrine which he considers crucial in the mid-century milieu of European thought, especially under the influence of German Idealism.

As with Balmes, the criticism is orientated fundamentally toward Kant but through Gunther and Hermes,[12] and there is a

10 Since an intellectual instinct assures us of the existence of bodies corresponding to our sensations, no "principle" is needed to serve as a basis of argument for this, although reason does confirm this instinct. *Ibid.,* I, 275. Speaking of both Balmes and Liberatore, Van Riet observes: "le rationalisme cartésien transposé par Leibniz constitue l'ambiance doctrinale de l'époque." *Op. cit.,* p. 47.

11 Joseph Kleutgen, S.J., (1811-1883), *Die Philosophie der Vorzeit* (Zweite, verbesserte Auflage: Innsbruck: F. Rauch, 1878). First published in 1860-1863, it was translated into Italian by Cardinal Reisach (*La filosofia antica esposta e difesa* (Rome: 1866-67) and into French by Constant Sierp of the Picpus Fathers (*La philosophie scolastique exposée et défendue,* (Paris: Gaume et Duprey, 1868-1870). The section on Principles is in volume one of the original German, pp. 439-586, especially p. 458 to p. 476, in which pages are found paragraphs No. 292-302. Van Riet says: "Kleutgen est vraiment un initiateur du néothomisme. Il semble ignorer les travaux de Balmés, de Liberatore et de Sanseverino." *Op. cit.,* p. 70. But compared with them he is more of a Neo-Suarezian than a Thomist; at a deeper level than that of textual references and eclectic excerpts, they are all essentially orientated to the primacy of essence.

12 George Hermes (1775-1831) and Anton Günther (1783-1863) were German priests and theologians whose writings ultimately were condemned, the former in 1835-36 and the latter in 1857, for a rationalization of theology that threatened the distinction between philosophical knowledge and faith. Joseph Schulte points out that Hermes, in trying to prove the existence of God along lines of theoretical reason in contradiction to Kant's approach from a postulate of practical reason, used the

wider scope given the problems than that of the philosophy lecture room. Unlike Balmes, whose problems were drawn at the level of general culture and civilization, Kleutgen works against the more specialized background of speculative Scholastic theology. The depth and range of the latter's use of Scholastic philosophy, despite its Suarezian cast, made him much more of a real originator of the revival than Balmes. But both were orientated toward the problem of certitude and faced metaphysics inward to the data of psychological reality.

But it was in this mid-nineteenth century that the eclectic Scholastic met a problem unknown to manual writers of the 1750 era. Because the break with rationalism was not at first clearly made, the basic context into which Kleutgen and others fitted their piecemeal drawings from St. Thomas was characterized by the old dichotomy between sense and reason, narrowed now to the problem of relating singular, individual facts with the necessity and universality of knowledge.

With metaphysical knowledge still restricted to the limits of conceptual abstraction, principles continued to play a great role in the metaphysical enterprise. The only difficulty now was that Kant had wrought havoc with "principles" by pushing the inevitable logic of rationalism to conclude that it is the mind ultimately independent of its object that supplies whatever values principles have in knowledge. All of the manuals struggle with this problem, always short of facing it on the fundamental level of existential judgment and the object of metaphysics. Kleutgen and Liberatore are classic examples of half a century and more of Scholastic writing in which the answer to Kant is often built out of the same materials and takes the same ground which furnished him strength and coherence.

Kleutgen's two volumes are divided into nine dissertations which begin with the question of knowledge and certitude and extend through the topics of being, philosophy of nature, and doctrine on the soul, to the existence and attributes of God and His creative act, to a numbered total of 1,047 sub-sections.

Principle of Sufficient Reason. This Principle, said Hermes, must be accepted as true together with all propositions subordinate to it; with this Principle and the consciousness that I know, together with the thought, *something is there*, theoretical reason can demonstrate that God exists. Cf. Joseph Schulte, "George Hermes," *The Catholic Encyclopedia* (New York: Appleton, 1912), VII, 276-279.

"Principles" are the subject of the fourth discourse; its four chapters take up (1) the doctrine of Descartes on principles; (2) the knowledge of ideal truth (universal concepts); (3) the knowledge of the existence of real things; (4) how we know the essence of real things. In the chapter on the knowledge of ideal truths, Kleutgen sets out to study the doctrine of the Scholastics "on principles understood in the strict sense of the word, consequently, on the general truths which serve as the foundation of all our thoughts."[13]

Two reproaches made by Gunther against Scholastic philosophy contend that while much has been said about principles and their certitude, nothing has ever been given on the relations between principles and on the foundation of their certitude. One answer to this reproach is by way of flat denial. Aristotle and the Scholastics (St. Thomas, Suarez, Sylvester Maurus, for example) have not failed on this point; the supremacy of the Principle of Contradiction is well known, and the first principles of metaphysics are founded in the propositions which rest on being and its transcendental properties.[14]

Following Suarez, Kleutgen points out that: "it is the concept of its object that constitutes the supreme principle of a science. You begin from this concept to study scientifically the essential attributes of this object, and all the other truths taught about it."[15] What guarantees that the affirmation of attributes really belongs to the object of the concept, that the notes are identical with the concept, is the Principle of Identity. But this Principle is not absolutely the first, since what it directly guarantees to be true can also be validated indirectly by showing the impossibility of the contrary. This latter procedure is an indirect demonstration that rests upon the Principle of Contradiction and therefore, Kleutgen concludes, the Principle of Contradiction is prior to that of Identity in the sense that it is a more ultimate validation of what that Principle directly guarantees.

Kleutgen then takes up the further reproach that this only confirms the fact that Scholastics are exclusively occupied with principles of the *understanding*, which proceed by abstraction "and have lost sight of the principle of *reason,* which belongs to things,

13 Kleutgen, *Die Philosophie der Vorzeit,* I, 455.
14 *Ibid.,* I, 457-458.
15 *Ibid.,* I, 458-459.

that is, the *principle of causality*."¹⁶ But Kleutgen is not bothered about any attempt to credit modern philosophy and Leibniz in particular with having introduced, besides the Principle of Contradiction, a positive principle of Sufficient Reason. This newcomer principle does not reflect discredit on Scholasticism because it is only saying in a different way what the Scholastics always said. Formulated as: *Nothing becomes or comes to be without a sufficient reason,* the Principle says nothing more than what was formerly said by the well-known axiom: *There is no effect without a cause,* although it may be said with more exactness in the new formula.

But since this Principle of Sufficient Reason can and ought to be understood of all being and all knowledge, says Kleutgen, it can be formulated thus: *Nothing can be (and consequently cannot be affirmed) without a sufficient reason.* "In this general formula it is incontestably among the number of first principles."¹⁷

Kleutgen then goes on to show by example that, granted the Scholastics did not speak expressly of a principle so formulated, their whole theory of knowledge by causes, following Aristotle, and of demonstration, as commented on by St. Thomas, implies the Principle of Sufficient Reason. The four causes and the interrelation of finality and formality in creatures, as well as the unity of essence, existence, and finality in God are profundities of the Principle of Causality which Scholastics knew and taught. But what else does this principle signify if not that

> . . . we must not only affirm nothing without a sufficient reason,
> but more than that, to be able to pretend to a true science, we
> must affirm it only by the reason or by the cause by which it
> *is* what we affirm?¹⁸

Let it stand, he continues, that modern philosophy merits credit for having perfected the theory of the laws of thought by a more profound study of the Principle of Causality. That does not justify reproaching Scholasticism; that does not give "the right to reproach the old school for not having recognized in its theory, as a condition of true science, thought which pentrates to the cause."¹⁹

Thus, principles are judgments whose truth we know in themselves—we find in the very concepts which are combined to form a judgment the reason of this combination itself. These first prin-

---

¹⁶ *Ibid.*, I, 459.   ¹⁸ *Ibid.*, p. 462.
¹⁷ *Ibid.*, p. 459.   ¹⁹ *Loc. Cit.*

ciples of all science are founded on simple elements without which complex concepts cannot be had, such as being, unity, and cause. Of such simple things there is either no knowledge at all or there is true knowledge.[20]

Hermes' contention that such judgments arise immediately in our own minds and not in virtue of a perception is based on his false Kantianism, declares Kleutgen. The simple truth is that we believe the whole to be greater than the part, that every effect presupposes a cause, and that everything that is has a sufficient reason only because we perceive and comprehend that the relation expressed in these judgments between subject and predicate exists in reality. Although it is this knowledge that produces the necessity of adherence, Kleutgen's conceptual-analysis theory of judgment means that this knowledge comes from the *concepts* of subject and predicate, which themselves are the constituent elements of the judgment whereby it is called immediate.[21]

Kant, he continues, always understood the definition of an analytic judgment too literally and in too restricted a sense. To say that the predicate is contained in the subject of an analytic judgment is not to say that by analysis of the subject itself one could obtain the concept of the predicate since one does not as yet possess it. But it means—and again Kleutgen is true to the primacy he accords abstract essence—that one finds by this analysis the *reason* for attributing the predicate to the subject, or, what is the same thing, that by consideration alone of the concepts of the subject and predicate, one can perceive and comprehend the reality of the relation expressed in the judgment.

Kleutgen thus finishes the section refuting Hermes' *a priori form* theory of the principle of causality, a theory which affirms that the necessity of the relation between subject and predicate (effect and cause) exists in the mind before any representation of the predicate (cause) is possible. The necessity of thinking that every being has a cause is imposed on us before we have acquired any concept of cause. Kleutgen summarizes Hermes as follows: "The need to understand, which determines the reason to form the concept of cause, contains at the same time the necessity of thinking the principle of causality or of sufficient reason, although this principle had not been thought of previously."[22] This neces-

---

[20] *Ibid.*, p. 467.   [21] *Ibid.*, pp. 469-470.   [22] *Ibid.*, I, 473.

sity for conceiving a sufficient reason, a cause, is a need of the mind; otherwise it could not comprehend the possibility of a thing nor accord it reality.

To which Kleutgen answers that this necessity, far from generating first the idea of cause, presupposes on the contrary that we have this concept and know evidently that without a sufficient reason, or cause, nothing is possible. In other words, we know with certitude the Principle of Causality.

Again, although the Scholastics made no special study of the question of causality, it is clear how they would have explained the origin of this principle. The idea of cause, like all ideas, is formed by abstraction from experience, "particularly from the experience we have in ourselves."[23] The evident consciousness of phenomena within ourselves, of the activity of thought, evidently implies the concept of sufficient reason or cause, and even of an agent or efficient cause, that is, of cause in the strict sense.

Attentive examination and definition of the concepts thus obtained in our own inner experience yield an understanding of this principle that *all that is has its raison d'être, or sufficient reason.*[24] Nothing is able to become by itself, and the concept of being or existence does not suppose necessarily *becoming;* there is a being which is the sufficient reason of its existence. Just as the concept of being does not necessarily imply a beginning of existence, so the concept of *reason* or foundation does not suppose production.

> A being can be a principle or a sufficent reason without being a cause in the proper sense of the word, which supposes the production of a thing distinct from the agent-being. If then we understand these concepts: being and principle or sufficient reason in the sense explained, we cannot doubt the truth of the principle: every being has a sufficient reason.[25]

What the principle actually affirms, concludes Kleutgen, is merely that all existing being exists either by itself or by another. This judgment presupposes nothing else except the negative principle that what is cannot exist by nothing, or what is cannot be by what is not.[26]

---

23 *Ibid.,* I, 474-475.
24 "Ebenso bedarf es aber auch nur einer Erörterung der Begriffe, um den allgemeineren Satz, dass alles, was ist, seinen Grund habe zu erkennen." *Ibid.,* I, 475.
25 *Loc. Cit.*
26 *Loc. Cit.*

Liberatore and the Nineteenth-Century
Format for Sufficient Reason

Liberatore's much-discussed process of evolution toward Thomism is generally conceded to have come to term about 1850, almost ten years after he began writing his manuals.[27] But as late as 1857 his *Institutiones* carry the aura of the eclectic background from which the author had progressed. It is not until after 1860 that the new light, a more faithful presentation of St. Thomas, grows bright, with closer attention paid, as promised in the 1860 Preface, to the "dialectical form of dispute and arrangement of subject matter."

Selecting the edition of 1864 as a kind of water-shed of tendencies before and after that date, we shall view: 1. the general context and position in the manual of the Principle of Sufficient Reason, and some variations therein from past and future arrangements; 2. the actual doctrine on the meaning and use of the Principle as an axiom of philosophical reasoning. This doctrinal context remains substantially the same in all of the editions from 1857 to the end of the century regardless of other changes in make-up, expansion of other doctrine, or restriction of actual use of the principle. Neither changes in his own personal insights and development, nor such exterior factors as the regulations from his religious superiors in the matter of seminary studies, nor the passing parade of philosophical opponents who were so many moving targets for

[27] Matthew Liberatore, S.J., (1810-1892) joined the Society of Jesus in 1826 after being ordained a priest in Salerno. The fact that he was appointed to replace Dominic Sordi, S.J., at Naples in 1834 plus the content of his early manuals seems sufficient to indicate that he did not begin his career as a Thomist. Sordi and Taparelli were removed because of certain difficulties about the teaching of Thomistic doctrine there. Liberatore must have been at least neutral in this regard to have been selected as a replacement. Later transferred to Rome with the staff of the newly founded *Civiltà Cattolica*, he came under the influence of other staff members devoted to a revival of St. Thomas' doctrine: Curci, Calvetti, Taparelli, and Seraphin Sordi. His *Institutiones logicae et metaphysicae* first appeared at Naples in 1840; by 1855 eight editions in Latin, nine in Italian and one at Louvain had appeared. Pelzer says the early eclectic trend, characterized by the influence of Cousin, begins to change by the time the first edition of the *Elementi di filosofia* appears in 1846. Before that time there was no mention of hylomorphism, no potency and act doctrine, and a rejection of the real distinction. Cf. A. Pelzer, "Les initiateurs italiens du néo-thomisme," *Revue néo-scolastique de philosophie*, XVIII (1911), 230-254; Paul Dezza, S.J., *Il Neotomisti Italiani del XIX secolo* (Milan: Fratelli Bocca, 1942); A. Masnovo, *Il neo-tomismo in Italia* (Milan: Vita e Pensiero, 1923). By 1855 the change to Thomistic philosophy had been accomplished. We make our first quotations here from his 1857 edition and make further reference to those of 1864, 1869 (*Compendium*), 1872, 1833, and 1897.

manual authors eager to keep their students abreast of current problems seems to have touched the core doctrine on the Principle of Sufficient Reason.[28]

Arrangement and Context of the Manual

In 1857, Liberatore drew references and material from a rather wide circle of non-Scholastic sources. The edition of the *Institutiones* of that year carries as a frontispiece quotation, Bacon's ant-and-bee aphorism on the nature of philosophical work. At the beginning of the section on the definition of philosophy he quotes from Cicero, Wolff, Genovesi Gallupi, and Romagnosi and disputes Laromiguière's contention that such variety makes a definition impossible, arguing that the divergencies are more apparent than real.[29]

A quotation from Kant's *Critique of Pure Reason* helps along the Prolegomenon to the *Logic*; "phenomenon" is a word often used, and there is a brief summary of the history of philosophy. Part one of the *Logic* is developed according to the elements of the reasoning process: simple apprehension and idea; judgment and proposition; deduction and the syllogism, ending with a discussion of forms of reasoning such as Enthymeme, Sorites, etc. which lack some of the integrity and simplicity of the syllogism, that fullest and the most simple expression of reason. Last but not least comes induction, classified as essentially syllogistic, a contention which seems aimed partly at refuting Bacon's aspersion cast on the syllogism by showing that even his vaunted induction is syllogistic.

Metaphysics, says Liberatore in his Prolegomenon, takes its division from the three types of objects that make up being: God, soul, and natural bodies, a division which was also the basis of Bacon's

---

28 An example of regulatory legislation on the content of the manuals which touched our Principle is the ordination for the three-year course in philosophy sent to the various Provinces of the Society of Jesus by the General, Peter Beckx in 1858, after the twenty-second General Congregation: "6. De principio et causa, quo loco etiam de principio causalitatis et rationis sufficientis quaeratur; de variis causarum speciebus, ubi non solum de causa efficiente et finali, sed etiam de formali atque materiali, nec non de causa universali et particulari, necessaria et libera agendum est." *Ordinatio pro Triennali Philosophiae Studio ex deputatione Congr. Gen. XXII* Ab A.R.P.N. Petro Beckx. Cf. George M. Pachtler, S.J., *Ratio studiorum et institutiones scholasticae Societatis Jesu per Germaniam olim vigentes collectae concinnatae dilucidatae* (Berlin: A. Hofmann & Co., 1887-94), IV, 562.

29 Liberatore, *Institutiones philosophicae* (Editio decima novis curis emendata et aucta; Rome: Civiltà Cattolica Press, 1857), I, 2.

partition of philosophy.[30] General metaphysics or what Wolff called ontology considers those *notions* which supply the principles and elements of the other parts of philosophy. Part three of metaphysics is devoted to causes. A fourth and final chapter discusses Axioms. Broken up into five articles, this treatment remained substantially the same in doctrine and arrangement for half a century;[31] only the relative position in the textbook undergoes some change from edition to edition.

By 1864, several important modifications appear in the editions of Liberatore's *Institutiones*. Bacon has been replaced by Beckx on the frontispiece where, instead of the aphorism of the bees, one reads an 1860 permission to print, granted by the General of the Jesuits after an examination of the work by theologians.[32] Because of what Liberatore calls the insanity of Idealism, as represented more commonly by Malebranche and Berkeley, and in the Transcendental sense by Kant and Fichte, he inserts into the *Logic,* after his treatment of the veracity of the senses, an article "On the Existence of Bodies." Although this soon disappeared from later editions, we may note how the Principle of Sufficient Reason is used here in a practical function as part of a philosophical argument. There are four summary propositions in this article, each built on our Principle. They are stated as follows:

1. The Sufficient Reason of representative knowledge of bodies cannot be the internal conformation of the mind.
2. The Sufficient Reason of representative knowledge of bodies cannot be the will of the knowing subject itself.
3. The Sufficient Reason of representative knowledge of bodies cannot be the divine influx, as postulated by the Idealists.
4. The Sufficient Reason of representative knowledge of bodies is the real existence itself of those bodies.[33]

With the completion of this article, Liberatore then proceeds to the veracity of consciousness, intelligence, and reason, respectively, from which he moves through an article on skepticism to chapter four on the criterion of truth. A chapter on universals is

---

[30] *Ibid.,* pp. 58-59. Here he refers to his own *Elementi di filosofia;* Logica cap. 4, art. 1 e 2; item cap. 2, art. 2, "ubi hanc materiam fusius aliquanto tractavi."

[31] *Ibid.,* I, 60-61.

[32] *Ibid.,* I, 127.

[33] Liberatore, *Institutiones philosophicae ad triennium accommodatae* (Editio tertia; Rome: Civiltà Cattolica Press, 1864), pp. 130-133; "Ad triennium accommodatae" evidently reflects the Ordination mentioned above in N. 28.

written into the new edition before the author comes, in chapter five, to that consideration of Axioms which in 1857 appeared at the end of the *Ontology* but from 1860-64 onwards is always found at the end of part two of the *Logic*.

This chapter is word for word, paragraph for paragraph, the same matter as the earlier edition even as to the printer's type. The only revisions or changes are in sentence structure, a few minor omissions, and the inclusion of numbered propositions that summarize the thesis of a particular block of paragraphs. To this section we shall return for further analysis of its contents.

Liberatore sees the subject of causes as especially pertinent to ontology both because of the connection with the concept of being (every being is either a cause or from a cause) and because the other sciences, to which it supplies the principles, are engaged especially in the investigation of causes. Although there is substantially the same write-up here as in the older edition, there is some rearrangement and addition of matter. The first new proposition is in article two, "On efficient cause," which states that *The notion of efficient cause is real and deduced from the observation itself of phenomena.*[34] Article three on material and formal cause is a new one in the *Ontology* format, and there is a cautious doctrine of matter as potency and the mutual causality between it and form.[35]

We may now turn to the details of Liberatore's doctrine on the Principle of Sufficient Reason.

Liberatore's Principle of Sufficient Reason

In his 1857 edition, Liberatore introduces his chapter on axioms which appeared then at the end of the *Ontology*. It connects the subject with the chapter on being and its associated notions and states that the study of axioms is a *study of judgments which are formed from these notions* which pertain to being either in itself or in its principal divisions. In the later editions, where the subject of Axioms practically concludes *Major Logic,* the emphasis is on the judgmental nature of axioms and the consideration begins with their definition as "those judgments which are not only *per se* evident, but also possess universality and thus constitute the principles of the sciences."[36] He then draws on logic for a previous

---

[34] *Ibid.,* p. 360.
[35] Cf. again the 1858 Ordination above.
[36] *Ibid.,* p. 192.

division made of immediate judgments into those whose truth appears from the very nexus of the ideas themselves and those which are founded in facts and experience.

Judgments which are formed from a resolution of the idea of subject or predicate and are not dependent on experience are rightly called *analytic* and *a priori* just as the other kind, dependent on experience and formed by combining attribute and subject, are correctly named *synthetic a posteriori* judgments.[37]

Analytic *a priori* judgments, such as *the whole is greater than its parts* or *nothing which begins to be, exists by its own power (virtute sua)*, pertain to matter in which the attribute is so absolutely necessary to the subject that the judgment itself is necessary and universal. Such judgments, unlike the experiential *a posteriori* synthetic ones, make up the axioms or principles of science.

However, there is a way in which these experiential judgments may become scientific contrary to what Wolff and others held about restricting the certitude exclusively to the cases examined and being satisfied only with probability for the remainder. There are, says Liberatore, axioms which, although built upon an induction made from an incomplete enumeration of the series, nevertheless enjoy the universality of real certainty.[38]

These axioms are arrived at by bringing the individual facts or synthetic *a posteriori* judgments, each of which is only particular, under the universality of an analytic *a priori* judgment which alone has this quality of itself and can communicate it. Such axioms may be called *inductive a posteriori* principles.

This participating or sharing of the singular in the universal is accomplished by means of the Principle of Causality, or, if you prefer, by the Principle of Sufficient Reason into which the Principle of Causality itself is resolved.[39]

[37] *Ibid.*, p. 193. "Iudicia omnia, quae synthetica sunt, *a posteriori* vocamus, idque iure meritoque. Ut enim contra Kant mox videbimus, nullum est syntheticum iudicium, quod experimentale non sit. Has vero denominationes ad iudicia mediata, quae ratiocinio deducuntur, transferre facile erit. Nam si iudicium mediatum sit eiusmodi, ut per ratiocinium purum ex duobus iudiciis analyticis deducatur; nemini dubium esse potest, quin ipsum quoque analyticum censendum sit." *Ibid.*, n. 1.

[38] In these later editions induction is given an article in the *Minor Logic* as before, with explanation in terms of the axiom that says *The same physical causes always produce the same effect,* or, *The Laws of nature are constant.* Ibid., p. 91. Their explanation comes later. Cf. next note.

[39] *Ibid.*, p. 195. "Vi enim huius principii phaenomena particularia, quae ob-

Liberatore then takes up the question as to whether or not there is any principle to which all the others can be reduced. He notes Leibniz' assertion of two distinct realms with their respective principles of Contradiction and Sufficient Reason, which he himself classifies according to the terms: analytic and synthetic, respectively. Since this doctrine of Leibniz is not stated clearly enough, and in regard to the Principle of Sufficient Reason can be especially absurd if twisted from its right meaning, "the whole question therefore should be accurately reflected upon."[40]

First of all, it is not a question of seeking a single principle which alone is known in itself and all the others demonstrated therefrom. Something is always given to start with in either kind of judgments; the most simple demonstration assumes something admitted before the reasoning process begins, such as the rules of the syllogism itself.

Rather, it is a question of what certain judgment is implicit, as it were, in all other judgments and expresses a general condition characteristic of any assent of the mind. Understood in this way, it is clear that the Principle of Contradiction, *nothing can be and not be at the same time,* is the one in question, for as the idea of being is implicit in every concept, then in every judgment there should be implied that judgment which follows immediately from the idea of being.

All that the Principle of Contradiction asserts is that repugnance which exists between being and its negation, non-being, a repugnance that extends to every order of being. It is not only most evident and absolutely universal as a condition and implicit component of every judgment, but it is also most necessary, for it contains the first law of intellectual judgment without which all thought is corrupted and lost.[41]

Restricting consideration to analytic judgments alone, another prerogative of the Principle of Contradiction appears in the fact that it is a kind of common formula into which the truth of these judgments can ultimately, although indeterminately, be resolved.[42]

servantur, ad naturam omnibus communem, aut ad ordinem a Deo in rebus constabilitum, tamquam ad propriam causam, revocantur; atque adeo ipsis applicantur duo illa principia, quae innuimus in Logica: *Causae naturales eosdem semper producunt effectus. Leges naturae sunt constantes." Ibid.,* p. 196.

40 *Ibid.,* p. 197.
41 *Ibid.,* p. 198.
42 *Ibid.,* pp. 198-199.

The impossibility of thinking the contrary of what the mind, in analytic judgment, sees to be a necessary nexus between two ideas is seen to be present because it is seen that the same thing cannot be and not be at the same time.

Thus, the Principle of Contradiction expresses a common law by which the mind is governed in any analytic judgment. For example, to affirm that "the whole is greater than the part" or that "an effect demands a cause" is ultimately to affirm nothing else except that a whole cannot be at the same time "whole" and "not whole," nor an effect both an effect and a non-effect. Indirectly, then, by reduction to absurdity, analytic judgments can be demonstrated by the Principle of Contradiction.

As to synthetic judgments or contingent truths, the opinion of Leibniz that they are reduced to the Principle of Sufficient Reason must be rejected. While it is true that the objects of contingent truth demand not only a reason but also a cause of their existence, it is most false to say that we are moved implicitly to assent to them because of the Principle of Sufficient Reason.[43] The true reason and foundation of such assent is in experience itself, whether internal or external. Conscience or sensation, not the principle that there is nothing without a sufficient reason, makes you certain of your own existence or the fact that it is day time. Our knowledge proceeds *a posteriori* and from the intuition of the facts themselves, rather than *a priori* and from causes.

However, where it is not a question of this kind of contingent truths but of those which are carried by induction to a universality, then it must be admitted that at least indirectly the Principle of Sufficient Reason is at work.[44] In detecting the cause of phenomena to be either the very nature of the subject itself or a law established by God, induction, and the Principle of Causality play a part. But the Principle of Causality, *there is no effect without a cause,* is nothing else than a certain contraction of the Principle of Sufficient Reason, which is why in ordinary usage, it is often confused with it.

[43] *Ibid.,* p. 199. Propositio 3.ᵃ *Iudicia synthetica nequeunt resolvi in principium rationis sufficientis, tamquam in formulam generalem motivi, quo ad iis assentiendum impellimur."*

[44] "Propositio 4.ᵃ *Si non de quibuslibet veritatibus contingentibus sermo sit, sed de iis quae inductione ad universalitatem evehuntur: hae principio rationis sufficientis indirecte saltem nituntur." Ibid.,* p. 200.

Therefore, in this interpretation, the Leibnizian doctrine may certainly be admitted. But, to remove all ambiguity, it should be stated as follows:

> Universal judgments, on which the reasoning process depends, rest upon two great principles; one of these expresses that of Contradiction: *non potest idem simul esse et non esse;* the other, the Principle of Sufficient Reason: *nihil est sine ratione suffi-cienti.* The first supports analytic axioms, the other, synthetic or experimental axioms. The former presupposes nothing except the intuition of ideas; the latter requires an intuition of facts along with a legitimate enumeration of particular cases, as explained in speaking of induction elsewhere.[45]

In the 1883 edition of his *Institutiones,* Liberatore drops completely these last two mentioned propositions above on the Principle of Sufficient Reason, namely on the resolution of judgments to the Principle of Sufficient Reason; he seems content to let it *operate* in the explanation of induction, without too many formal details of theoretic justification.

The rest of the chapter on Axioms is devoted to the Principle of Causality. Enunciated as *whatever becomes, has a cause* or, *every occurrence implies a cause,* or *there is no effect without a cause,* this Principle is not the same as that of Sufficient Reason. They differ in both subject and attribute. To be and to be effected or caused are not the same. Hence, *nothing is which does not have a sufficient reason why it is* and *nothing is effected without a cause* are not the same proposition, which is clear in the case of God, Who is, but is not caused in the sense of passing from non-existence to existence.

Neither is "sufficient reason" the same as "cause," since it is more general and signifies that whence it is, that something be rather than not be, whereas cause is more restricted and signifies some agent which produces the existence of something distinct from itself. Whatever has the notion of cause has also the meaning of sufficient reason, but not vice versa.

We need not follow Liberatore through the rest of this section on Axioms, which details the objections and defense of the Principle of Causality. Hume's objections are refuted in *Ontology* in the chapter on efficient cause by showing the difference in the notions involved. At this point in the *Logic* where the judgmental

45 *Ibid.,* p. 200.

nature of the Principle of Causality is being considered, Liberatore
asserts that whatever may be the origin of the notion of cause,
common conscious experience testifies that we have it and that
we make causal judgments. A more pertinent adversary to the
doctrine here is Béguelin, who confuses the Principle of Causality
with that of Sufficient Reason and contends that it is incapable of
demonstration and uncertain.[46]

Although Liberatore refers in a footnote to Gerdil's dissertation against Béguelin, he leaves this dispute to the objections at the
end of the section and goes on to state the proposition that *The
Principle of Causality is indubitable.* He proves this first by
common sense and an appeal to the insanity of any other position,
then by an analysis of the terms, which is really an explication of
concepts, he says, rather than a reasoning process.[47] The notion of
a thing which passes from a state of possibility to existence is a
notion involving something added to mere possibility. This in
turn involves the notion of a thing that adds this complement, ex-

[46] *Ibid.*, p. 204. Against Béguelin's argument that there is a "transitus to real
existence, whose notion is most obscure, in cases of causality or sufficient reason,
whereas in the Principle of Contradiction it is a case of ideal existence, and therefore certainty is possible, Liberatore answers that in the abstract enunciation of
necessary nexus between contingent being and its cause, one can infer the existence of the cause. The point of his argument is to show that the nexus or
identity is between *two abstract ideas*, i.e., the idea of a contingent being and the
idea of a cause, and therefore the judgment is analytic; therefore it is certain
because it is not involved in that obscurity attached to real existence and the
singularity of existent individuals. After all, he concludes, that is the way the
Principle of Contradiction works: "positio quod aliquid *realiter* existet deducitur
etiam *realiter* illud ipsum non posse non esse." The Principle of Contradiction,
as well as the Principle of Causality, involves ideal existence, "quatenus hanc
respicit *abstracte* et *independenter* ab actuali existentia rerum creatarum . . . Etsi
enim nil creatum exsisteret, semper tamen verum esset hoc axioma: *nihil fieri
nec fieri posse sine causa.*" But it is false to think that the Principle of Contradiction regards only the idea and not the objective existence of its truth. "In cog-
nitionibus enim directis non percipimus ideas, sed obiecta idearum." Moreover
the idea of existence is the clearest and the best known of all; but whether clear
or obscure, it is very evident that "per existentiam aliquid superaddi nudae
possibilitati, ac proinde aliquam necessario requiri causam, quae rem antea possi-
bilem ad exsistentiam transferat." *Ibid.*, Objection I, pp. 206-207.

Nor is there a vicious circle involved in defending the Principle of Sufficient
Reason, because it is an axiom *per se notum* and needs no demonstration, and if
it were not, then Béguelin himself would be reduced to skepticism. In demonstrating it, that is, giving a sufficient reason for its truth, it does not call upon
itself, but depends on some other principle, which is the sufficient reason of the
illation but is not itself the Principle of Sufficient Reason. *Ibid.*, Objection II,
p. 207.

[47] *Ibid.*, p. 205.

istence, and "therefore the necessity and existence of a cause regarding the thing which began to be or to become is necessarily connected with its notion."[48]

Liberatore completes the chapter on Axioms with two articles on the principal adversaries to the objectivity of the causal axiom. They are: Kant with his synthetic *a priori* judgments, which are repudiated as repugnant to the human mind and not justified by the examples,[49] and Hume and Reid with their psychological-association doctrine, which is rejected by asserting the existence of rational principle over and above experience.[50]

Concluding Survey of the Century's Textbook Production

The choice of Liberatore's manual context and doctrine on the Principle of Sufficient Reason made in the previous section of this chapter could perhaps be defended with page and line reference to show that most of the textbook authors contemporary with and subsequent to him had imitated him on that topic in their own manuals. But it is enough here merely to say that the majority of nineteenth-century (and many twentieth-century) manuals are essentially *similar* to his, without meaning to assert any direct causal connection of borrowings and influence. A brief survey of these other manuals is the object of this final section of the chapter.

Since the differences between these writers and Liberatore are not very great generally on this subject, the survey will tend more to a bibliographical accounting than a doctrinal analysis. How-

[48] *Ibid.*, pp. 204-205. The whole argument is bolstered, finally, by a little help from the geometry of being which is based on adding existence to possibility to get existents. The Principle of Causality follows proximately from the Principle of Contradiction because, on the basis of Béguelin's contention that the truth of mathematical axioms comes from their dependence on the Principle of Contradiction but that contingent being does not have this dependence, Liberatore takes Béguelin's mathematical assertion and argues that if any contingent existent appears without an efficient cause, then it receives existence either from its own possibility (which Béguelin seems to hold) or from nothing. But since existence is greater than bare possibility, then the lesser suffices for the more, and there is a contradiction even for the mathematical Béguelin, since he has pointed out that the principle, *the whole is greater than the part,* is equivalent of the *greater cannot be the less,* and is thus a deduction from the Principle of Contradiction. The argument holds all the more if you say the new being comes from nothing. *Ibid.,* p. 205.

[49] *Ibid.*, pp. 209-213.

[50] *Ibid.*, pp. 213-218.

ever, by noting the over-all context of these manuals in terms of their commitment to St. Thomas, origin in a particular seminary or religious order, or any major divergence from the generally accepted pattern, a final insight will be afforded for those features which characterize the Principle of Sufficient Reason. In some cases, as usual, the evidence is entirely negative: some manuals of this period made no use of the Principle whatsoever.

Before 1879

Using Leo XIII's Encyclical of 1879, *Aeterni Patris,* as a natural mid-point, the sequence of manuals falls naturally into two divisions: before and after the Encyclical—a distribution which is hampered somewhat by the overlapping of editions and the lack of any clear-cut distinction in some manuals to indicate the influence of the Encyclical on their composition. Some authors and editors continued to issue earlier works with no explicit reference to the new importance accorded St. Thomas as a guide in philosophy. But in general, such Thomistic phrases as "secundum principia St. Thomas Aquinatis," "ad mentem Angelici Doctoris," etc. appeared frequently in the titles.

But previous to the Encyclical, of course, some manuals laid claim to a basis in St. Thomas, as, for instance, Cardinal Giuseppe Prisco's text published at Naples in 1864, *Elementi di filosofia speculativa secondo le dottrine degli scolastici specialmente di San Tommaso d'Aquina;*[51] L'Abbé Cacheux's Paris product of 1858, "honorably mentioned by the Academy of Moral and Political Sciences," *De la philosophie de St. Thomas d'Aquin;*[52] and the *Prima principia scientiarum seu philosophia Catholica juxta divum Thomam ejusque interpretatores respectu habito ad hodiernam disciplinarum rationem* (1866) by Michael Rosset, philosophy professor in the major seminary at Cambray, later (1876) a Bishop.[53]

The work of Cacheux, a rather weird mixture of quotations from St. Thomas and a "Cartesian" orientation to psychology as

[51] Cardinal Giuseppe Prisco (1836-1923), *Elementi de filosofia speculativa secondo le dottrine degli scolastici specialmente di San Tommaso d'Aquina* (Naples: Fibreno, 1864-65). He also refers to Béguelin, comments on Sanseverino.

[52] L'Abbé Cacheux, *De la philosophie de St. Thomas d'Aquin* (Paris: Charles Douniol, 1858).

[53] Michael Rosset, *Prima principia scientiarum seu philosophia Catholica juxta Divum Thomam ejusque interpretatores respectu habito ad hodiernam disciplinarum rationem* (Paris: Vives, 1866).

the basis for metaphysics, has no formal Principle of Sufficient Reason. Rosset, who takes Suarez as a genuine interpreter of the writings of St. Thomas, refers to it among five causal axioms; he does not include it among the usual three principles (contradiction, excluded middle, and identity) flowing out of the notion of being at the beginning of his *Ontology*. Prisco gives it a paragraph at the end of his section on the Principle of Contradiction, noting the origin of the question in Leibniz and pointing out that Sufficient Reason can be understood in regard to being, to nature or tendency, and to perfection or completion.[54] In his *Theodicy,* under the metaphysical argument, the contingency of the world is taken to mean that which does not have within it the sufficient reason of its existence.

One of the most famous manuals of the century was the three-volume work of Cajetan Sanseverino, *Elementa philosophiae Christianae cum antiqua et nova comparatae,* which appeared in 1862 and was later completed, as well as issued, in a *Compendium* by the author's disciple and friend at Naples, Nuntio Signoriello.[55]

Like Liberatore, his friend, fellow-townsman, and colleague in the movement to restore Scholasticism and in particular the doctrine of St. Thomas, Sanseverino came to Thomism after a period of eclectic philosophizing which was particularly Cartesian in contrast to Liberatore's early affinity for Cousin. Sanseverino's "conversion" occurred somewhat later than Liberatore's, and he too seems to have left traces of the evolution of his thought in his writings.[56] He seems to have identified a return to Scholasticism with a renewed use of some of the format and matter we have seen current in textbooks stemming from German rationalism. At least

[54] Prisco, *op. cit.,* p. 19.

[55] Cajetan Sanseverino (1811-1865), *Elementa philosophiae Christianae cum antiqua et nova comparata* (Naples: Apud Officinam Bibliothecae Catholicae, 1873-76); *Institutiones seu elementa philosophiae Christianae cum antiqua et nova comparatae* a Nuntio Can. Signoriello continuatae et absolutae (Editio novissima; Naples: Apud Officinam Bibliothecae Catholicae Scriptorum, 1875); *Philosophia Christiana cum antiqua et nova comparata in compendium redacta ad usum scholarum clericalium* (Editio sexta; Naples: Apud Officinam Bibliothecae Catholicae Scriptorum, 1881). For details on these works, the writing which preceded them, the author's background and the story of his conversion from Cartesianism, consult Van Riet, *op. cit.,* pp. 56-62, and the historians of the Thomistic revival.

[56] "Depuis 1840, en effet, les rapports sont fréquents et cordiaux entre le collège des jésuites et le lycée. Professant les mêmes cours, préoccupés des mêmes problèmes, Liberatore et Sanseverino ont dû, sans aucun doute, se faire maintes confidences sur l'évolution de leur pensée." Van Riet, *op. cit.,* p. 61. Sanseverino

his reactions and points of disagreement are more directly related to Wolff, Storchenau, Tamagna, etc. than is the case in the manuals of Liberatore and others.

At any rate, in Sanseverino, the Principle of Sufficient Reason has its time-honored place at the very beginning of the *Ontology,* whose first chapter concerns Being viewed absolutely and proceeds through the notions of being and nothing to the principles which derive therefrom. The Principle of Contradiction is primary, for the usual reasons, and "Leibniz' Principle of Sufficient Reason" as distinct from this, is true and valid not only for contingent truths but also for necessary ones; it is a principle of these truths also, but not a first principle. The validity of the Principle of Sufficient Reason for necessary truths depends on the fact that all existents are ordered by the divine mind and "where order is, there is *ratio.*"[57]

From Bülffinger's interpretation of Leibniz' meaning of sufficient reason, Sanseverino concludes that what is called the principle of sufficient reason signifies nothing else than that "nothing in the order of nature exists without some motive which determines its existence and from which it can be understood why it is rather than is not."[58]

As a final question on the subject, Sanseverino asks if the Principle of Contradiction is subjective. He answers affirmatively, in the sense that the intellect forms it not from things which are in nature but from the abstract notions of being and non-being.[59] Since he has taken great pains to show that the Principle of Sufficient Reason reduces to that of Contradiction, it is clear that it too

founded *La Scienza et la Fede,* a review in which many of his articles on modern philosophy appeared. In these articles and in his series in the *Bibliothèque catholique* there is little reference to St. Thomas. Pelzer quotes a paragraph from Sanseverino which illustrates his eclectic position on Catholic philosophy, claiming as he did, accord with "les cours philosophiques de Dmowski, de Pacetti, de Liberatore et de Bonelli, qui sont employés également dans les écoles de Rome; avec les traités d'Ubaghs, de Cock, de Peemans en usage à l'Université de Louvain; avec les opuscules des louvanistes Tits, Moeller, Laforêt; avec les cours de Mgr. Bouvier, de Lacoudre, de Lequex, de Gabelle de Balterou en usage dans divers séminaires de France; avec le cours de Rothenflue jadis employé au Collège, aujord'hui dissous, de Fribourg; enfin avec le cours élémentaire que Balmès a écrit pour l'Espagne." Pelzer, *op. cit.,* p. 247.

[57] Sanseverino, *op. cit.,* p. 12. This phrase does not appear in the larger works, where the emphasis brings out the details of sufficient reason as motive.

[58] *Elementa philosophiae Christianae,* II, 42.

[59] *Ibid.,* p. 46.

is subjective. Thus, Sanseverino, who at other points is against Wolff's division of knowledge into empirical and rational, preserves the dichotomy intact and is one more contributor to the primacy-of-essence orientation of the Scholastic manuals of 1850-1900.[60]

An outstanding example of an old textbook hardly, in any sense, Thomistic in its doctrine, which appeared in a new edition almost on the eve of *Aeterni Patris,* was the *Institutiones philosophicae* of Salvator Tongiorgi, S.J. Written originally in 1861, it was adopted by the seminaries of Bruges and Liège and was widely regarded as a kind of successful *rapprochement* with modern science. Its author considered modern science as having extended the limits of metaphysics and brought about those new divisions originally made by Wolff but now, most opportunely, taken up by all.[61]

Called the "Balmes of Italy," Tongiorgi in places repeats the Spaniard word for word on the doctrine of certitude and the three primitive truths. For him, only the Principles of Identity, Contradiction, and Excluded Middle, in that order, flow out of the notion of being. But at the end of his treatment of causes, two-thirds of the way through his *Ontology,* the usual importation is made of the Principle of Sufficient Reason, to which he devotes an article subordinating to it the Principle of Causality, which applies only in the order of existence, and distinguishing *ratio* according to the orders of essence, existence, and evidence or cognoscibility, thus granting it greater extension than "cause."[62] Sufficient Reason is the "connection of the principle with the *principiatum in actu secundo,*" but in cases of existential sufficient reason careful distinction must be made between necessary and free causes. Both principles are evident; Béguelin is answered by showing that the concept, "having an efficient cause" is contained in the concept, "beginning of existence."[63] Somewhat abbreviated, this same doctrine appears in a *Compendium* of this larger work, the *Institutiones,* printed in 1878.

[60] The basic division of his work is into "Subjective" and "Objective" philosophy.

[61] Salvatore Tongiorgi, S.J., (1820-1865), *Institutiones philosophicae* (Brussels: H. Goemaere, Logica: 1864; Ontologia-Cosmologia: 1862). Cf. II, 4. Tongiorgi taught at the Roman College (Gregorian University) during the last ten years of his life.

[62] *Ibid.,* II, 153-155.

[63] *Ibid.,* II, 154, 158.

In the same Balmesian tradition, Tongiorgi's successor, Dominic Palmieri, S.J., after nine years of teaching philosophy at the Roman College, produced in 1874 an *Institutiones philosophicae* which, although it is anti-Thomistic in its fundamentals, he adjusted, somewhat extrinsically, to the current revival of Thomism by means of a short and pious dedication to St. Thomas.[64]

Other examples in this decade (1870-1880) of manuals prior to the Encyclical which exhibit no formal Thomistic commitment in their titles are the *Institutiones philosophicae* of John Baptist Rastero,[65] the *Philosophiae speculativae summarium* of Anthony Maria Bensa,[66] both diocesan seminary professors. The latter does not mention the Principle of Sufficient Reason, while Rastero gives it only brief development. Two Dominicans of this period, Zigliara and Lepidi, will be considered in the survey of manuals by members of that order at the end of this section.

Finally, two outstanding Thomistic titles appearing before 1880 were: first, an anonymous five-volume set from the Abbey press at Monte Casino entitled *Institutiones philosophicae ad mentem Angelici Doctoris S. Thomae Aquinatis ordinatae non solum ad theologiam scholasticam perdiscendam, sed etiam ad faciliorem veterum, ac recentiorum philosophorum lectionem;*[67] and second, a translation by the Patriarch of Venice, Dominic Agostini, of *Lezioni de filosofi ordinate allo studio delle altre scienze* written by John Marie Cornoldi in 1872 and going through two more editions and into English (1876) and French (1878) translations. Agostini called his 1878 translation *Institutiones philosophicae speculativae*

[64] Dominic Palmieri, S.J., (1829-1909), *Institutiones philosophicae quas tradebat in Collegio Romano Societatis Iesu* (Rome: Typis Cuggiani, Santini et Soc. I: Logica Ontologia, 1874-1876). Thesis XX in the *Ontology* reads: "I Praestituto principio rationis sufficientis, II evidentissime evincitur principium causalitatis, quod satius hac forma proponitur, 'quod incipit existere habet causam sui efficientem' III Semper proinde constat causam aliquam existere quoties rem novam incipere experientia manifestat. IV Erravit ergo Humius negans obiectivum valorem conceptui causae efficientis." p. 431.

[65] John Baptist Rastero, *Institutiones philosophicae* (Genoa: Ex Typographia Iuventutis, 1874).

[66] Anthony Maria Bensa, *Philosophiae speculativae summarium* (Paris: Jouby and Roger, 1877).

[67] *Institutiones philosophicae ad mentem Angelici Doctoris S. Thomae Aquinatis ordinatae non solum ad theologiam scholasticam perdiscendam, sed etiam ad faciliorem veterum, ac recentiorum philosophorum lectionem* (Monte Casino: Ex Typis Abbatiae, 1875).

ad mentem Sancti Thomae Aquinatis.[68] There is no use made of the Principle of Sufficient Reason in this work.

The Benedictine work, arranged somewhat differently from the Liberatore format, includes physics in philosophy and while referring to Liberatore and other contemporaries, seems to draw on tradition further back along the line of textbook evolution. Principles are considered at the beginning of ontology but the Principle of Sufficient Reason and the question of the two realms of truth, says the author, need not be considered here because the question at this point is precisely on the first principle of demonstration, and demonstration is concerned with necessary truths.[69] At the end of the *Ontologia*, he returns to the question of Sufficient Reason in connection with "Existents and Futures," simply asserting that *nothing exists without a sufficient reason of its existence* with a warning against the Leibnizian sense that destroys free will and a rather long note vindicating the presence among the ancients of this Principle against the modern contention that it is something new.[70] Not only was it known to Archimedes, Cicero, Plato, and St. Thomas,[71] but it is natural to the mind not to admit anything unless there is a reason for it, although in matters of revelation that reason is the testimony of divine authority. As to the dispute between Clarke and Leibniz, the sufficient reason of the existence of created things, says this author, must ultimately be resolved in the Divine will. In his *Natural Theology* be uses the five proofs of St. Thomas for the existence of God.

From 1879 (Aeterni Patris) to 1900

Gonzalez, in his much quoted history of philosophy,[72] singles out the works of three Sulpicians as examples of the new Thomistic

---

[68] John Maria Cornoldi (1822-1892), *Institutiones philosophiae speculativae ad mentem Sancti Thomae Aquinatis*, trans. Dominic Agostini (Bologna: Mareggianiana, 1878). This work began as *Lezioni di filosofia, ordinate allo studio delle altre scienze. Parte speculativa* (Florence: L. Manuelli, 1872); in 1875 a second edition was called *Lezioni di filosofia scolastica* and the third edition of 1881 was *La filosofia scolastica speculativa di S. Tommaso d'Aquino.*

[69] *Institutiones philosophicae* (Monte Casino, III, 120, n. b.

[70] *Ibid.*, p. 306, n. 3.

[71] "Et s. Thomas (I, q. 32, art. 1 ad 2) expresse nominat rationem sufficientem: 'Dicendum, ait, *quod ad aliquam rem dupliciter inducitur ratio. Uno modo ad probandum* sufficienter *aliquam radicem; sicut in scientia naturali inducitur* ratio sufficiens *ad probandum, quod motus coeli semper uniformis velocitatis etc.*" *Ibid.* Compare this with Chapter one, note 2, *supra*.

[72] Gonzalez, *op. cit.*, IV, 457 ff.

trend in philosophy manuals resulting from the impetus given by
Leo XIII. The Abbé Vallet, S.S., wrote his *Praelectiones philosophicae* for publication at Paris in 1880;[73] four years later the
*Manuductio ad scholasticam, maxime vero Thomisticam philo-
sophiam* of Abbé Dupeyrat appeared, and a fifth edition came out
in 1898;[74] and more important than these two, says Gonzalez, was
the 1889 *Traité de la philosophie scolastique* of Abbé Élie Blanc
of Lyons.[75]

Dupeyrat devotes two theses in his *Ontology* to the Principle of
Sufficient Reason, one stating that it is true *in se,* the other that it
has no primacy in any order.[76] In the *Scholia* he points out that the
principle has an opportune use in the investigation of the laws of
nature because whoever is detecting in experience of phenomena
their laws and causes should always keep before his eyes the principle that there is nothing without a sufficient reason so that he will
accept as cause of his facts only that which renders the sufficient
reason thereof. In his *Logic* he has already stated that hypothesis
and the hypothetical method of proceeding to discover truth rest
on the Principle of Sufficient Reason: *Nihil fit frustra in natura,
nihil existit sine ratione sufficiente.*[77]

Although his first edition appeared in 1878, the 1888 edition of
Propaedeutica philosophica theologica of another seminary professor, Francis Egger, Domestic Prelate and Rector of the Seminary
at Brescia, may be mentioned here with the additional note that a
fifth edition of this work appeared in 1898 still carrying notice to
the reader of the author's avowed purpose of following especially,
after St. Thomas, the footsteps of Suarez. In this work the Principle
of Sufficient Reason is merely mentioned rather than used.[78]

[73] Abbé Vallet, S.S., *Praelectiones philosophicae ad mentem S. Thomae Aquinatis Doctoris Angelici* (fifth edition; Paris: Ouby and Roger, 1887).

[74] Abbé Dupeyrat, S.S., *Manuductio ad scholasticam, maxime vero Thomisticam
philosophiam* (fourth edition; Paris: Lecoffre, 1894).

[75] Abbé Élie Blanc, *La philosophie traditionnelle et scolastique. Précis pour
le temps présent* (2nd ed.; Lyons-Paris: Librairie Catholique Emmanuel Vitte,
1928). Cf. also C. Alibert, S.S., *Manuel de philosophie pour la préparation au
Baccalauréat à l'usage des séminaires & des colleges ecclésiastiques* (Lyons-Paris:
Delhomme & Briguet, 1883). "Il n'est pas de terme plus général que ce mot de raison
des choses: c'est le seul, à notre sens, qui traduit dans son entier l'objet de la
science, qui en exprime à la fois l'*étendue et l'unité,* qui lui soit *adéquat.*" *Ibid.,*
p. 6.

[76] Dupeyrat, *op. cit.,* I, 206.

[77] *Ibid., pp.* 147, 148.

[78] Francis Egger, *Propaedeutica philosophica theologica* (5th ed.; Brescia:

By the end of the decade, the *Institutiones logicales secundum principia S. Thomae Aquinatis ad usum scholasticum* (1888) of Tillman Pesch, S.J., had appeared. Under *Logica Realis* in volume two there is a presentation of the Principle of Sufficient Reason which seeks to stay as much as possible on middle ground in the question of identifying it with the Principle of Causality and relating it to the Principle of Contradiction.[79] The English Jesuit, John Rickaby, published the first edition of his famous work in this same year of 1888. Called *The First Principles of Knowledge*,[80] it is divided into two parts: The nature of certitude in general, and special treatment of certitude. Chapter ten of part one is called "The primary facts and principles of the logician." After explaining the primary fact, the primary condition, and the primary principle of all knowledge in a way reminiscent of Balmes, Palmieri, and Tongiorgi, he points out that to assert such primacy does not deny that there are other primacies. In fact,

> . . . in addition to them, the principle of identity is primary, so is the principle of sufficient reason, that nothing can be without an adequate account for its existence; and so is the principle of evidence that what is evident must be accepted as true.[81]

It would be both tedious and not particularly useful, he continues, to compile a catalogue of all the self-evident truths; but if called upon to emphasize any beyond the three mentioned primary ones, "it will be the Principle of Sufficient Reason, so often violated by pure empiricists, and yet so vital to all philosophy."[82] Rickaby

Wegerian, 1898). Cf. pp. 263-264. He says the Principle of Sufficient Reason is built upon the notion of *ratio*, primarily indicating a concept of the mind, secondarily the thing corresponding to this concept. *Ratio* can sometimes mean the essential notes in the mind, sometimes the elements or essentials in the thing. The Principle is an axiom so immediately evident and universal in both the logical and the ontological orders that to deny it is to deny the Principle of Contradiction; whatever is must have its essence; whatever is understood must have its notes through which understanding comes.

[79] Tilmann Pesch, S.J., *Institutiones Logicales secundum principia S. Thomae Aquinatis ad usum cholasticum accommodavit. Paris II: Logica Maior; Volumen I complectens logicam criticam et formalem* (Freiburg i. B.: Herder, 1889).

[80] John Rickaby, S.J., *The First Principles of Knowledge* (London: Longmans, Green, and Co., 1919). "Avec Rickaby, le traité d'epistémologie paraît pour la première fois en traité autonome; le nom même de 'logique' est délaissé pour celui de 'premiers principes de la connaissance'; le plan est modifié . . . ce traité . . . est assurément un des meilleurs de XIXᵉ siècle." Van Riet, *op. cit.*, p. 115.

[81] Rickaby, *op. cit.*, pp. 174-175.

[82] *Ibid.*, p. 175.

is noteworthy also for his orientation toward the English Non-Scholastic philosophers and refers to the interpretation of our Principle by Bain, Mill and Mansel.

Another Jesuit, Van der Aa, in Belgium, may be mentioned for his use of strict thesis form (state of the question and proofs) proving that the Principles of Sufficient Reason and Causality are immediately evident and analytic and cannot be denied without falling into skepticism. All reasoning and all certitude presuppose the Principle of Sufficient Reason in such a way that, if it could be denied, certitude would be impossible. However, neither of these principles is made by him to flow out of the concept of being with the standard three, Identity, Contradiction, and Excluded Middle. But since being differs from non-being, this being from that being, and existent being from possible being, this difference cannot be because of nothing. Therefore it is due to something either intrinsic or extrinsic "which is called the sufficient reason."[83] The causal principle is clear because, being a mere possible before existence, something cannot determine itself to exist and so, "as in all analytic judgments," it is easy to conclude in the abstract from existence of effect to existence of cause.

From 1890 to 1900. In the last ten years of the century, four distinct groups of manuals may be indicated and a word said about the appearance of the Principle of Sufficient Reason in each. By choosing as the basis of distinction the somewhat extrinsic classification of authors according to membership in a religious order, we have Jesuit, Dominican, Benedictine, and diocesan seminary manuals—this latter including Mercier at Louvain and some Sulpician professors.

1. Among the Jesuits a further division may be made on the basis of "Thomistic" and "Suarezian" tendencies which at this stage of the evolution of the Neo-Scholastic textbook generally agree in eliminating the Principle of Sufficient Reason from their systematic development. John Joseph Urraburu, S.J., and Sanctus Schiffini, S.J., illustrate this for the Suarezians; De Maria, S.J., and Remer, S.J., for the Thomists.[84]

---

[83] John Van der Aa, S.J., *Praelectionum philosophiae scholasticae brevis conspectus* (2nd ed.; Louvain: Fonteyn, 1888). Both the Principle of Causality and the Principle of Sufficient Reason are immediately evident and analytic. Cf. I, 230.

[84] De Maria, Michael, S.J., *Philosophia Peripatetico-Scholastica ex fontibus Aristotelis et S. Thomae Aquinatis expressa et ad adolescentium institutionem accommodata* (Editio quarta; Rome: Ex Pontificia Officina Typographica, 1913). Vol. I.

Urraburu, it is true, in his *Institutiones philosophicae quas Romae in Pontificia Universitate Gregoriana tradiderat,* devotes a brief consideration to the Principle of Sufficient Reason.[85] But it is not without significance that this comes after 1,161 pages of logic in volume one and 1,101 pages of ontology in volume two, during which he gets along quite nicely without it. That it appears at all in the article on causes, at the end of the *Ontology,* seems due more to custom than to need. He simply states the Principle, shows it to be wider than the Principle of Causality and as self-evident.

> For if *ratio* be taken for the essence of a thing or for the determinant to existence, it is clearly evident that nothing can be without a suitable and proportionate essence and nothing can exist unless there is something which determines its existence; otherwise it would be indifferent to existence and from indifference nothing follows.[86]

A scholion condemns Leibniz' restriction of the Principle to "contingent truth or synthetic judgments" and promises future reference to the subject under the topic of an *optimum* world in Natural Theology.[87]

Schiffini, whose *Principia philosophica ad mentem Aquinatis quae in Pontificia Universitate Gregoriana tradebat,* first appeared in 1886 but enjoyed further editions and enlargements into the new century, devotes a passage at the end of the book to the Principle of Sufficient Reason, i.e., *Nihil est sine ratione sufficiente.* He concludes that the Principle holds true, if you are saying there is no being without its corresponding concept, but if you are discussing dependence, then the Principle is resolved into the causal axiom and applies only where causality is in question. "Speaking simply, what is insufficient is not a cause."[88]

2. Among the following seminary professors, the Principle of Sufficient Reason held a varied place. Benedict Lorenzelli, Archbishop of Lucca, who wrote *Philosophiae theoreticae institutiones*

Vincent Remer, S.J., *Summa praelectionum philosophiae scholasticae quas in Universitate Gregoriana habuit* (Prati: Giachetti, 1895).

[85] John Joseph Urraburu, S.J., *Institutiones philosophicae quas Romae in Pontificia Universitate Gregoriana tradiderat* (Valladolid: Typis Viduae ac Filiorum a Cuesta, 1891), II, 1101.

[86] *Ibid.,* p. 1102.

[87] *Loc. Cit.*

[88] Sanctum Schiffini, S.J., *Principia philosophica ad mentem Aquinatis quae in Pontificia Universitate Gregoriana tradebat* (Turin: Ex Typographia Fratrum Speirani, 1886), pp. 748-749.

secundum doctrinas Aristotelis et S. Thomae Aquinatis traditae in Pont. Collegio Urbano de Propaganda Fide in 1890 and makes one of the sharpest brief criticisms of the Principle found anywhere during its history, refused primacy to "that principle formulated by Leibniz" because:

> . . . it is founded in the concepts of effect and cause, which suppose the concept of being: moreover, because it is not the best known to all nor applicable to every being, since not every being has the *ratio* of a something caused, for God has no cause of Himself.[89]

In his second volume, he gives a brief criticism of the Principle's misuse in the proof for the existence of God, an observation as pertinent as it was neglected by other authors. He points out that Leibniz (in the *Theodicy*, I, 7) changed the nature of the Thomistic argument,[90] by arguing as he does that

> . . . *the world is contingent;* but the sufficient reason of the contingent is the necessary and the eternal, therefore the necessary and the eternal is to be supposed over and above the world. And it was because of this that this proof, to which Leibniz gave an absolute value, was admitted by Kant only as to its form and not its matter, both because the contingency of the whole universe is not evident and because, in the conclusion, occurs the *ratio* of eternal and extra-mundane, which does not seem to be clearly indicated from the corruptibility of any things, and which seems induced rather *a priori* from the ontological argument.[91]

The illation here, thinks Lorenzelli, seems to lead only to some kind of immanent principle in the world and leaves true Theism open to the accusation of proving the existence of God from the supposition of the universal contingency of the world and then proving this contingency from the creation of that same world. Whereas St. Thomas, Lorenzelli adds, drew his argument not from the contingency of the whole universe, which is not manifest according to all its parts, but from the manifest contingency proper to some sensible things or some substances of the universe.

---

[89] Benedict Lorenzelli, *Philosophiae theoreticae institutiones secundum doctrinas Aristotelis et S. Thomae Aquinatis traditae in Pont. Collegio Urbano de Propaganda Fide* (Rome: P. Cuggiani, 1890), I, 231.

[90] *Ibid.*, II, 432.

[91] *Ibid.*, pp. 432-433.

At Innsbruck at about this same time, Max Limbourg presented the more usual doctrine that the Principle of Sufficient Reason establishes the analytic nature and complete certitude of the Principle of Causality,[92] while in France, the Sulpician, M. Brin, reviewed in his *Philosophica scholastica ad mentem S. Thomae Aquinatis exposita et recentioribus scientiarum inventis adopta* (1893) the discussion among philosophers on the primacy of principles and the theory of three principles flowing from the notion of being. He added thereto the Principles of Sufficient Reason and Causality, and made them all dependent on Contradiction. This work was issued early in the new century in a fourth edition by A. Farges and D. Barbedette, who also appear under this same title as the authors.[93]

Meanwhile, Mercier's works began to appear and in the famous *Cours* itself the Principle of Sufficient Reason receives scant attention. In the *Logic* there is no mention of it when he treats of those directive rules of thought we call first principles, which are the most simple and universal judgments the intellect can pronounce and are usually listed as the Principle of Identity, Contradiction, and Excluded Middle.[94] In the *Métaphysique générale* or *Ontologie,* he takes up again the notion of first principles after treating of being and its transcendentals. The Principle of Sufficient Reason is specifically excluded as a first principle since it reduces either to a form of the Principle of Identity or to Causality.[95]

[92] Max Limbourg, *Begriff und Einteilung der Philosophie.* Historisch-Kritische Untersuchung (Innsbruck: F. Rauch, 1893). Bound under this are the following: *Quaestionum Dialecticarum Libri Tres privato auditorum facultatis theologiae usui accommodati,* 1896; *Quaestionum Logicarum Libri Quattuor,* 1894; *Quaestionum metaphysicarum Libri quinque,* 1893. Cf. Thesis 131 of this latter, page 344 ff.: Declarato principio rationis sufficientis ponitur, principium causalitatis analyticum esse atque certissimum.

[93] M. Brin, S.S., *Philosophia scholastica ad mentem S. Thomae Aquinatis exposita et recentioribus scientiarum inventis adopta* (Editio quarta penitus recognita curantibus DD. A. Farges et D. Barbedette; Paris: Berche and Tralin, 1893). The twelfth edition of 1908 does not carry Brin's name on the title page. Instead, A. Farges and D. Barbedette are indicated as authors.

[94] Cardinal Désiré Mercier, *Cours de philosophie: Logique* (septième édition; Louvain: Institut supérieur de philosophie, 1922), p. 200.

[95] Mercier, *Cours de philosophie: Métaphysique générale ou ontologie* (septième édition; Louvain: Institut supérieur de philosophie, 1923), p. 266, explains the Principle of Sufficient Reason as follows: "Ce principe, que l'autorité de l'illustre Leibniz a rendu célèbre, s'énonce: Tout être a sa raison suffisante. Raison, *ratio* chez les scolastiques, correspond souvent à *perfection formelle, forma.* Or il est évident que tout être possède en lui-même, sa perfection formelle, sa raison. Il a

3. Before concluding this chapter with a summary of the Dominican manuals of the time, the Benedictine, Joseph Gredt, must be placed in this survey. His famous *Elementa philosophiae Aristotelico- Thomisticae* (1929) first appeared in two volumes in 1899-1901.[96] Principles *per set nota* are those in which the connection between subject and predicate appears immediately from an understanding of the terms, such as "being," "non-being," "whole," "cause," etc. The Principle of Contradiction is first in order followed by the Principle of Sufficient Reason. There are seven Principles in all: Excluded Middle, Identity, Difference, *Dictum de omni,* and *Dictum de nullo.* This is in logic.

In metaphysics there is a thesis establishing the objective reality of the concept of cause and a scholium indicating that the Principles of Causality and Sufficient Reason are both *per se* known and absolutely evident.[97]

4. Dominican philosophy manuals were relatively few in the last half of the nineteenth century, although historians of philosophy trace some of the roots of the century's revival of Thomism, even among the Jesuits, to two Dominican manuals from previous centuries: the *Philosophia juxta inconcussa tutissimaque D. Thomae dogmata quatuor tomis comprehensa* (1671) of Anthony Goudin, O.P., and the *Summa philosophica ad mentem Angelici Doctoris S. Thomae Aquinatis* (1777) of Salvatore Roselli, O.P.[98] Both

donc en lui-même sa raison suffisante immédiate. Ceci n'est, d'ailleurs, qu'une des multiples impressions du principe d'identité. Un être est blanc par sa blancheur, la raison nécessaire et suffisante pour qu'il soit blanc c'est qu'il possede la blancheur. La raison suffisante de l'existence de l'Être nécessaire c'est qu'il est. Mais le principe de raison suffisante s'entend souvent dans le sens de raison adéquate *extrinsèque.* Il est, dans ce cas, postérieur au principe de causalité et n'est pas en rigueur de termes un principe premier."

96 Joseph Gredit, O.S.B., *Elementa philosophiae Aristotelico-Thomisticae* (Rome: Desclée, Lefebvre et sociorum, 1899-1901). In the later editions, logic and natural philosophy precede metaphysics. But the doctrine on Sufficient Reason is substantially the same in both early and late editions and amounts to what we have seen as the doctrine of Liberatore regarding induction as a syllogistic process from the Principle of Causality and Sufficient Reason.

97 Gredt, *op. cit.,* I, 129-130. Cf. Joseph Gredt, O.S.B., *Elementa philosophiae Aristotelico-Thomisticae* (5th ed.; Freiburg i. B.: Herder, 1929). In this latter work, causality receives considerably more space than in the first edition. The Principle of Sufficient Reason includes the intrinsic sufficient reason of *essendi* as well as the extrinsic sufficient reason of *fiendi* (here Sufficient Reason is merely the causal principle). Both of these principles are reduced to the Principle of Contradiction in that they can be demonstrated indirectly *per absurdum.*

98 Vincent Buzzetti (1777-1824) was the teacher at the seminary in Piacenza of the three Sordi brothers who later entered the restored Society of Jesus and

of these works circulated widely and appeared in new nineteenth-century editions.[99] Neither shows any trace of the Principle of Sufficient Reason, although a *Compendium summae philosophiae* made of Roselli's larger work in 1837 notes Storchenau's division of principles according to necessary and contingent truth.

> It is enough to say here that the Principle of Sufficient Reason is reduced to the Principle of Contradiction and it is false to restrict it to contingent things. St. Thomas . . . admits only one principle of demonstration as absolutely prime, namely, the Principle of Contradiction.[100]

In 1868 the Spanish Dominican, later Cardinal, Zephyrinus Gonzalez, produced at Madrid in three volumes his *Philosophia elementaria ad usum academicae ac praesertim ecclesiasticae juventutis opera et studia,* designated by Van Riet as a fundamental textbook used by the great Belgium Cardinal, Mercier, in the early period of his teaching.[101] Aside from a neat note on the theological use of Sufficient Reason and a mild use of it in the *Cosmology,* the Principle is not featured in Gonzales' work. He lists the Principles of Contradiction, Identity, and Excluded Middle in Logic (a selection later found in Mercier). While his *Ontology* begins with *notio entis,* it proceeds next to potency and act and then to principles of being and knowledge, where the synthetic *a priori* judgment of Kant is rejected, the Principle of Contradiction asserted as the first principle of demonstration, and the Principle of Causality identified as an analytic judgment. Here we find the note mentioned above:

together with Taparelli greatly influenced the restoration of Scholastic and in particular Thomistic philosophy in that order. Buzzetti was influenced while in theology by an exiled Spanish Jesuit, Baltasar Mesdeu (1741-1820), who helped him abandon Locke's sensationalism taught at the Vincentian college in Piacenza and turn to Scholasticism. But it was his reading of Roselli and Goudin which determined him to Thomism. Cf. Bonansea, Masnovo and Van Riet as cited above in n. 1, 3, and 27.

[99] Salvator Marie Roselli, O.P., *Summa philosophica ad mentem Angelici Doctoris S. Thomae Aquinatis* (Rome: Puccinelli, 1777). Balmes and Liberatore are indebted to Roselli. Anthony Goudin, O.P., *Philosophia juxta inconcussa tutissimaque D. Thomae dogmata quatuor tomis comprehensa* (Editio novissima; Orvieto: S. Pompei, 1860).

[100] Salvator Maria Roselli, O.P., *Compendium summae philosophiae* (Rome: Urban College, 1837), I, 8.

[101] Cardinal Zephyrinus Gonzalez, O.P., *Philosophia elementaria ad usum academicae ac praesertim ecclesiasticae juventutis opera et studio* (4th ed.; Madrid: Lezcano et C., 1882).

There are those who confound the principle of causality: *whatever becomes has a cause,* or in other words, *there is no effect without a cause,* with the principle of sufficient reason: *whatever is, has a sufficient reason of itself.* But this is wrong, because not everything that is, is caused; God exists and is his own sufficient reason of existing, but he is not caused nor is he a cause of Himself. Hence the notion and principle of sufficient reason have a wider extension than the notion and principle of causality.[102]

Some ten years later (1876), Cardinal Zigliara's *Summa philosophica in usum scholarum* was printed at Rome,[103] while at Louvain, during the years from 1875 to 1878, appeared a three volume set, *Elementa philosophicae christianae,* by Albert Lepidi, O.P. This latter author notes in his *Logic,* in the chapter on principles in a section on the reasoning process, that Leibniz proposed two first principles. He dismisses the Principle of Sufficient Reason as follows: "This second principle is too vague and obscure; perhaps it can be treated as belonging to the two logical principles treated above."[104] These principles stated that *The intellect is a faculty and efficient power of manifesting and knowing truth; Whatever is distinct and evidently represented to the intellect, must be affirmed as true.*[105] Zigliara does not *use* the Principle of Sufficient Reason.

Finally at the end of the century (1898) a Dominican manual appeared in which considerable space is devoted to our Principle. This is the *Elementa philosophiae* of Jerome Maria Mancini, O.P.[106] In the *Critica* portion of his *Logic,* the sixth question treats of the supreme criterion of truth, and article three under the subject of first principles of demonstration discusses synthetic principles.

---

[102] *Ibid.,* II, 49, n. 1.

[103] Cardinal Thomas Maria Zigliara, O.P. *Summa philosophicae in usum scholarum* (11th ed; Paris: Delhomme and Briguet, 1898).

[104] Albert Lepidi, S.P., *Elementa philosophiae christianae* (Paris: P. Lethielleux, 1875-79).

[105] *Ibid.,* I, 273. He has two other principles of which he calls one, psychological, *I think;* and the other, ontological, *It is not possible for the same thing under the same aspect to both be and not be.* I, 270.

[106] Jerome Maria Mancini, O.P., *Elementa philosophiae ad mentem D. Thomae Aquinatis Doctoris Angelici ad triennium accommodata* (Rome: Ex Typographia Polyglotta S. C. de Propaganda Fide, 1898).

Here we find the "Liberatore" doctrine on the influx of analytic principles necessary to give universality to induction. This principle, says Mancini, can be no other than "the principle of similar cause, that is, *similar effects demand a similar cause; or,* at least, the Principle of Sufficient Reason itself: nothing is or becomes without a sufficient reason."[107]

Leibniz' doctrine, he continues, that analytic judgments rely on the Principle of Causality, and synthetic ones, on the Principle of Sufficient Reason, is absolutely false as to this latter point unless you mean synthetic and universal judgments. It is ridiculous that "for anyone to know with certainty the truth of this or that fact, it is necessary to call on some analytical principle in which that fact is contained as a part in its whole." Rather, universal synthetic judgments rely on the Principle of Sufficient Reason in the sense that "they presuppose it as a true knowledge by the mind, which by means of reasoning bestows universality upon them." This settled, he states as a proposition that *Universal synthetic judgments are ruled indirectly by the Principle of Sufficient Reason; but particular synthetic judgments are resolved in experience.*[108] A corollary also scores the falsity of Leibniz' Principle of Sufficient Reason because of the determination involved therein that is destructive of liberty.

In his *Ontology,* Mancini faces the question of identity between the Principle of Causality and that of Sufficient Reason and says that, according to the common way of speaking, they are taken for one and the same. But if pressed for precision, it must be said that they differ in two ways: first, the Principle of Sufficient Reason enunciates a truth which is found even in God; secondly, it signifies more than the Principle of Causality and extends to everything which is able to be determinative of another, and is not restricted, as is the causality principle, to the relation and dependence of an effect on a cause.

Here our presentation of the Principle of Sufficient Reason as used by some Scholastics from 1750 to 1900 comes to an end, and we turn now to a final summary and brief critique. The choice of Dominican manual writers for the conclusion of this chapter and as final evidence in our long list of textbooks examples is not without significance.

[107] *Ibid.,* I, 180.
[108] *Ibid.,* pp. 180-181.

First of all, these writers from Goudin and Roselli to Mancini are a kind of microcosm of the world of textbooks passed in review; as in the larger picture, there is a beginning from the old Peripatetic tradition in which no trace has been found and no place seems available for the Principle of Sufficient Reason. Then there are the examples of a mild use and later of some commitment to its importance, especially in the epistemology of induction. Despite their devotion to St. Thomas and what may perhaps be a closer following in general of Thomistic sources, the primacy-of-essence orientation continues, and the Principle of Sufficient Reason functions in that context.

Secondly, there is a kind of prophetic fitness about bringing this study of the Principle to a close in the shadow of Dominican writings. One of the great exponents and popularizers of our Principle in the years after 1900 was Reginald Garrigou-Lagrange, O.P. His rationalistic use and development of the Principle of Sufficient Reason in *God: His Existence and His Nature,* not to mention other books and periodical writing,[109] have helped to secure it that place in Scholastic philosophy manuals today which makes critical evaluation of its meaning and use difficult without some insight into its history such as these pages try to supply.

---

[109] Reginald Garrigou-Lagrange, O.P., *Dieu, Son Existence et Sa Nature: Solution thomiste des antinomies agnostiques* (3rd ed.; Paris: C. Bauschesne, 1920), (1st ed.; 1915). Translated into English by Dom Bede Rose, O.S.B., from the Fifth French Edition, in 1939. Cf. *infra,* ch. 6, n. 8.

Chapter VI

ཆུ་ Critique and Conclusion

SINCE THIS STUDY is in the nature of a pioneer attempt at viewing the bibliography of a century and a half of Scholastic philosophy manuals, the proportion allotted to the historical data of authors and texts is quite high. This, together with the very nature of the Principle of Sufficient Reason as it appears in the manuals under examination, constituted a peculiar problem.

Because in itself "sufficient reason" can mean a number of things, the Principle of Sufficient Reason must be related to the contextual framework of its use in order to establish its relevant intelligibility. To attempt this in detail for each appearance in the textbooks would expand these pages to an absurd length; yet to neglect this contextual reference completely would result in a mere repetition of instances which the simplicity of our Principle's formulation and the accommodating neutrality of its meaning would render both monotonous and sterile.

A solution to this problem was found in a method of procedure: first, an examination of the historical data on the Principle's use with special attention paid to the context accorded it in Leibniz and Wolff, thus affording some insight into those features which characterize it as a principle wherever it occurs. Then, with the outline of this context sketched in general, individual instances of the Principle of Sufficient Reason's appearance were cited with some further indication of the background peculiar to each textbook or group of manuals. In this way, critical comment has been held to a minimum until completion of the historical survey, and thus a balance was sought between a somewhat exhaustive accounting of sources and a satisfactory appraisal of content. Now, the historical survey completed, it remains to draw together in a unified critique the evidence available from the foregoing exploration of the actual textbook situation.

A First General Conclusion

By way of organizing the following matter, a primary general conclusion of this historical investigation may be stated as follows: *no one individual author or group of authors examined ever completely broke out of that primacy-of-essence context in which, as a matter of fact, the Principle of Sufficient Reason is most relevant and useful.* As exemplified in Leibniz and systematized into a geometry-of-being by Wolff, this context is found to be present throughout the period of textbook history from 1750 to 1900.[1]

Clearly, there are many differences between the Leibnizian-Wolffian system and those of Catholic manual-writers. In their borrowings, these latter left behind the absurdities of the Monadology while influences older than either Leibniz or Wolff have shaped their doctrine and other aims and purposes controlled their selection and organization of content material. But at rock-bottom they are sufficiently alike on: 1. the starting-point and object of metaphysics, 2. the consequent theory of method and format, 3. the doctrinal position on the nature of judgment in relation to the "notions" of being and cause, and 4. the place of sensation in systematic metaphysics to justify this procedure of comparison and co-presentation.

This is not a technique of name-calling, nor is it an attempt to establish metaphysical guilt by association. Rather it is a legitimate use of a "pure position" to help specify the philosophy in question and to find a systematic way through areas in which there is a great mixture and cross-blend of method and doctrine.

This short critique of the Principle of Sufficient Reason, therefore, will proceed toward making this general conclusion more

[1] Some striking examples of the continuation of this context beyond 1900 may be found in the following: Gustavus Pecsi, *Cursus brevis philosophiae* (Esztergom [Hungaria]: G. Buzarovits, 1906), I, 198-199; C. Willems, *Institutiones philosophicae* (Treves: Ex Officina ad S. Paulinum, 1915), I, 309, 341, 403, 508; Zacharias Van de Woestyne, O.F.M., *Cursus philosophicus in breve collectus* (Mechlin: Typographia S. Francisci, 1921), I, 74, 509-512; Francis Marxuach, S.J., *Compendium dialecticae, criticae et ontologiae* (Editio Altera; Barcelona: Eugenius Subirana, 1929), pp. 195-196; Peter Descoqs, S.J., *Schema theodiceae* (Paris: Beauchesne, 1941), I, 21, 48-49; Raphael Martinez del Campo, S.J., *Cursus philosophicus Collegii Maximi Ysletensis Societatis Iesu, Pars VI, Theologia Naturalis* (Mexico City, A. Alvarez, 1943), pp. 9, 12. A good example of a twentieth century textbook attempting to restore Thomistic existential reference to metaphysics and to take cognizance of recent textbook history on such points as the Principle of Sufficient Reason is F. X. Maquart, *Elementa philosophiae seu brevis philosophiae spceulativae synthesis ad studium theologiae manuducens* (Paris: Andreas Blot, 1938), III-I, 220-243.

explicit, breaking it down into precise points of evidence. As a guide in this process, two characteristics of the Principle will be stated and relevant data presented under each one. These data will establish the primacy-of-essence orientation of the Principle's usual meaning and interpretation as well as indicate its practical application in systematic metaphysics.

The two characteristics of the Principle as it appears during this century and a half of philosophy manual writing are: 1. its amazing neutrality in formulation and, as a consequence, 2. its migratory pattern within the textbook format. During the last half of the nineteenth century, the Principle of Sufficient Reason was given a crucial function at three points in the Neo-Scholastic manuals which were not prominent in the earlier texts and which will be expanded briefly here under this second characteristic. These points are: (a) the explanation of induction; (b) the origin and nature of first principles, especially that of causality, and (c) the proof for the existence of God.

Neutrality of the Principle's Formulation

As one consequence of the narrow line separating the Principle of Sufficient Reason from the ordinary idea or concept, there is a peculiar neutrality about *"ratio sufficiens"* which must be removed by contextual reference. "Sufficient reason" acquires its meaning more from the context in which it is used than from any established definition attached to the words themselves. This characteristic has enabled it to fit into more than one systematic context and, within a given system, to perform a variety of functions. Since *"ratio"* or "reason" thus takes its content from its context, the ambiguity of "sufficient reason" makes it fair game for any system builder, be he rationalist, idealist, or eclectic scholastic, who wishes to open logic to metaphysics or metaphysics to logic.

Eusebius Amort early in the eighteenth century and Archbishop Lorenzelli late in the nineteenth, bearing witness to this feature, presented the core of critical comment on the Principle of Sufficient Reason when they branded it as essentially vague and obscure, fundamentally equivocal in its basic concepts: "sufficient" and "reason." Amort, contemporary with the beginnings of Wolff's rise to prominence, observed that *ratio* is an equivocal term chosen by Wolff because the context of the Leibnizian system makes *causa* almost meaningless in the traditional sense of the transmission of *esse* from substance to substance. For Amort, this equivocation disqualifies the Principle of Sufficient Reason as a *principle* because, by definition and purpose, principles are supposed to be self-evident and ultimate.[2] In the centuries that followed many a page was to be written in an effort to escape this vagueness and remove this disqualification since this is the first task for anyone desiring to use the Principle of Sufficient Reason in systematic philosophy.

One simple expedient for clarifying the meaning, so that the ambiguity of "reason" might be removed (or suppressed), was by means of selected definitions. But with definitions restricted to the univocity of clear and distinct ideas, precise commitment to a general systematic context is necessary. Moreover, since the nominal meaning usually assigned "reason" here is "that whence it is understood why something is rather than is not, or is of such a kind rather than another," the "that" in this explanation must be given some ultimate grounding in the real. Hence, to explain "sufficient reason" involves the necessity both of explaining the origin of the Principle of Sufficient Reason and of indicating wherein its intelligibility ultimately is resolved. This is precisely the hinge whereby an author can make the Principle face in one of two directions. Either it is intelligible in terms of existential experience and thereby analogous rather than equivocally neutral; or it is rendered explicable and coherent in terms of selected definitions enjoying formal consistency in the order of abstract essence.

As a matter of wording and formulation, the Principle of Sufficient Reason in itself is orientated away from an existential starting point toward something in some way beyond and deeper than the being of our experience. This is also true as a matter of historical context and background. Early in its career the Principle became involved in the apologetic against skepticism and the denial of God's existence; later, an epistemological context gave it importance as a bridge between subjective ideas and their objective content.[3]

[2] Cf. Eusebius Amort (1692-1775), *Philosophia Pollingana ad normam Burgundicae* (Augsburg: Vieth, 1730), p. 579, who observes by way of critical comment: "4. Ea, quae sunt vel fiunt, sua non destituuntur ratione, unde intelligitur, cur sint vel fiunt. N.B. Potuisset Wolfius dicere, *non destituuntur sua causa,* sed, quia ex Systemate Leibniziano supponitur omnia vivere, sentire, & intelligere, noluit praejudicare huic sententiae, sed potius uti termino aequivoco, dicendo, *non destituuntur sua ratione.* Uti vero terminis aequivocis in ipsis scientiarum principiis, est contra Methodum."

[3] In Osterreider there appeared an interpretation of Sufficient Reason in terms

In either case, the Principle worked as a kind of philosophical *Deus ex machina* to rescue the realities of *being* from absorption into a mere projection of subjective necessities and intelligibilities. When authors such as Tamagna and Liberatore in his later works drew the content of the Principle of Sufficient Reason from existential experience, they concluded that the Principle is identical with the Principle of Causality, at least in the world of created being.

This Janus-like openness of the Principle of Sufficient Reason to meaning from either the existential or the essential order helped render it so permanent in the history of recent philosophy. We must now examine the evidence for our further conclusion that, as a matter of fact in the period under study, the content of the formal Principle has generally been drawn from the abstract conceptions of the essential order. The meaning of this Principle formulated as *Nothing is without a Sufficient Reason* has been determined consistently by the primacy of the essential, the possible, the logical.

In Leibniz and Wolff this primacy-of-essence position is much more coherent and pure than in those Scholastics who have at least the negative influence of theology and a tradition of "realism" holding them to spontaneous existential reference. None the less, it may be asserted that in general the attempt by Scholastic manual-writers to construct or, at least, present a philosophical system was guided by the primacy which they too gave the essential, the logical, the deductive. Their orientation, even when "corrected" by other factors, led them on basic points to the same position as that held by Leibniz and Wolff. On such fundamentals as the nature of judgment, the conceptions of being and cause, principles of being, the potency-and-act correlation, explanation of abstraction, and the origin of knowledge, these manuals differ from their great originals more on the reason why they assume the positions they do than on the essentials of doctrine itself.

Since these are the points that determine the pure context of the Principle of Sufficient Reason and settle the direction it must

of motive or end, with an orientation of the question toward theological considerations involving freedom. In Altieri and Tamagna an epistemological context for the principle began to take shape. These two authors also pointed up the distinction between *reason* and *cause,* Tamagna eliminating "sufficient reason" from the physical order as signifying anything distinct from cause itself. His distinction between essential reason and existential cause was part of the process of breaking Scholastic philosophy manuals out of the realm of essences.

face for acquiring systematic content, their outline in Leibniz and
Wolff, although accompanied by details abhorrent to Catholic authors, is a classic exposé of doctrine that is not only at the heart of
eighteenth-century rationalism and its genetic antecedents, but
also is the persistent core-element in most of the Scholastic manuals
written even to our day. Leibniz' own monadological system is
more of a consequence than a cause of the primacy-of-essence position. Hence, the following fundamentals of this doctrine, which
remain even when the monadological details can be sloughed off
by successors of Leibniz and Wolff, may be gathered from Leibniz
and held as test points for evaluating the context of the Principle
of Sufficient Reason even in Scholastic manuals.

One result of the early philosophical decisions of Leibniz in
rejecting the traditional four causal principles was to give himself
a world of univocal being. Worked out in the details of the *Monadology* where the monad was both being and mind, individuation
became a question of psychic content, a concept based on a force-
theory of substance instead of a metaphysical doctrine of matter
and form in substantial unity. Differences were a question of degree, not of kind; there were no principles of being in the technical sense of an "ens quo" or co-principle in the order of substantial
essence. Prime matter became second matter with its usual result-
ant, extension, included among *phenomena bene fundata*.

Form was a functional concept applied to the dominant monad
of an aggregate, and all that "co-principle" could mean was the
subordination of distinct acts or monads in an adapted but non-
determining relation. Finality was achieved by means of the Principle of Sufficient Reason, which supplied *knowledge* of the fact
that the universe had an end outside the system itself. Within the
contingencies of existence, efficient causality became "sequence"
in a line of reasons.

Explanation in terms of the intelligibility of the four causes now
lacked not only two of the four but was also crippled by a concept
of the universe in which the remaining two, efficient and final
causes, were separated by the dichotomy of matter and spirit, the
contingent and the necessary. Hence, physics and metaphysics
could be reduced to unity only at a point outside the series.

In the order of substance-accident relations and at the level of
operation in transient action, "efficient causality" took its meaning
from a theory of windowless monads brought into metaphysical

union by means of pre-established harmony and the dynamistic subject-predicate concept of substance. This reduced causality to implication, an embodied, implicit subject-predicate nexus whose dynamism is the *ratio* or cause of the real multiplicity of perceptual states within the substance.

This multiplicity never reduced utterly to unity within the monads because God is the only substance of one idea or perception perfectly clarified. Thus, being was univocal as *activity*, and differences in being were ultimately a distinction of degree, not of kind. The ultimate *ratio* of contingent existents was non-contradiction or the possible, and the ultimate *ratio* in contingent events was pre-established harmony, which is itself ultimately explicable only in terms of the possible. The possible world was a world of essences and in making existence an exigency of the essence, Leibniz succeeded in making it logical, that is, demonstrable, in its intelligibility.

Thus the final and crucial consequence of this situation was the undisputed primacy granted essence over existence. Under this primacy, the existent was so implicated in a world of essence that, for the Thomist who examines this best possible world of Leibniz, there is no satisfactory distinction between essential actuality and the reality of existential coming-to-be.

With essence equated to the possible and the possible as the non-contradictory, logic and the non-repugnance of essence to existence constitute the real. In the absence of the act of existence and a theory of judgment through sense experience, the ultimate intelligibility of the contingent world of experience is not in its existential act but in a relation to the possible. Thus, the structure of philosophical science, which in a Thomistic system rests on the judgment of existence, is completely inverted.

This means that intelligibility is everywhere but in being itself, and, systemwise, Leibniz is hard put to save his monads from collapsing into the unity of a one-substance universe. In such a universe the non-contradiction of identical truth tends to become a One which is beyond being because there is no being, only essence with an exigency for existence. Again to the Thomist, it appears that existence must remain outside of metaphysics, since it is incapable of being integrated into the system, and the system is itself the only source of intelligibility.

So also with Wolff, whose originality lies more in the way he conceived his theory of method in reference to the practical needs of philosophy textbooks than in any new and startling change in the original deposit of primacy-of-essence doctrine. His mathematical theory of method in philosophy is best applied where this basic doctrinal orientation is present. Only in the order of essence and the univocity of formal concepts is there demonstration from clear and distinct ideas, *modo geometrico,* to the extent that metaphysics, with its four parts, is a pure science independent of the senses.

For Wolff and those who step into his dichotomy of reason and experience, metaphysics is a "geometry of being" which attempts a mathematical deduction of *something* from clear and distinct ideas in the order of essence. This *something* is the possible, the non-contradictory, and certainly it is related to the real world. But it is the compatibility of notes in a concept, the necessities of formal logic, and not the being of existential sense experience that can be systematized into an intellectual science of pure concepts or eternal truths. For Wolff these latter derive ultimately from our own innate power or ideas and, for most Scholastics of our period, from the analysis of abstract concepts founded in the real. This science thus treats of the possibility or the essence of things in a realm of reason distinct from the experimental world of fact known by induction from natural historical knowledge.

The ultimate test of whether we have "something" or "nothing" is not judgment or sensation but the Principle of Contradiction. In a particular case it is by means of this principle that we know whether or not there is a corresponding notion present. Since, for example, there is no contradiction in the notion of a space terminated by three lines, a triangle is something, an *aliquid;* "triangle" has a corresponding notion of "space terminated by three straight lines." Later, as we have seen in Liberatore, the Principle of Sufficient Reason will function in this general context to determine even whether something existential corresponds to sensation or to provide factual knowledge with the universality and necessity of science.

The German Jesuits of the eighteenth century followed this same contextual pattern. Although they saw that *being* itself is intelligible and while they had no use for innate ideas and the primacy of an *a priori* reason as such, nevertheless, they were implicitly committed to this position. For them as for generations of Scholastics before and after, the judgmental act of knowledge was always a union of two ideas, a putting together of concepts in a logical union assumed to be self-evidently ontological. Hence, metaphysics began with the explication and demonstration of clear and distinct notions and proceeded to the construction of demonstrable propositions enchained to these original notions.

As Stattler saw, being is intelligible; but, in this primacy-of-essence context, it is also conceptual and must ultimately be rendered intelligible *by principles possessed prior to the experience of being itself.*[4] Variation was possible as to the selection and relative position of these principles, but discussion of this question,

---

[4] The manuals certainly reject innate principles and emphasize that experience is necessary to their formation. But in their general commitment to conceiving being as an intelligibility grasped in abstraction rather than in a perpetual judgment, they are caught in the dichotomy between reason and experience that reserves intelligibility exclusively to the order of abstract essence. The *here and now experience of being* is rendered intelligible by principles formed from a *consideration of being in the abstract.* Hence, whether they say that the principles are formed once by a formal consideration of notions and then applied in subsequent experience, or that the principles are formed here and now in each experience by consideration of the notions derived therefrom, in either case there is a gap between *principles and intelligibilities so derived* and the *being exercising the existential act* necessarily left behind in the abstractive process. Cf. Stattler, *Philosophia methodo scientiis propria explanata,* 1-2, 3-4, "Definitiones Ontologicae *notiones directrices* appellandae sunt; eo quod per eas appareat, quo dirigendae cogitationes sint, ut in proposito quovis quaestionis argumento reperiatur, quod quaeritur. E.G. *horologii essentiam* invenire optas? & ecce! Ontologia generalem *essentiae entis compositi* notionem tibi offert, unaque ex eadem eruta principia; ex quorum applicatione essentiam horologii in specie, ceu entis item compositi, valeas invenire; scilicet partes singulas maximas & minimas, & compositionis illarum modum, id est, proportiones mutuas, nexum atque ordinem, examinandum esse &c."

"Ces axiomes en effet sont des formes abstraites, générales; ils sont stériles par eux-meme et ne sauraient engendrer une seule vérité. Il leur faut un contenu auquel ils s'appliquent, et nous verrons plus tard qu'il appartient à l'experience de le donner." De Decker, *Cours élémentaire de philosophie,* II, 15.

Peter Hoenen, S.J., *Reality and Judgment according to St. Thomas,* trans. Henry F. Tiblier, S.J., (Chicago: Henry Regnery Co., 1952), points out the dead-end to which this position leads when he says, "Consider for a moment the effort of the great Balmes, which ended in the hopeless conclusion, 'The principle of evidence is not evident.' The reason is that a consideration and analysis of the abstract formula, 'That which is evident is true,' cannot of itself lead to any other conclusion."

Other examples of this attempt to derive judgments from ideas may be found in the following: Gustavus Lahousse, S.J., *Praelectiones logicae et ontologicae quas in collegio maximo Lovaniensi S. J. habebat* (Louvain: C. Peeters, 1888), pp. 502-504. Henri Renard, *The Philosophy of God* (Milwaukee: Bruce Publishing Co., 1952), p.1 5, n. 18. Cf. also n. 12 *infra.*

in manual after manual, leaves the fundamental assumption unex-
amined and unchallenged, i.e., that first principles of knowledge
are exclusively the first principles of demonstration.

As long as the dichotomy between sense data and the work of
reason is unresolved, the method of metaphysics, instead of showing
within experience itself a real necessity imposed on intellect by
actual existents, accents the formal necessity of truth and becomes
fundamentally demonstrative, that is, deductive. Starting points,
instead of being inductive insights into the real, are understood
in terms of fruitful deduction from concepts, the origin and nature
of which in turn depend on a world whose intelligibility is restricted
to formal causality. The function of principles then is to guarantee the fruitfulness of conceptual analysis, but concepts themselves
are divided as to their existential origin and essential intelligibility.
Logical principles guarantee the fruitfulness of certitude which is
a subjective adherence to formal consistency; metaphysical principles guarantee the fruitfulness of truth, that is, the objectivity of
knowledge content. The Principle of Sufficient Reason is made
to order for either function.

Like Leibniz, who claimed for the Principle of Sufficient Reason the happy facility of putting a quick end to many metaphysical
disputes, Scholastic authors also used its ambiguity to avoid basic
philosophical problems.[5] Generations of manual-writers imitated
Wolff in his efforts to put his duo-verse of experience and reason
back together again, *without ever facing the existential problem
of the union in terms of being or the act of knowledge.* As did
Wolff, they asserted that the abstract disciplines themselves, such
as first philosophy and moral and civic philosophy, derive their
fundamental notions and principles from experience. They declared for the same holy matrimony between reason and experience
in all branches of knowledge as he did, and this reference to experience was a great advance over the old-style Peripatetic prior
to the Wolffian revolution whose *a priori* Scholasticism, whether

---

[5] "Principium illud summum: *nihil esse sine ratione,* plerasque Metaphysicae
controversias finit. Illud enim videtur negari non posse a Scholasticis, nihil fieri,
quin DEUS si velit rationem reddere possit, cur factum sit potius quam non sit.
Quin etiam de futuris conditionatis circa quae scientiam mediam introduxere Fon-
seca et Molina, idem dici potest." Conturat, *Opuscules et fragments inédits de
Leibniz,* p. 25. One of the deceptive things about ending metaphysical disputes in
this way is the sometimes unnoticed concomitant overthrow of an act-potency metaphysics itself.

in the name of Thomas, Scotus, or Suarez, often began with textual quotation and worked out from there to the "real."

Leibniz, Wolff, and the Scholastic manual-writers were realists as opposed to any subjective idealism. The mind is conscious of changes in itself occasioned by sense knowledge of the other however varied may be the explanations of this occasioning. Yet their idealism and the existential reference of this rationalism were more a result of common sense than of systematic exposition.[6] In their *systematic* failure to account for the union of reason and experience existentially, they not only failed to rescue metaphysics from the sterility of the essential order but also were incapable of answering those who declared it an impossibility.

Consequently, in this context, the Principle of Sufficient Reason was tied from the beginning to an epistemological weakness which lies in the assumption that it and its meaning ultimately reduce to principles of the mind, that is, to the order of reason, of essence, of the necessary and universal, distinct from the singular existent, although of course related to it. The *real* real was the real of essence, to which existence came as a kind of complement and fulfillment, while remaining, like sensation, always subordinate and ultimately unimportant systematically because unintelligible systematically, since it was not essence and, therefore, not conceptual and deductive. As we shall see, it was still no solution for this state of affairs to give *esse* a role in the system by making it conceptual.[7]

---

6 The *systematic* unimportance of existence is seen in the very arrangement of the textbooks themselves in which (1) the treatment of existence generally comes after the systematic presentation of realities of the order of essence, or of being entirely in terms of essence. (2) The definition of existence, i.e., its intelligibility, is considered of minor importance because it is such an obvious and self-evident *notion*. (3) "Being" is a concept and it is the result of an abstraction. These characteristics lead the Thomist to say that as far as the system is concerned in these manuals, the singular existent is left an *ignotum X* to the extent that sensation and perceptual judgment are not prsented as first principles of knowledge. Cf. John E. Gurr, S.J., "Genesis and Function of Principles in Philosophy," *Proceedings of the American Catholic Philosophical Association,* XXIX (1955), 121-133.

7 This is why when Kant appeared and pointed out that in this situation there is no ultimate escape from the order of abstract essence and an intelligibility derived from the mind itself, the interminable discussion in the later Neo-Scholastic manuals as to the analytic versus the synthetic nature of the Principles of Contradiction, Causality, and Sufficient Reason revolved around a magnificent *petitio principii.* The basic error lay in the Wolffian noetic of clear and distinct ideas, which conceived the act of judgment in terms of a subject-predicate union of concepts. Kant forced an answer, *yes* or *no,* to the alternative: is the mind *constitutive* or *reproductive* of the

Nor was anything accomplished by authors like Pesch and Tongiorgi who postulated the Principle of Sufficient Reason as an obvious starting point to be accepted without question by men of good will. But this brings us to one final facet of the Principle's characteristic adaptability. To solve Kant's objection to the extramental validity of the Principle of Causality appeal was made to the "undeniable" Principle of Sufficient Reason. But this was only a further narrowing of the meaning of metaphysics to be that science which studies *objective* being, in contrast to logic which studies *subjective* being. When *being* is understood in terms of essence, the science of being is the science of ideas that have objective reference. But this reference itself must be in terms of ideas and, to avoid an infinite regress in ideas of ideas, something must be agreed upon that actually resolves the process into existential reference.[8]

This is the role accorded First Principles and in particular the Principle of Sufficient Reason. Once again, in conceiving metaphysics as concerned not with objective being as such but with the *objectivity* of ideas of the objective, the primacy-of-essence orientation has played its part to furnish further consent to the ever-open terminology, "sufficient reason."

object of its acts. The resounding *no* of Scholastic manuals to *a priori constructs* often enough amounted to *yes*, because of their serious misreading of the judgmental act of knowing *being* as if it were an abstraction primarily resolved in *quiddities*. Ultimately, they did nothing more than *assert*, on the authority of common sense, the important distinction between conceptual being and actual existence. One function of "principles" was to give systematic foundation to this assertion or, in some instances, to "prove" a relation between the conceptual and the existential. Descartes' distinction of the objects of human cognition into "things" and "eternal truths" (*Principiorum Philosophiae*, I, 48, 49) has a long history.

    8 "The *principle of sufficient reason*, on which the proofs for the existence of God are based, is not, like the principle of substance, a simple determination of the principle of identity, but resolves itself into this principle by an appeal to the impossible." R. Garrigou-Lagrange, O.P., *God: His Existence and His Nature; A Thomistic Solution of Certain Agnostic Antinomies*, trans. from the fifth French edition by Dom Bede Rose, O.S.B. (St. Louis: B. Harder, 1939), I, 181. Two points about this author's presentation of the Principle of Sufficient Reason are worth noting: (1) His use of Africanus Spir, *Pensée et réalité*, trans. H. Penjon (Lille: au siège des Facultes, 1896) as an aid in presenting the argument for reducing Sufficient Reason to Identity. (Spir was a thorough-going proponent of idealistic monism). Garrigou-Lagrange's understanding of the Principle of Sufficient Reason and its relation to the Principle of Identity must be rescued from tendencies which logically at least reduce his explanations to the very position he seeks to refute: intelligibility is *imposed* on phenomena by the mind itself. (2) Despite the copious use of quotations from St. Thomas, the intelligibility of being and of cause are explained by this author as though grasped by abstraction. Cf. George Klubertanz, S.J., "Being and God According to Contemporary Scholastics," *The Modern Schoolman*, XXXII (1954), 1-17.

But just as Leibniz was always faced with the threat of his system collapsing into the Spinozan unity of substance, so also the objectivity of this principle-philosophy of the Scholastic manuals was under constant pressure of being reduced to the universality and necessity of Kant's *a priori* forms and synthetic *a priori* judgments. Under the second characteristic of the Principle of Sufficient Reason, its migratory pattern in the manuals, we will now consider in particular three crucial pressure points of this immanent systemic tendency: *induction, origin of principles,* and *the proof for the existence of God.*

Migratory Pattern Within the Manuals

By migratory pattern is meant in general the *variation in location* and consequently of the applied use of the Principle of Sufficient Reason within the textbook format. For example, at the beginning of its history, it always appeared first in ontology along with the Principle of Contradiction; by the end of the nineteenth century it is relegated to the treatment of causes at the end. Between these extremes there were further variations. Wolff, refusing the Principle the autonomy granted it in its own realm of contingent truth by Leibniz, subordinated it to the Principle of Contradiction; Stattler reversed this situation to make the Principle of Sufficient Reason primary. Other authors kept the traditional tract on First Principles at the beginning of ontology but moved the whole unit further into the developed system after considering certain concepts necessary for rendering the Principles themselves intelligible or functional.

In Liberatore's manuals its range of position is wide. In 1842 he is still working out of the old "twin-pillar-of-philosophy" concept of Principles as originated by Wolff, and he continues the practice of the previous century of placing the Principle of Sufficient Reason, with that of Contradiction, at the beginning of ontology. By 1857 it is at the end, under causes; eight years later its formal treatment is removed completely from the *Ontology* and placed at the end of *Major Logic* in connection with axioms expressed in judgments. Generally, in other authors of the nineteenth century, the Principle of Sufficient Reason is discussed at the end of metaphysics or ontology.[9]

[9] For examples of how the starting-point and method of metaphysics influences the use and position of the Principle of Sufficient Reason, to the point even of

Here again, a kind of summary law of migration governs this position-pattern and may be stated as follows: *in proportion as the system employing the Principle of Sufficient Reason eliminated, at least from explicit consideration, the existential causality traditionally associated with the intrinsic factors, Matter and Form, Substance and Accident, and the extrinsic influence of efficient and final causality in being, to that extent the Principle of Sufficient Reason enjoys a position of primacy and prestige at the heart of metaphysics and the consequent development of a system.*

Since this fluidity of the Principle is due to its immersion in the flexible order of ideal being, this "law" of migration is but a further confirmation of our first general conclusion as to the primacy-of-essence context. In addition to this horizontal migration of the Principle within the format of textbook philosophy, it also has undergone a kind of vertical change in its applied use at three points of textbook doctrine, as mentioned above. A brief critique of Sufficient Reason at these three points will lead us to a final summary and conclusion.[10]

Induction

Induction poses the problem of explaining universality and necessity in singular existent facts of experience. This problem and its solution in Liberatore (generally accepted by other authors of the period) has already been indicated: singular existential fact is endowed by means of a syllogistic process with the universality

eliminating it as a systematic exigency, cf. the Cartesian manuals presented in part two of chapter four, *supra*. Thus, Cochet, Mey and Para (n. 55 to 60, ch. 4) with their emphasis on psychology and a subjective starting point have no need of a Principle of Sufficient Reason.

[10] One of the most startling examples of the Principle's mobility of function appears in the following contrast between an early and late edition of Esser's manual. In the 1933 edition, the Principle of Sufficient Reason thesis declares it to be "analyticum et maxime universale," with two corollaries stating it to be "objectivum, metaphysice certum et necessarium." The arguments are drawn from an analysis of the subject and predicate involved, i.e., "ens" and "ratio sufficiens." Gerard Esser, S.V.D., *Metaphysica generalis in usum scholarum* (Techny, Ill.: Typis Domus Missionum ad St. Mariam, 1933), pp. 256-258. In the second edition of this work published in 1952 there is an unequivocal statement of exactly the opposite thesis: "Verumtamen *principium rationis sufficientis neque esse universale neque per se ipsum evidens* duplici *argumento probatur, uno directo, altero indirecto.*" *Ibid.* (1952), p. 355. The proof here consists in rejecting the arguments used in 1933. He makes the Principle of Sufficient Reason a verbal collection ("quaedam verbalis collectio" (p. 358) of the Principle of Identity and a Principle of Real Reason (essence is real reason for the properties that flow from it). *Ibid.*, p. 358.

and necessity required for scientific knowledge and peculiar to the order of essence. This process proceeds from a major premise which is itself an analytic principle, usually and ultimately the Principle of Causality or, in other words, the Principle of Sufficient Reason.[11] Leaving induction as such to other studies and without minimizing the complexity of the problem posed therein, we only need to note here that this solution of the manual authors is the late nineteenth-century form of that dichotomy between experience and reason characteristic of rationalism. Applied to metaphysical induction, it is the Neo-Scholastic form of that geometry-of-being conception of metaphysics which Wolff popularized as ontology, and which came to be identified with Scholasticism in general.

In this context, intelligibility ultimately is rooted in the abstractions of the essential order where the analysis of concepts occupies first place. The actual point of departure in inductive experience of the singular, which these manuals of course in no way deny, is *endowed* with intelligibility rather than made to yield it. After all, intelligibility, as we have so frequently seen our authors assert, belongs to the ideal world or to possible being, the truth of whose laws does not depend upon the existence of things sensible.

Lest one should object that this criticism is nothing more than the demolition of a straw man since these later manual authors were well acquainted with the Thomistic doctrine on abstraction, it must be noted that their explanation of induction is a failure because they make it a kind of appendage to the syllogistic process. Induction involves the *deduction of universality and necessity from a principle possessed prior to and independently of the experience supposed to yield this intelligibility.*[12] Once again, the Principle

---

11 A careful distinction must be kept between the "Principle of Causality" as a kind of generic summary of specific instances involved in the abstractive process and a description of intelligible necessities embedded in some concrete exemplification and grasped in judgment. The manuals generally used the Principle in the former sense.

12 Cf. Liberatore's explanation of induction in ch. 4, *supra,* especially n. 49 and 51. Other examples: "Inductio est ratiocinatio, in qua de genere vel specie universe affirmatur, vel negatur, quod de contentis sub eodem inferioribus singillatim antea affirmatum, vel negatum fuit . . . Inductio nititur hoc principio: *genus vel species idem est cum inferioribus sub se contentis: quidquid ergo universe de singulis omnino inferioribus affirmari vel negari potest, id etiam simpliciter de toto genere vel specie, sub quo illa inferiora continentur, affirmandum vel negandum est.*" Stattler, *Philosophia,* I-1, 178-179.

"Inductio est argumentatio, qua probatur aliquid inesse omni, quia inest singulis . . . Hic arguendi modus efficax est . . . innititur enim *principio dictum de omni.*"

of Sufficient Reason functions in a primacy-of-essence-over-existence context.

Such a use of the Principle is important and necessary for these writers because to conceive induction as an insight or discovery of intelligible necessities in singular existents would be a sin against the very geometry-of-being on which rationalism is built. Just as idealism, to survive as a system, must treat the sensuous as conceptual, so rationalism must treat being as conceptual and the mind makes its passage from the singular to the general *in* the order of essence, not in the structure of the existential object of perception.

The "Concept of Being" and First Principles

It is especially at this point, where inductive experience yields the intelligibility of *being* itself, that the whole of metaphysics as a science is determined toward the logical and formal orientation of ontological geometry. Here the manuals are unanimous in explaining both the conception of being and of existential causality as resulting from an abstraction; no amount of distinctions of degrees or expanding of notions to include inferiors and differences suffices to make this knowledge judgmental. Despite their explicit mention and fervent avowal of the existential reference of this idea, *being,* it remains an abstraction from the existent singular and its intelligibility belongs to the order of abstract essence.

So also with existential causes. The intelligibility of "cause" and "effect" are formal definitions understood in conceptual analysis and applied to, rather than perceived in, the existing world. This, as a matter of systematic exigency, involves the authors of textbooks in various attempts to explain the part that existence has in a theory of judgment based on such a conception and thereby to validate these analytic judgments and the principles expressed therein. As we have seen in Liberatore, for example, the Principle of Causality is a general *a priori* principle whose validity is sustained by an analysis of the concepts "cause" and "effect." Thus conceived as analytic in nature, and in view of the concept of being itself, it is safely anchored to the Principle of Contradiction and enmeshed in the universality and necessity of the order of essence.

Historically, a further explanation of this devotion to analytic judgments, besides the age-old conception of judgment as an act

Berthold Hauser, S.J., *Elementa philosophiae ad rationes et experientiae ductum* (Augsburg: J. Wolff, 1755-1758), I, 243-244.

of combining concepts, was the dilemma posed by Kant. In Kant's theory, the function of judgment was limited either to clarifying ideas or constructing objects of thought.[13] On this restricted basis he founded his distinction of judgments into *analytic*—the predicate appears from a mere analysis of the notion of one subject— and *synthetic*—there is an addition to our idea of the subject. If this addition is factual as based on experience, the judgment is *synthetic a posteriori;* if it is universal and necessary, such as in the Principles of Contradiction and Causality, then it comes from the structure of the mind itself and is *synthetic a priori.* This means that factual judgments of experience do not have that universality and necessity necessary for principles, and that *a priori* synthetic judgments are not true in the sense of representative of extra-mental reality because their universality and necessity are imposed by the mind rather than derived from the object.

Attempting to use Kant for their own purposes, the post-Kantian Scholastic manuals took the other horn of the dilemma, since they could not accept either kind of synthetic judgment, and tried to show that first principles are analytic and therefore both necessary and true. This explains, at least in part, why our Principle of Sufficient Reason, as distinct from the Principle of Causality, is derived by analysis from the concept of being and the Principle of Causality itself is verified by analysis of the concepts involved, namely, "cause" and "effect." The manuals were equally consistent in explaining an old and favorite example, *the whole is greater than its parts.* This relationship is perceived, according to them, not in the perception of some *singular sensible whole* but in the analysis of the idea "whole" and "part" whereby it is seen that these concepts contain the idea of one as greater than the other, under pain of violating the Principle of Contradiction, which has itself been derived from analysis of the concepts of *being* and *non-being.*

Thus, the fundamental criticism of this primacy-of-essence explanation of First Principles is that it tries to derive judgments (of existential reality) from concepts which, by the definition of abstraction itself, have left the existent singular behind and are constituted intelligibilities in the order of abstract essence. These manuals therefore leave "realism" in possession of an abstract con-

---

[13] Immanuel Kant, *Critique of Pure Reason,* trans. Norman Kemp Smith (London: Macmillan and Co., 1950), pp. 42-43.

cept of being as a starting point of metaphysics and are then faced with the unrealistic necessity of logically analyzing this concept (or concepts such as "cause" and "effect") into further principles at a methodological moment prior even to any experience of their content and application. Such a procedure, aimed at deducing the existence of a real identity otherwise not apparent under the logical diversity of subject and predicate, leaves *being* outside of metaphysics because these first principles are formulated independently of the analysis of *existential* experience of being as grasped in a perceptual judgment.[14]

But what drew this whole question of the origin of First Principles and the function of the Principle of Sufficient Reason into prolonged discussion was the difficulty which this quidditative notion of the existential judgments of *being* and *cause* posed for the proof for the existence of God.

The Proof for the Existence of God

The Major. Briefly, the situation was this. If the Principle of Causality is analytic—true but sterile, as Kant said—it was difficult to see what it could add to the demonstration of God's existence. This demonstration was usually formulated in terms of a major premise asserting, as the Principle of Causality, that the contingent is caused and a factual minor premise saying that the world is contingent, drawing therefrom the conclusion that the world is caused.

But if, as Scheltens points out so well,[15] the experience and affirmation of the contingency of the world are incapable by themselves alone of bringing us to the affirmation of God's existence, what additional force accrues from their association with a purely analytic judgment that entails no enrichment of our knowledge beyond the realm of formal manipulation of concepts? For the concepts, as abstractions, have by their nature left existence behind and bear only on the essential, the possible, the logical. The contingent being of experience is the starting point of the demonstration and argues to a cause which is not itself contingent. But how

14 Cf. n. 4, 6, 12 *supra.*

15 G. Scheltens, O.F.M., "La preuve de l'existence de Dieu dans la philosophie néoscolastique. Sa méthode—sa structure," *Franciscan Studies,* XIV (1954), pp. 293-309. Cf. also Francis X. Meehan, "Professor Scheltens and the Proof of God's Existence," *Progress in Philosophy: Philosophical Studies in Honor of Rev. Doctor Charles A. Hart,* ed. by James A. McWilliams, S.J., (Milwaukee: Bruce Publishing Co., 1955).

can the demonstration proceed to a conclusion from this starting point if forced to rely on an abstract principle whose intelligibility lies outside the sense-experienced being supposed to yield the demonstrated conclusion?

To escape this difficulty, many nineteenth-century Scholastic authors distinguished between *a priori* analytic judgments in the strict sense and in the wide sense, these latter supposed to be more fruitful in existential reference. But this, as Amédée de Margerie pointed out at the International Scientific Congress held in Paris in 1888, is really saying that the Principle of Causality in this wide sense was actually a synthetic principle. Hence, any reduction of it to the Principle of Contradiction was inconceivable and a *petitio principii* since, by definition, a synthetic principle is irreducible.[16]

One way out of this difficulty was to get a tighter hold on the fruitfulness of *a priori* analysis by introducing a deductive process. Tilmann Pesch, for instance, from a position reminiscent of Tongiorgi's doctrine that the truth of first principles is known to consciousness, held the Principle of Sufficient Reason as *per se notum* and proved the validity of the Principle of Causality by deducing it from Sufficient Reason.[17]

But those who accepted de Margerie's contention that the Principle of Causality was synthetic and therefore incapable of being objectively validated by reduction to the Principle of Contradiction sought to establish a new point of resolution. Here two groups of authors divide. According to one, the resolution lies in personal experience of the causal influence the *Ego* exerts on its own acts; with the other, there is simply an assertion of the immediate evidence of the Principle of Causality and a denial of any need to reduce it to further foundations.[18] These latter admitted the synthetic *a priori* nature of the Principle of Causality and insisted such a *joining* of concepts in synthetic *a priori* judgments was immediately evident from an understanding of the terms. They had no

16 Amédée de Margerie, "Le principe de causalité est-il une proposition analytique ou une proposition synthétique a priori?" *Congrès scientifique international des Catholiques tenu à Paris en 1888* (Paris Congrès, 1889), I, 276-286. This same thesis is defended by Jacques Laminne, "Le principe de contradictione et le principe de causalité," *Revue néo-scholastique*, XIX (1912), pp. 453-488.

17 Cf. Pesch, *Institutiones logicales*, II, 2, 55, 57, 61, 65, 375. Tongiorgi, *Ontologia*, pp. 158-159.

18 For a recent summary and evaluation of this question cf. Joseph Owens, C.SS.R., "The Causal Proposition—Principle or Conclusion?" *The Modern Schoolman*, XXXII (1955), 159-171, 257-270, 323-339.

answer to the objection that such a joining of terms was purely arbitrary because they had no theory of existential judgment to explain the mind's grasp of causal necessities in the singular existents of experience. The former group of *"Moi*-analysts" belongs mostly to the twentieth-century, particularly in the decades from 1920 to 1935.

Both attempts met failure at the point where the primacy given to essence makes existential reference impossible. For both groups, causality is an abstraction and its content held in a univocal concept. The analysis-of-concepts judgment of the principle cracks on this *abstractive* nature of the object under analysis; the analysis of subjective experience fails because of the *univocity* involved: at most they grasp cause of being not *qua being* but *qua thinking subject.*[19]

The Minor. Similar difficulties plague the minor of the syllogism purporting to demonstrate that God exists. As Prémontval pointed out to contemporary Wolffians, the precise point to be established is that the world is contingent. To conclude from the fact that we do not know the beings of our experience as necessary existents to their *de facto* contingency comes perilously close to assuming a perfect equation between human knowledge and the essence of things; some intelligibility must be pointed out in being itself whereby it presents itself as contingent.

What is wrong then, when the Principle of Sufficient Reason is employed to deduce contingency or dependence in this context, is that what is understood by sufficient reason is not existential causality but simply "every condition or cause necessary for the existence of a being and without which that being is inconceivable." In the order of essence or formal logic this meaning of sufficient reason gives the Principle an iron-clad consistency and coherence that are undeniable and can be demonstrated by the Principle of Contradiction. For it is impossible that a being have and not have every condition or cause necessary for its existence, and without which it is inconceivable.

Clearly, "the existence of A supposes all the conditions requisite for the possibility of this existence."[20] But this teaches us nothing

[19] De Coninck, for instance, begins his analysis in that concrete knowledge by identity which is consciousness of one's own reality. Cf. Antoine De Coninck, "Le principe de raison d'être est-il synthétique?" *Revue philosophique de Louvain,* XLVII (1949), pp. 71-108.

[20] Scheltens, *op. cit.,* p. 299.

about the *de facto* existence of any particular being other than its conceivability. Applied to the world of our experience it merely says that, on condition that the world is conceivable only as dependent on God, it is necessary that God exist in order for the world to exist. The purely logical use of the Principle of Contradiction is no help here. To argue that a caused thing would not be what it is without a cause and therefore is caused or the Principle of Contradiction is violated overlooks the point that an uncaused caused thing would not merely be other than what it is, but that it would not be at all.[21]

Thus Prémontval's objection remains: prove not merely that the world is *conceivable* only as dependent on God, but that it *is* dependent, i.e., that God exists and that a denial of His existence contradicts my existential experience and not merely the laws of logical conceivability in the abstract order of essence. It remains to be shown that the world without God is not only inconceivable but contradictory of being itself. To establish contingency something more is required than appeal to an abstract *a priori* principle of the order of formal logic; once contingency is established, recourse to an abstract synthetic principle is superfluous for the movement toward affirming God's existence.

Summation and Conclusion

In final summary, the Principle of Sufficient Reason may be viewed either in relation to the metaphysical experience of concrete singular being or as belonging to the abstract conceptual order of logic; its meaning-content derives from either of these two points of resolution.

(1) Viewed *metaphysically*, the term "principle" must be disengaged from any connotation of fruitfulness in the deductive order which clings to it from long association with the dichotomy between reason and experience characteristic of rationalism.[22] Since being is either *ens a se* or *ens ab alio*, the Principle of Sufficient Reason, applied to the former, cannot mean that God is the source of His own existence or that His essence entails His existence. This is simply a form of the ontological argument; "source"

[21] D. J. B. Hawkins, *Being and Becoming: An Essay Towards a Critical Metaphysic* (London: Sheed & Ward, 1954), pp. 164-165.
[22] Etienne Gilson, "Les principes et les causes," *Revue Thomiste*, LII (1952), pp. 39-63.

is either meaningless or it refers to the essence as if it existed at least in logical priority to its existence.[23] All that can be meant by saying that God is His own sufficient reason is that He requires no causal explanation.[24]

Applied to contingent being, *ens ab alio,* all that the Principle says is that such being needs a causal explanation. "What does not have a sufficient reason in itself" remains a purely nominal definition of the *contingent* until "sufficient reason" is given some existential causal meaning. In practice, therefore, it becomes a doublet for the Principle of Causality. But in those systems where "Causality," a kind of generic concept, is replaced by the analogous intelligibility of existential causes in a potency-act metaphysics, there is simply no need for a Principle of Sufficient Reason.[25]

Once the break is made with the old rationalistic tradition that experience expressed in *a posteriori* judgments can only reveal singular truths of fact and must be "button-holed" into the abstract order of the *a priori* rational for its *real* intelligibility, the whole nature and function of principles such as Sufficient Reason, Causality, and even Contradiction so conceived must be reassessed.

(2) From the point of view of *logic,* the proposition that *everything has a sufficient reason* likewise requires explanation.[26] Considerable discussion is eliminated by those who, following Kant's conception of mind-structure, assign a purely subjective origin to the intelligibility of all propositions. The difficulty here, of course, is that the metaphysical world of existential experience also dis-

---

23 Hawkins, *op. cit.,* p. 174.

24 With an eye to theological consequences, many of the manual authors complicated the formulation of the Principle of Sufficient Reason. Not content with a principle of causality that explains the world in relation to God, the First Cause, they sought to formulate it in such a way that it explains God as well; thus they tried to include Him and His creation under the principle that there is nothing without a sufficient reason why it is.

25 Gilson, *op. cit.,* p. 59.

26 The *psychological,* in contrast to both the logical and the metaphysical, explanation of the Principle of Sufficient Reason does not appear as such in strictly "Scholastic" manuals, although it can be found in some Catholic authors who view a state of intellectual curiosity, for instance, as a psychological expression of the Principle of Sufficient Reason. This principle is conceived as a dynamic law making new thoughts burgeon forth, whereas the Principle of Identity or of Contradiction is a static law. Examples of manual authors who take this approach into consideration are: C. Bonnet, S.J., *Ontologia* (ad usum privatum) (Wetteren [Belgium]: J. De Meester & Fils, 1923), pp. 38, 99, 269; Gaston Sortais, S.J., *Traité de philosophie* (Paris: Lethielleux, 1922), I, 289.

appears, and the Principle of Identity, as a mold into which all thought must ultimately be poured for coherence and meaning, is ultimate.

Sometimes *everything has a sufficient reason* is taken to mean that for every judgment there must be some motive of assent, and this in turn leads either inward to the *a priori* forms of the mind or outward to the intelligible necessities of being itself. Again, a further precision of meaning for the Principle of Sufficient Reason can be that every true proposition is either demonstrable or self-evident. Depending upon the starting point and object of the accompanying metaphysics, this again can have existential reference whereby the Principle of Sufficient Reason relates being and truth in the sense that the former is said to possess truth as source and final guarantee of knowledge that is true.

But in this reading, and it may have been what Stattler had in mind, the Principle of Sufficient Reason is a form of *Omne ens est verum*: it is saying that being is intelligible. And that returns us to a distinction made quite early in these pages between the ordinary concept or notion of Sufficient Reason and the technical Principle itself. To say that being is intelligible belongs more to the former; to make the Principle of Sufficient Reason a true description of the real order, it must be understood in terms of other and more ultimate realities.

Suggestions for Further Research

In the course of this study, additional lines of investigation have opened out from the main area of concentration. Further research, therefore, along the byways of textbook philosophy may be suggested at the following three points:

1. Considerable material remains to be examined as to the merely implicit origins of the Principle of Sufficient Reason in the period from 1550 or earlier to 1700. For instance, there was the sixteenth-century controversy on the nature of moral freedom and choice which was well known to Leibniz.

2. Within the period chosen here (1750-1900), monograph studies of the following topics as developed by the manual-authors would be useful: the starting-point and object of metaphysics; theories of method and format, especially as found in practical lay-out of the textbooks and explained in their introductions; Scholastic manual doctrine on the nature of judgment; the place of sensation

as a principle in metaphysics, and the attempted marriage of experience and reason in textbook systems.

3. On a more specifically historical level, further study would collect valuable information on the textbook writers' relation to modern philosophy, their understanding and use, for instance, of Descartes, Leibniz, Kant, and the empiricists such as Locke and Condillac. The influence of these latter in bringing philosophy back to that existential reference in concrete experience which rationalism had left confused, if not entirely omitted, could be traced to some of the early originators of the Thomistic revival. Monographs on this matter could well be written from the point of view of the true and valid insights which were in the grasp of non-Scholastic philosophers, rather than with exclusive emphasis on the *logical* consequences of their errors for faith and morals.

A useful study would be to determine the time-schedule of Kant's appearance in the manuals as an important point of doctrinal reference and reaction.

Finally, it could also be shown to advantage how current apologetical pressure, generated by social and political, and even scientific and theological circumstances, contributed to the determination of textbook content and presentation, and how the authority of St. Thomas was pulled into a Wolffian context and used to support rationalistic Scholasticism. This would be particularly valuable for those students of textbook philosophy who are appalled at times at the way the manuals vary among themselves and within themselves on points which seem to be settled once and for all in one edition or in one section only to be minimized or reversed entirely in others.

These and other considerations of the historical circumstances and apologetical exigencies surrounding the authors of philosophy textbooks may help their readers to avoid that temptation to substitute skepticism for metaphysics and fideism for theology which is part of every man's effort to think the Faith.

Bibliography

1. Sources

Alibert, C., S.S. *Manuel de philosophie pour la préparation au Baccalauréat à l'usage des seminaires & des collèges ecclésiastiques.* 3 vols. Lyons: Delhomme & Briguet, 1888.

Altieri, Laurentius, O.F.M.Conv. *Elementa philosophiae in adolescentium usum ex probatis auctoribus adornata.* (Editio tertia.) 3 vols. Venice: T. Bettinelli, 1779.

Amicus, Bartholomeus, S.J. *In universam Aristotelis philosophiam notae ac disputationes.* Naples: L. Scorigium, 1623.

Amort, Eusebius. *Philosophia Pollingana ad normam Burgundicae.* Augsburg: Vieth, 1730.

Babenstuber, Louis, O.S.B. *Philosophica Thomistica Salisburgensis.* Augsburg: G. Schlisteri, 1706.

Balmes, James. *Curso de filosofia elemental.* Paris: Rosa, 1850.
———. *Fundamental Philosophy.* Translated by Henry F. Brownson. 2 vols. New York: D. & J. Sadlier & Co., 1856.
———. *Obras Completas.* Edited by P. Casanovas, S.J. Madrid: Biblioteca de autores cristianos, 1950.

Baumeister, Friedrick Christian. *Historia doctrinae recentius controversae de mundo optimo.* Leipzig: Richter, 1741.
———. *Institutiones metaphysicae ontologiam, cosmologiam, psychologiam, theologiam denique naturalem complexae methodo Wolfii adornatae.* (Editio nova.) Wittenburg: S. Zimmermann, 1744.
———. *Philosophia recens controversa complexa definitiones theoremata et questiones nostra aetate in controversiam vocata.* Leipzig: Marcheana, 1741.

Baumgarten, Alexander G. *Acroasis logica in Christianum L. B. de Wolff dictabat.* (Editio secunda.) Halle: Hemmerde, 1723.
———. *Metaphysica.* (Editio sexta.) Halle: Hemmerde, 1768.
———. *Metaphysik.* Halle: Hemmerde, 1766.

Béguelin, Nicolas de. "Mémoire sur les premiers principes de la métaphysique," *Histoire de l'Académie Royale de Sciences et Belles Lettres,* XI (1755), 405-423.

Bensa, Anthony Marie. *Philosophiae speculativae summarium.* 2 vols. Paris: Jouby et Roger, 1877.

Blanc, Elie. *La philosophie traditionnelle et scolastique. Précis pour le temps present.* (2nd ed.) Lyons: Libraire Catholique Emmanuel Vitte, 1928.

Blatairou, J. *Institutiones philosophicae ad usum seminariorum.* 3 vols. Bordeaux: J. Dupy, 1848.

Bonelli, Aloysius. *Institutiones logico-metaphysicae.* Editio quarta. 2 vols. Rome: Ex Typographia Bonarum Artium, 1846.

Bonnet, C., S.J. *Ontologia* (ad usum privatum). Wetteren (Belgium): J. De Meester & Fils, 1923.

Boscovich, Roger, S.J. *De continuitatis lege, et ejus consectariis pertinentibus ad prima materiae elementa, eorumque vires.* Rome: Salomoni, 1754.

————. *Philosophiae naturalis theoria redacta ad unicum legem virium in natura existentium.* Vienna, 1758.

Branchereau, Louis, S.S. *Praelectiones philosophicae in majori seminario Claromontensi primum habitae.* (Editio secunda.) Paris: J. Leroux et Jouby, 1855.

Brin, M., S.S. *Philosophia scholastica ad mentem S. Thomae Aquinatis exposita et recentioribus scientiarum inventis adapta.* (Editio quarta penitur recognita curantibus.) Eds. A. Farges et D. Barbedette. Paris: Berche et Tralin, 1893.

Bruckert, James. "G. G. Leibnitii vita." Ex tom. V. ejusdem philosophiae historia deprompta (*Gothofredi Guillelmi Leibnitii opera omnia*) Ed. William Dutens, Vol. I. Geneva: Fratres de Tournes, 1768.

Buffier, Claude, S.J. *Les principes de raisonement exposéz en deux logiques nouveles. Avec des remarques sur les logiques qui ont eu le plus de réputation de notre temps.* 2 vols. Paris: Pierre Witte, 1714.

————. *Oeuvres philosophiques du Père Buffier de la Compagnie de Jésus.* Ed. Francisque Bouillier. Paris: A. Delahays, 1843.

————. *Traité des premières veritéz et de la source de nos jugements, ou l'on examine le sentiment des philosophes sur les premières notions des choses.* Paris: V. Monge, 1724.

Bülffinger, George. *Dilucidationes philosophicae de Deo, anima humana, mundo et generalibus rerum affectionibus.* Tubingen: J. & C. Cottae, 1725.

————. *De origine et permissione mali, praecipue moralis, commentatio philosophica. Sectio Prima cautelas dijudicandae rei necessarias; Secunda definitiones fundamenta systematis, objectionum occupationes; Tertia expositionem originis & permissionis ipsam; Quarta usus doctrinae morales; Epilogus universam in compendio tractationem exhibet.* Frankfurt: T. Mezlerum, 1724.

Cacheux, Abbé. *De la philosophie de St. Thomas d'Aquin.* Paris: Charles Douniol, 1858.

Cochet, Jean. *La métaphysique qui continent l'ontologie, la theologie naturelle et la pneumatologie.* Paris: J. Desaint & C. Saillant, 1753.

Combalot, Abbé. *Élémens de philosophie Catholique.* Louvain: Vanlinthout et Vandenzande, 1833.

Compton-Carleton, Thomas, S.J. *Philosophia universa.* Antwerp: J. Meursiun, 1649.

Cornoldi, John M., S.J. *Institutiones philosophiae speculativae ad mentem Sancti Thomae Aquinatis.* Translated by Dominic Agostini. Bologna: Mareggianiana, 1878.

De Decker, J.-V., S.J. *Cours élémentaire de philosophia.* 4 vols. Namur: F. Douxfils, 1850.

Delboeuf, Joseph. *Essai de logique scientifique; prolégomènes suivis d'une étude sur la question du mouvement considérée dans ses rapports avec le principe de contradiction.* Liége: J. Desoer, 1865.

De Maria, Michael, S.J. *Philosophia Peripatetico-Scholastica ex fontibus Aristotelis et S. Thomae Aquinatis expressa et ad adolescentium institutionem accommodata.* (Editio quarta). Vol. I. Rome: Ex Pontificia Officina Typographica, 1913.

Descartes, Rene. *Correspondance de Descartes.* Eds. C. Adam and G. Milhaud. 5 vols. to date. Paris: Alcan, 1936 ff.

————. *Oeuvres de Descartes.* Eds. C. Adam and P. Tannery. 12 vols. Paris: Cerf, 1897-1905.

Des Champs, Jean. *Cours abrégé de la philosophia Wolffienne.* 2 vols. Amsterdam: Arkstee et Merkus, 1743-47.

Descoqs, Peter, S.J. *Scheme theodiceae. Liber primus de Dei cognoscibilitate.* Paris: Beauchesne et ses fils, 1941.

Dionysius a. S. Joanne in Galdo. *Philosophiae universae institutiones.* 2 vols. (2nd ed.) Rome: C. Puccinelli, 1846-1847.

Dmowski, Joseph Aloysius, S.J. *Institutiones philosophicae.* 3 vols. Uden: P. N. Verhoeven, 1840-1841.

Doney, Abbé. *Nouveaux élémens de philosophie, d'après la méthode d'observation et la règle du sens commun.* Brussels: Demengeot et Goodman, 1830.

Dupeyrat, A., S.S. *Manuductio ad scholasticam, maxime vero Thomisticam philosophiam.* 2 vols. (Editio quinta.) Paris: Victor Lecoffre, 1894.

Egger, Francis. *Propaedeutica philosophica-theologica.* (Editio tertia.) Brescia: Wagerian, 1888.

Erber, Antonius, S.J. *Cursus philosophicus methodo scholastica elucubratus.* 3 vols. Vienna: J. Trattner, 1750-1751.

Esser, Gerard, S.V.D. *Metaphysica generalis in usum scholarum.* Techny, Ill.: Mission Press, S.V.D., 1952.

Euler, Leonard. *Lettres à une princesse d'Allemagne sur quelques sujets de physique et de philosophie.* 3 vols. St. Petersburg: 1768-1772.

Eymery, M., S.S. *Exposition de la doctrine de Leibnitz sur la religion, suivie de pensées extraites des ouvrages du même auteur.* Paris: Tournachon-Molin et H. Seguin, 1819.

Fabre, Abbé Jules. *Cours de philosophie ou nouvelle exposition des principes de cette science.* Tome premier. Paris: Durand, 1865.

Feder, John G. *Institutiones logicae et metaphysicae.* (Editio quarta.) Göttingae: J. Dietrich, 1797.

Ferrar, Joseph Anthony, O.F.M.Conv. *Philosophica Peripatetica adversus veteres, et recentiores praesertim philosophos firmioribus propugnata rationibus Joannis Dunsii Scoti Subtilium principiis.* 3 vols. (Editio secunda.) Venice: T. Bettinelli, 1754.

Fortunatus a Brixia, O.F.M. *Dissertatio physico-theologica, de qualitatibus corporum sensibilibus.* Brescia, 1741.
————. *Philosophia mentis methodice tractata atque ad usus academicos accommodata.* 2 vols. Brescia: J. Rizzardi, 1741-42.

Garrigou-Lagrange, Reginald, O.P. *God, His Existence and His Nature: A Thomistic Solution of Certain Agnostic Antinomies.* Translated from the fifth French edition by Dom Bede Rose, O.S.B. 2 vols. St. Louis: B. Herder, 1939.

Genovesi, Antonio. *Elementa metaphysicae mathematicum in morem adornata.* (Editio secunda.) Naples: B. Gessari, 1756.

Gerdil, Cardinal Hyacinthus Sigismond. "Reflexions sur un mémoire de Monsieur Béguelin concernant le principe de la raison suffisante de la possibilité du système du hazard," *(Opera Edite ed Inedite del Cardinale Giacinto Sigismondo Gerdil,* Vol. I. (8 vols. Florence: G. Celli, 1844-1851.

Gonzalez, Cardinal Zephyrinus, O.P. *Philosophia elementaria ad usum academicae ac praesertim ecclesiasticae juventutis opera et studio.* (Quarto editio.) 2 vols. Madrid: Lezcano et C., 1882.

Goudin, Antoine, O.P. *Philosophia iuxta inconcussa tutissimaque D. Thomae dogmata quatuor tomis comprehensa.* (Editio novissima.) 3 vols. Orvieto: S. Pompei, 1859-1860.

Gredt, Joseph, O.S.B. *Elementa philosophiae Aristotelico-Thomisticae.* 2 vols. Rome: Desclee, Lefabvre et Sociorum, 1899-1901.

Hauser, Berthold, S.J. *Elementa philosophiae ad rationis et experientiae ductum conscripta atque usibus scholasticis accommodata.* 7 vols. Augsburg: J. Wolff, 1755-1758.

Kant, Immanuel. *Critique of Pure Reason.* Translated by Norman Kemp Smith. London: Macmillan and Co., 1950.

Klaus, Michael, S.J. *Prima ac generalis philosophia, seu metaphysica quinque partibus comprehensa: doctrina primarum veritatum, ontologia, cosmologia, psychologia, et theologia naturalis.* Vienna: J. Trattner, 1775.

Kleutgen, Joseph, S.J. *Die Philosophie der Vorzeit.* (Zweite Auflage.) 2 vols. Innsbruck: F. Rauch, 1878.

—————. *La philosophie scolastique exposée et défendue.* Translated by Constant Sierp, de la congrégation des Sacrés-Coeurs, dite de Picpus. 4 vols. Paris: Gaume Frères et J. Duprey, 1868.

Kortholt, Christian. *"Disputatio de philosophia Leibnitii Christianae religioni haud perniciosa,"* (*Gothofredi Guillelmi Leibnitii opera omnia,* ed. William Dutens, Vol. I.) Geneva: Fratres de Tournes, 1768.

Lahousse, Gustavus, S.J. *Praelectiones logicae et ontologiae quas in collegio maximo Lovaniensi S.J. habebat.* Louvain: Car. Peeters, 1889.

Laromiguière, M. *Lecons de philosophie sur les principes de l'intelligence, ou sur les causes et sur les origines des idées.* (4th ed.) Paris: Brunot-Labbe, 1826.

Laurentius, Augustus, S.J. *De triplici ente cursus philosophicus in tres tomos divisus: I. De ente logica; II. De ente physica; III. De ente metaphysica.* 3 vols. Liége: W. Streel, 1688.

Leibniz, Gottfried Wilhelm. *G. W. Leibniz, textes inédits d'après les manuscrits de la bibliothèque provinciale de Hanovre.* Ed. Gaston Grua. Paris: Presses Universitaires de France, 1948.

—————. *Jurisprudence universelle et Théodicée selon Leibniz.* Ed. Gaston Grua. Paris: Presses Universitaires de France, 1953.

—————. *Lettres de Leibniz à Arnauld d'après un manuscrit inédit. Avec une introduction historique et des notes critiques.* Ed. Genevieve Lewis. Paris: Presses Universitaires de France, 1952.

—————. *Leibniz Selections.* Ed. P. Wiener. New York: Scribner, 1951.

—————. *Opera omnia, nunc primum collecta.* Ed. L. Dutens. 6 vols. Geneva: Fratres de Tournes, 1768.

—————. *Opuscules et fragments inédits de Leibniz.* Ed. Louis Couturat. Paris: Alcan, 1903.

Lepidi, Albert, O.P. *Elementa philosophiae christianae.* 3 vols. Paris: P. Lethielleux, 1875-1879.

Liberatore, Matthaeus, S.J. *Institutiones philosophicae ad triennium accommodatae,* (Vol. I.) Rome: Alexander Befani, 1872.

Limbourg, Max. *Quaestionum dialecticarum libri tres privato auditorum facultatis theologiae Oenipontanae usui accomodati.* Innsbruck: F. Rauch, 1896.

————. *Quaestionum metaphysicorum libri quinque.* Innsbruck: F. Rauch, 1893.

Lorenzelli, Benedict. *Philosophiae theoreticae institutiones secundum doctrinas Aristotelis et S. Thomae Aquinatis traditae in Pont. Collegio Urbano de Propaganda Fide.* 2 vols. Rome: P. Cuggiani, 1890.

Maestrus de Meldula, Bartholomeus, O.F.M.Conv., and Bellutus de Catan, Bonaventura, O.F.M.Conv. *Philosophiae ad mentem Scoti cursus integer.* Venice: N. Pezzana, 1708.

Mancini, Jerome Maria, O.P. *Elementa philosophiae ad mentem D. Thomae Aquinatis Doctoris Angelici ad triennium accommodata.* 3 vols. Rome: Ex typographia Polyglotta S. C. de Propaganda Fide, 1890.

Mangold, Joseph, S.J. *Philosophia rationalis et experimentalis hodiernis discentium studiis accommodata.* Ingolstadt: Cratz & Summer, 1755-1756.

Manier, S. S. *Compendium philosophiae ad usum seminariorum.* 3 vols. Paris: Lecoffre, 1867.

Mansuetus a S. Felice, O.S.A. *De discordia systematis rationis sufficientis cum libertate humana cum libertate, omnipotentia, & sapienta divina cum mysteriis gratiae, & praedestinationis. Dissertationes VII Philosophico-Theologicae.* Cremona: L. Manini, 1775.

Maquart, F. X. *Elementa philosophiae seu brevis philosophiae speculativae synthesis ad studium theologiae manuducens. Tomus III: Metaphysica. I. Metaphysica defensiva seu Critica.* Paris: Andreas Blot, 1938.

Martínez del Campo, Raphael, S.J. *Cursus philosophicus collegii maximi Ysletensis Societatis Iesu. Pars VI. Theologia naturalis.* Mexico City: A. Alvarez, 1943.

Marxuach, Francis, S.J. *Compendium dialecticae, criticae et ontologiae.* (Editio altera.) Barcelona: E. Subirana, 1929.

Mayr, Anton, S.J. *Philosophia Peripatetica antiquorum principiis et recentiorum experimentis confirmata.* Geneva: Gosse, 1746.

Mercier, Cardinal Desiré. *Critériologie générale ou théorie générale de la certitude.* (Septième édition.) Louvain: Institut supérieur de philosophie, 1918.

—————. *Logique.* (Septième édition.) Louvain: Institut supérieur de philosophie, 1922.

—————. *Métaphysique générale ou ontologie.* (Septième édition.) Louvain, Institut supérieur de philosophie, 1923.

Mey, Claude. *Essai sur métaphysique; ou, principes sur le nature et les operations de l'esprit.* Paris: Desaint & Saillant, 1753.

Migeot, Antoine. *Philosophiae elementa quinque distincta partibus, studiosae juventuti in collegio bonorum puerorum universi Remensis tradita.* 2 vols. Paris: Le Clerc, 1784.

Négrier, C. F. *Elementa philosophiae, quae juxta novam methodum digessit.* (Vol. I.) Paris: Brunot-Labre, 1826.

Noget-Lacoudre, A. *Institutiones philosophicae in seminario Bajocensi habitae, anno 1839-1840. Tomus secundus. De ontologia generali et speciali.* (Editio tertia.) Paris: Mequignon Junior et J. Leroux, 1844.

Osterrieder, Herman, O.F.M.Conv. *Metaphysica vetus & nova, logicae criticae nuper editae tanquam pars altera adjuncta, usibusque philosophiae tyronum sic accommodata, ut hi, solis istis duabus partibus mediantibus, etiam sine physica ad SS. theologiam aut jurisprudentiam absque difficultate ascendere valeant.* Augsburg: M. Rieger, 1761.

Palmieri, Dominicus, S.J. *Institutiones philosophicae quas tradebat in Collegio Romano Societatis Iesu.* 3 vols. Rome: Typis Cuggiani, Santini, et Soc., 1874-1876.

Para du Phanjas, Abbé. *Theorie des êtres insensibles, ou cours complet de métaphysique, sacrée et profane, mise à la portée de tout monde. Avec une table alphabétique des matières, qui fait de tout cet ouvrage, un vrai dictionaire de métaphysique ou de philosophie.* 3 vols. Paris: L. Cellot & A. Jombert, 1779.

Pecsi, Gustavus. *Cursus brevis philosophiae.* 3 vols. Esztergom (Hungaria): Typis Gustavi Buzarovits, 1906.

Perrard, J. Ferreol. *Introduction à la philosophie, ou nouvelle logique francaise, pour préparer les jeunes gens à subir l'examen de Bachelier ès-Lettres.* (Nouvelle edition.) Paris: T. Berquet, 1822.

Pesch, Tilmann, S.J. *Institutiones logicales secundum principia S. Thomae Aquinatis ad usum scholasticum accommodavit. Pars II: Logica Maior; Volumen I complectens logicam criticam et formalem.* Freiburg i. B.: Herder, 1889.

Phillipus a Sanctissima Trinitate, O.C.D. *Summa philosophiae ex principiis Aristotelis et d. Thomae juxta legitimam scholae Thomisticae intelligentiam.* Lyons: S. Jullieron, 1648.

Poncius, John, O.F.M. *Philosophiae ad mentem Scoti cursus integer.* Lyons: L. Arnaud & P. Borde, 1672.

Prémontval, André Pierre Le Guay de. *Du Hazard sous l'empire de la Providence, pour servir de préservatif contre le doctrine du Fatalisme moderne.* Berlin: J. C. Kluter, 1755.

Prisco, Cardinal Giuseppe. *Elementi di filosofia speculativa secondo le dottrine degli scolastici specialmente di San Tommaso d'Aquina.* Naples: Fibreno, 1864-1865.

Rastero, John Baptist. *Institutiones philosophicae.* 2 vols. Genoa: Ex Typographia Iuventutis, 1874.

Rattier, M. *Manuel élémentaire de philosophie ou abrégé du cours complet de philosophie.* Paris: Gaume Frères, 1844.

Redlhamer, Joseph, S.J. *Philosophiae tractatus primus seu philosophia rationalis ad praefixam in scholis nostris normam concinnata. Philosophiae tractatus alter, seu metaphysicam, ontologiam, cosmologiam, psychologiam, et theologiam naturalem complectens ad praefixam etc.* 2 vols. Vienna: J. Trattner, 1755.

Remer, Vincent, S.J. *Summa praelectionum philosophiae scholasticae quas in Universitate Gregoriana habuit.* 2 vols. Prati: Giachetti, 1895.

Renard, Henri, S.J. *The Philosophy of Being.* (2nd ed.) Milwaukee: Bruce Publishing Co., 1947.

—————. *The Philosophy of God.* Milwaukee: Bruce Publishing Co., 1952.

Renouvier, Ch. *Manuel de philosophie moderne.* Paris: Paulin, 1842.

Rickaby, John, S.J. *The First Principles of Knowledge.* "Stonyhurst Philosophical Series." London: Longmans, Green, and Co., 1919.

Roselli, Salvator Marie, O.P. *Summa philosophica ad mentem Angelici Doctoris S. Thomae Aquinatis.* 3 vols. Rome: Puccinelli, 1777.

—————. *Compendium summae philosophiae.* 3 vols. Rome: Urban college, 1837.

Rosset, Michael. *Prima principia scientiarum seu philosophia Catholica juxta Divum Thomam ejusque interpretatores respectu habito ad hodiernam disciplinarum rationem.* 2 vols. Paris: Vives, 1866.

Rothenflue, Francis, S.J. *Institutiones philosophiae theoreticae in usum praelectionum.* Freiburg i. S.: L. Piller, 1842.

Sagner, Caspar, S.J. *Institutiones philosophicae ex probatis veterum, recentiorumque sententiis adornatae in usum suorum dominorum auditorum. Tractatus III, seu Physica.* Prague: Academy Press, 1758.

Sanseverino, Cajetan. *Elementa philosophiae Christianae cum antiqua et nova comparatae.* 3 vols. Naples: apud Officinam Bibliothecae Catholicae, 1873-1876.

—————. *Institutiones seu elementa philosophiae Christianae cum antiqua et nova comparatae a Nuntio Can. Signoriello continuatae et absolutae.* (Editio novissima.) 3 vols. Naples: apud Officinam Bibliothecae Catholicae Scriptorum, 1885.

Schiffini, Sanctus, S.J. *Principia philosophica ad mentem Aquinatis quae in Pontificia universitate Gregoriana tradebat.* Turin: Speirani Bros., 1886.

Sortais, Gaston, S.J. *Traité de philosophie.* 3 vols. Paris: Lethielleux, 1922.

Spir, Africanus. *Pensée et réalité.* Translated by H. Penjon. Lille: au siege des Facultes, 1896.

Stattler, Benedict, S.J. *Philosophia methodo scientiis propria explanata.* 6 vols. Augsburg: M. Rieger & Sons, 1769-1772.

Storchenau, Sigismund, S.J. *Institutionum metaphysicarum libri IV.* (Editio altera.) 2 vols. Venice: J. Trattner, 1772.

Tamagna, Joseph, O.F.M.Conv. *Institutiones philosophiae.* (Editio secunda.) 3 vols. Rome: P. Junchius, 1780.

Thumming, Ludwig Phil. *Institutiones philosophiae Wolfianae, in usus Academicos adornatae.* (Editio nova.) Frankfurt, 1779.

Tongiorgi, Salvator, S. J. *Institutiones philosophiae.* 2 vols. Brussels: H. Goemaere, 1862-1864.

Ubaghs, Gerard. *Logicae seu philosophiae rationalis elementa.* Louvain: (5th ed.) Vanlinthout, 1860.

—————. *Ontologiae seu metaphysicae generalis elementa.* (5th ed.) Louvain: Vanlinthout, 1863.

—————. *Theodiceae seu theologiae naturalis elementa ad usum discentium accomodata.* (Louvain: Vanlinthout, 1863.

Urraburu, John Joseph, S.J. *Institutiones philosophicae quas Romae in Pontificia Universitate Gregoriana tradiderat.* 8 vols. Valladolid: Typis Viduae ac Filiorum a Cuesta, 1891.

Valla, Joseph. *Institutiones philosophicae auctoritate D.D. Archiepiscopi Lugdunensis ad usum scholarum suae diocesis editae.* 6 vols. Bassani: Remondin, 1817.

Vallet, Abbé, S.S. *Praelectiones philosophicae ad mentem S. Thomae Aquinatis Doctoris Angelici.* (5th ed.) 2 vols. in one. Paris: Ouby and Roger, 1887.

Van de Woestyne, Zacharias, O.F.M. *Cursus philosophicus in breve collectus.* 2 vols. Mechlin: Typographia S. Francisci, 1921.

Van der Aa, John, S.J. *Praelectionum philosophiae scholasticae brevis conspectus.* (2nd edit.) 5 vols. Louvain: Fonteyn, 1888.

Ventura de Raulica, James. *La philosophie chrétienne.* 3 vols. Paris: Gaume Frères et J. Duprey, 1861.

Willems, C. *Institutiones philosophicae.* 2 vols. Treves: Ex Officina ad S. Paulinum, 1915.

Wolff, Christian. *Cosmologia generalis methodo scientifica pertractata qua ad solidam, inprimis Dei atque naturae via sternitur.* (Editio novissima.) Verona: M. Moroni, 1779.

—————. *De differentia nexus rerum sapientis et fatalis necessitatis, nec non systematis harmoniae praestabilitae ab hypothesium Spinosae. Luculenta commentatio in qua simul genuina Dei existentiam demonstrandi ratio expenditur et multa religionis naturalis capita illustrantur.* Halle: Rengeriana, 1724.

—————. *Philosophia prima sive ontologia methodo scientifica pertractata qua omnis cognitionis humanae principia continentur.* (Editio novissima.) Verona: M. Moroni, 1779.

—————. *Philosophia rationalis sive logica methodo scientifica pertractata, et ad usum scientiarum atque vitae aptata.* (Editio novissima.) Verona: M. Moroni, 1779.

—————. *Psychologia empirica methodo scientifica pertractata, qua ea, quae de anima humana indubia experientiae fide constant, continentur.* (Editio novissima.) Verona: M. Moroni, 1779.

—————. *Psychologia rationalis methodo scientifica pertractata, qua ea, quae de anima humana indubia experientiae fide innotescunt, per essentiam et naturam animae explicantur, et ad intimiorem naturae ejusque auctoris cognitionem profutura proponuntur.* (Editio novissima.) Verona: M. Moroni, 1779.

—————. *Theologia naturalis methodo scientifica pertractata. Pars prior integrum systema complectens, qua exsistentia et attributa Dei a posteriori demonstrantur.* (Editio novissima.) Verona: M. Moroni, 1779.

—————. *Theologia naturalis methodo scientifica pertractata. Pars posterior qua exsistentia et attributa Dei ex notione entis perfectissimi et natura animae demonstrantur, et atheismi, deismi, fatalismi, naturalismi, Spinosismi aliorumque de Deo errorum fundamenta subvertuntur.* (Editio novissima.) Verona: M. Moroni, 1779.

Zigliara, Cardinal Thomas Maria, O.P. *Summa philosophica in usum scholarum.* (Editio undecima.) 3 vols. Paris: Delhomme et Briguet, 1898.

(Anonymous)

Elementa ontologiae ad usum alumnorum seminarii Sylvae-Ducensis. Gestel St. Michaelis: e Prelo Surdo-Mutorum, 1846.

Institutiones philosophicae ad mentem Angelici Doctoris S. Thomae Aquinatis ordinatae non solum ad theologiam scholasticam perdiscendam, sed etiam ad faciliorem veterum, ac recentiorum philosophorum lectionem. 5 vols. Monte Casino: Ex Typis Abbatiae, 1875.

Philosophiae Turonensis institutiones ad usum collegiorum atque seminariorum. Paris: Le Clerc, 1823.

2. Secondary Studies
A. Books

Balz, Albert G. A. *Cartesian Studies.* New York: Columbia University Press, 1951.

Bartholmèss, Christian. *Histoire philosophique de l'Académie de Prusse depuis Leibniz, jusqu'à Schelling, particulièrement sous Frédéric-LeGrand.* 2 vols. Paris: Marc Ducloux, 1850-1851.

Bréhier, Émile. *Histoire de la philosophie. Tome I: La philosophie moderne. I^{ne} partie: XVIIe et XVIIIe siècles.* Paris: Presses Universitaires de France, 1942.

Burnichon, Joseph, S.J. *La Compagnie de Jésus en France: Histoire d'un siècle 1814-1915. Tome Quatrième: 1860-1880.* Paris: Gabriel Beauchesne, 1922.

Butler, Cuthbert. *The Vatican Council: The Story Told from the Inside in Bishop Ullathorne's Letters.* London: Longmans, Green & Co., 1930.

Campo, Mariano. *Cristiano Wolff e il razionalismo precritico.* 2 vols. Milan: Vita e Pensiero, 1939.

Collins, James. *A History of Modern European Philosophy.* Milwaukee: Bruce Publishing Co., 1954.

Del Boca, Susanna. *Finalismo e Necessità in Leibniz.* Florence: Sansoni, 1936.

Dezza, Paul, S.J. *I Neotomisti Italiani del XIX Secolo.* 2 vols. Milan: Fratelli Bossa, 1942-1944.

Duhr, Bernard, S.J. *Geschichte der Jesuiten in den Ländern deutscher Zunge im 18. Jahrhundert.* (Vol. IV.) München-Regensburg: G. J. Manz, 1928.

Dumont, Paul. *Nicolas De Béguelin.* Paris: Felix Alcan, n.d.

Erdmann, John E. *A History of Philosophy.* Translation edited by Williston S. Hough. 3 vols. London: Sonneschein, 1892.

Fejer, Joseph, S.J. *Theoriae corpusculares typicae in universitatibus Societatis Jesu Saec. XVIII et Monadologia Kantiana. Doctrina J. Mangold, G. Sanger, R. J. Boscovich, B. Stattler.* Rome: Officium Libri Catholici, 1951.

Ferraz, M. *Histoire de la philosophie en France au XIXe siècle.* 3 vols. Paris: Didier et Cie, 1877-1880.

Gilson, Etienne. *Being and Some Philosophers.* Toronto: Pontifical Institute of Mediaeval Studies, 1949.

Gonzalez, Cardinal Zephyrinus, O.P. *Histoire de la philosophie.* Translated by P. de Pascal. 4 vols. Paris: P. Lethielleux, 1891.

Hawkins, D. J. B. *Being and Becoming: An Essay Towards a Critical Metaphysics.* London: Sheed & Ward, 1954.

Hecht, Francis Torrens, S.J. *Self-Evidence of God's Existence in Some Theologians, 1650-1750.* Unpublished Ph.D. dissertation, St. Louis University, 1954.

Hoenen, Peter, S.J. *Reality and Judgment According to St. Thomas.* Translated by Henry F. Tiblier, S.J. Chicago: Henry Regnery Company, 1952.

Jansen, Bernhard, S.J. *Die pflege der Philosophie im Jesuitenorden während des 17-18 Jahrhunderts.* Fulda: Parzeller, 1938.

Jones, W. T. *A History of Western Philosophy.* Vol. 2: *The Modern Mind,* Vol. II.) New York: Harcourt, Brace, 1952.

Klimke, Fridericus, S.J. *Institutiones historiae philosophiae.* 2 vols. Rome: Gregorian University, 1923.

Kulpe, Oswald. *Introduction to Philosophy.* Translated by W. B. Pillsbury and E. B. Tichener. New York: The Macmillan Co., 1897.

LaBelle, Henry Joseph, S.J. *The Tradition of the Three Degrees of Certitude in Later Scholastic Thought.* Unpublished master's thesis, St. Louis University, 1952.

Leo XIII. *De philosophia Christiana ad mentem S. Thomae Aquinatis doctoris angelici in scholis catholicis instauranda.* Encyclica epistola. Rome: 1879.

Masnovo, A. *Il neo-tomismo in Italia.* Milan: Vita e Pensiero, 1923.

Meehan, Francis X. "Professor Scheltens and the Proof of God's Existence," *Progress in Philosophy: Philosophical Studies In Honor of Rev. Doctor Charles A. Hart,* ed. by James A. McWilliams, S.J., Milwaukee: Bruce Publishing Co.. 1955.

Meyer, R. W. *Leibnitz and the Seventeenth Century Revolution.* Translated by J. P. Stern. Cambridge, England: Bower & Bower, 1952.

Nourrison, Jean Felix. *La philosophie de Leibniz.* Paris: Hachette, 1860.

Pachtler, George Michael, S.J. *Ratio studiorum et institutiones scholasticae Societatis Jesu per Germaniam olim vigentes.* 4 vols. Berlin: A. Hoffman, 1887-1894.

Pichler, Hans. *Über Christian Wolffs Ontologie.* Leipzig: Verlag der Dürr'schen Buchhandlung, 1910.

Pius XII. *Humani Generis.* Encyclical translated by Gerald C. Treacy, S.J. New York: The Paulist Press, 1950.

Sommervogel, Carl, S.J. *Bibliothéque de la Compagnie de Jésus.* (Nouvelle edition.) 10 vols. Brussels: Oscar Schepers, 1890-1900.

Touron, A., O.P. *La vie de S. Thomae d'Aquin, de l'Ordre des Frères Prêcheurs, Docteur de l'Eglise, avec un exposé de sa doctrine et de ses ouvrages.* Paris: Gissey, 1740.

Van Riet, G. *L'épistémologie thomiste.* Louvain: Editions de l'institut supérieur de philosophie, 1946.

Werner, Carl. *Franz Suarez und die Scholastik der letzten Jahrhunderte.* (Neue Ausgabe.) Regensburg: E. L. Manz, 1889.

Wilde, Norman. *Friedrick Henrich Jacobi: A Study in the Origin of German Realism.* New York: Columbia College, 1894.

Wundt, Max. *Die deutsche Schulmetaphysik des 17. Jahrhunderts.* Tübingen: J. Mohr, 1939.

————. *Die deutsche Schulphilosophie im Zeitalter der Aüfklärung.* Tübingen: J. Mohr, 1945.

B. *Journal Articles*

Bonansea, Bernardino M., O.F.M. "Pioneers of the Nineteenth-Century Scholastic Revival in Italy," *The New Scholasticism,* XXVII (1954), 1-37.

Couturat, Louis. "Sur la métaphysique de Leibniz," *Revue de métaphysique et de morale,* X (1902), 1-23.

De Coninck, Antoine. "Le principe de raison d'être est-il synthétique," *Revue philosophique de Louvain,* XLVII (1949), 71-108.

De Margerie, Amédée. "Le principe de causalité est-il une proposition analytique ou une proposition synthétique a priori?" *Congrés scientifique international des Catholiques tenu à Paris en 1888,* Paris, 1889, I, 276-286.

De Vries, J., S.J. "Geschichtliches zum Streit um die metaphysischen Prinzipien," *Scholastik,* VI (1937), 196-221.

————. "Zur Frage der Begründung des Kausalitäts-Prinzips," *Stimmen der Zeit,* CXXIII (1932), 378-390.

Gilson, Etienne. "Historical Research and the Future of Scholasticism," *The Modern Schoolman,* XXIX (1951), 1-10.

—————. "Les principes et les causes," *Revue Thomiste,* LII (1952), 39-63.

Gurr, John E., S.J. "Genesis and Functions of Principles in Philosophy," *Proceedings of the American Catholic Philosophical Association,* XXIX (1955), 121-133.

—————. "Some Historical Origins of Rationalism in Catholic Philosophy Manuals," *Proceedings of the American Catholic Philosophical Association,* XXX (1956), 170-180.

Klubertanz, George, S.J. "Being and God According to Contemporary Scholastics," *The Modern Schoolman,* XXXII (1954), 1-17.

Laminne, Jacques. "Le principe de contradiction et le principe de causalité," *Revue néo-scolastique de philosophie,* XIX (1912), 453-488.

Lamountain, George F. J. "A Note on the Traditionalism of Father Ventura de Raulica (1792-1861)," *The Modern Schoolman,* XXXIII (1956), 190-196.

Owens, Joseph, C.SS.R. "The Causal Proposition—Principle or Conclusion?" *The Modern Schoolman,* XXXII (1955), 159-171, 257-270, 323-339.

—————. "Theodicy, Natural Theology and Metaphysics," *Ibid.* XXVIII (1951), 126-137.

Pelzer, A. "Les initiateurs italiens du néo-thomisme contemporain," *Revue néo-scolastique de philosophie,* XVIII (1911), 230-254.

Scheltens, G., O.F.M. "Le preuve de l'existence de Dieu dans la philosophie néoscolastique, sa méthode—sa structure," *Franciscan studies,* XIV (1954), 293-309.

Schmitz, Kenneth L., "Natural Wisdom and Some Recent Philosophy Manuals," *Proceedings of the American Catholic Philosophical Association,* XXX (1956), 181-190.

Schulte, Joseph. "George Hermes," *The Catholic Encyclopedia,* VII, 1912.

Urban, Wilbur. "The History of the Principle of Sufficient Reason: Its Metaphysical and Logical Formulations," *Princeton Contributions to Philosophy,* I, 3 (1900), 1-87.

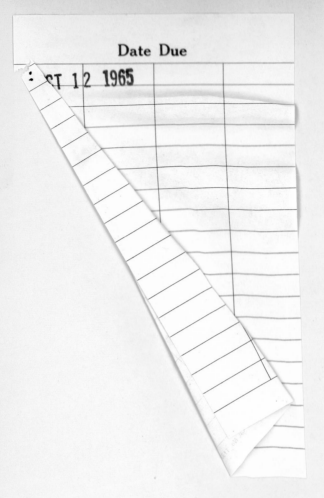